STATE AND LEGAL PRACTICE IN THE CAUCASUS

The timely drive to advance our understandings of legal pluralism is finding some of its richest material in the Caucasus past and present. This excellent volume, bringing together a model cohort of scholars from within the Caucasus and beyond, tells us why.

Bruce Grant, New York University, USA

In the large body of literature on "strong societies and weak states" the Caucasus has until now been neglected - this book fills this important gap. Some of the leading regional experts show us that even the Soviet state, though arguably strong if not "totalitarian", could never manipulate the local ethnic societies on an ideological whim. This volume opens a fruitful conversation on the modern uses of customary norms and informality.

Georgi Derluguian, New York University Abu Dhabi, United Arab Emirates and author of *Bourdieu's Secret Admirer in the Caucasus: A World-System Biography*

The contributors – some from the Caucasus and some from elsewhere, younger researchers as well as those who experienced the last years of the Soviet Union – bring an impressive diversity of theoretical stances and field experiences to bear on the themes of the state, politics and law in the lives of people from the South and North Caucasus. I believe this stimulating and useful collection will make a significant contribution to political and legal anthropology, as well as post-Soviet studies.

Kevin Tuite, Université de Montréal, Canada

The contributors to this book ask how people effectively deal with legal pluralism as an 'endemic condition of the Caucasus' and make sense of this co-existence of different legal frameworks, no matter if connected to a state or not. From a political anthropological perspective in their diverse field studies they are connecting micro with macro levels and thus challenge Eurocentric assumptions. A very inspiring book about an increasingly interesting region.

Oliver Reisner, Ilia State University, Georgia

Cultural Diversity and Law

Series Editor:

Prakash Shah, School of Law, Queen Mary, University of London, UK

Around the world, most states are faced with difficult issues arising out of cultural diversity in their territories. Within the legal field, such issues span across matters of private law through to public and constitutional law. At international level too there is now considerable jurisprudence regarding ethnic, religious and cultural diversity. In addition, there are several layers of legal control – from communal and religious regulation to state and international regulation. This multiplicity of norm setting has been variously termed legal pluralism, inter-legality or internormativity and provides a fascinating lens for academic analysis that links up to cultural diversity in new and interesting ways. The umbrella of cultural diversity encompasses various population groups throughout the world ranging from national, ethnic, religious or indigenous groupings. This series particularly welcomes work that is of comparative interest, concerning various state jurisdictions as well as different population groups.

Also in the series

Legal Reform and Business Contracts in Developing Economies
Trust, Culture, and Law in Dakar
Julie Paquin

Socio-Legal Integration
Polish Post-2004 EU Enlargement Migrants in the United Kingdom
Agnieszka Kubal

Law, Religious Freedoms and Education in Europe
Edited by Myriam Hunter-Henin

Islamic Law in Europe?
Legal Pluralism and its Limits in European Family Laws
Andrea Büchler

The Challenges of Justice in Diverse Societies
Constitutionalism and Pluralism
Meena K. Bhamra

State and Legal Practice in the Caucasus

Anthropological Perspectives on Law and Politics

EDITED BY

STÉPHANE VOELL
Philipps-University Marburg, Germany

AND

IWONA KALISZEWSKA
University of Warsaw, Poland

Routledge
Taylor & Francis Group
LONDON AND NEW YORK

First published 2015 by Ashgate Publishing

2 Park Square, Milton Park, Abingdon, Oxfordshire OX14 4RN
52 Vanderbilt Avenue, New York, NY 10017

Routledge is an imprint of the Taylor & Francis Group, an informa business

First issued in paperback 2020

British Library Cataloguing in Publication Data
A catalogue record for this book is available from the British Library

The Library of Congress has cataloged the printed edition as follows:
State and Legal Practice in the Caucasus: Anthropological Perspectives on Law and Politics / by Stéphane Voell and Iwona Kaliszewska.
pages cm
Includes bibliographical references and index.
1. Law – Caucasus Region. 2. Customary law – Caucasus Region. 3. Ethnological jurisprudence – Caucasus Region. I. Voell, Stéphane, editor. II. Kaliszewska, Iwona, editor.
KLA475.5.S727 2015
349.475 – dc23 2014029243

ISBN 978-1-4724-4690-9 (hbk)
ISBN 978-0-367-59958-4 (pbk)

Contents

Contributors

Levon Abrahamian: Institute of Archaeology and Ethnography, National Academy of Sciences of the Republic of Armenia, Yerevan (Armenia).

Makka Albogachieva: Peter the Great Museum of Anthropology and Ethnography, Department of Ethnography of the Caucasus, St Petersburg (Russia).

Sergey Arutiunov: Russian Academy of Science, Department of the Caucasus, Moscow (Russia).

Barbara Christophe: Georg-Eckert-Institute, Braunschweig (Germany).

Austin Cowley: Department of Geography, University of Colorado at Boulder (USA).

Lili Di Puppo: Faculty of Social Sciences, Department of Sociology, Higher School of Economics Moscow (Russia).

Elizabeth Cullen Dunn: Departments of Geography and International Studies, Indiana University at Bloomington (USA)

Natia Jalabadze: Ivane Javakhishvili Institute for History and Ethnography, Tbilisi (Georgia).

Lavrenti Janiashvili: Ivane Javakhishvili Institute for History and Ethnography, Tbilisi (Georgia).

Iwona Kaliszewska: Institute of Ethnology and Cultural Anthropology, University of Warsaw (Poland).

Elke Kamm: Department of Cultural and Social Anthropology, Philipps-University Marburg (Germany).

Ekaterina Kapustina: Peter the Great Museum of Anthropology and Ethnography, Department of Ethnography of the Caucasus, St Petersburg (Russia).

Yuri Karpov: Peter the Great Museum of Anthropology and Ethnography, Department of Ethnography of the Caucasus, St Petersburg (Russia).

Rail Safiyev: Freie Universität Berlin, Department of Political and Social Sciences, Berlin (Germany).

Gayane Shagoyan: Institute of Archaeology and Ethnography, National Academy of Sciences of the Republic of Armenia, Yerevan (Armenia).

Stéphane Voell: Department of Cultural and Social Anthropology, Philipps-University Marburg (Germany).

Evgenia Zakharova: Peter the Great Museum of Anthropology and Ethnography, Department of Ethnography of the Caucasus, St Petersburg (Russia).

Preface

The history of this edited volume began in Ireland in August 2010. Several of the authors met during the workshop called 'Law in the Caucasus: Anthropological Perspectives on Legal Practice' held at the European Association of Social Anthropologists (EASA) conference in Maynooth. At this time, the idea of organising a conference on the topics of law and the state in the Caucasus emerged.

A conference entitled 'Perceptions of the State and Legal Practice in the Caucasus Anthropological Perspectives on Law and Politics' was held in Batumi (Georgia) in November 2011. The event was funded by the Volkswagen Foundation and brought together anthropologists and anthropologically informed scholars working on the North and the South Caucasus. Researchers from different generations and backgrounds discussed how conceptions of order are enforced, used, followed and staged in social networks and legal practice in the Caucasus.

As is usually the case, an edited volume based on a conference does not necessarily reflect fully the event. For various reasons, the contributions of some participants did not make it into the present book. Apart from the authors in this volume, the following colleagues presented papers in Batumi: Irina Babich, Vladimir Bobrovnikov, Vladimir Dmitriev, Joni Kvitsiani, Lia Melikishvili, Nugzar Mgeladze, Ieva Raubisko, Mikhail Solonenko, and Andrea Weiss.

At the same time, during the preparation of the book we tried to include some regions and topics that were not addressed at the conference in Batumi and invited other authors to contribute. We are happy to have received additional papers from Levon Abrahamian, Gayane Shagoyan, Lilli Di Puppo, Barbara Christophe, Elizabeth Cullen Dunn and Austin Cowley. Unfortunately, we could not manage to get an equal share of papers pertaining to the North and the South Caucasus.

We are deeply indebted to the local organisers of our conference in Batumi. Nugzar Mgeladze and Manuchar Loria made arrangements for the use of rooms at Shota Rustaveli University. Without Ketevan Khutsishvili, who was also a respondent during the Batumi conference, and her support in regard to transportation, accommodation and budget issues, the conference would not have been possible.

The conference marked the end of the research project 'The Revitalisation of Traditional Law in Georgia', which was also funded by the Volkswagen Foundation. The project leaders Mark Münzel and Stéphane Voell want to thank the foundation for its support in recent years.

The English language editing of the book was done by Andreas Hemming, Eva Chatburn and Maryna Mews.

STÉPHANE VOELL & IWONA KALISZEWSKA
Marburg & Warsaw, April 2014

Chapter 1

Pluralism, Tradition and Perspectives on the State in the Caucasus: Introduction

Stéphane Voell and Iwona Kaliszewska

The usual way to open a text on the Caucasus is to cite the region's complexity and plurality. Typically, one quotes ancient writers mentioning the Caucasus a long time ago. The classical source is here the descriptions of the Caucasus as the 'Mountain of Tongues', a statement attributed to the Arab historian Al-Masudi (tenth century). But already in the fifth century BC the Greek historian Herodotus – often presented as history's first ethnographer – stated that 'the Caucasus has many various races of men dwelling in it' (History, I.203). The Greek geographer Strabo wrote on Dioscurias around the first century BC. It was founded by the Greeks in the sixth century BC on the site of present-day Sokhumi. He wrote that seventy tribes with different languages were living there side by side but with no interrelation with each other (Geography, XI.2.16). The Roman natural philosopher, Pliny the Elder, reported years later from the same town that the Greek navigator Timosthenes (third century BC) counted three hundred nations in Dioscurias. The Romans, Pliny continues, in order to conduct business in this town on the Black Sea, still needed 'one hundred and thirty interpreters for the purpose of transacting business' (The Natural History, VI.5).

Bruce Grant and Lale Yalçın-Heckmann (2007) see this linguistic pluralism, but also the associated cultural, religious, political and economic pluralisms, as part of the prominent 'Caucasus Paradigms'. The picture painted of the Caucasus in the literature is, they argue, a complex and heterogeneous image characterised by topics such as 'violence, savagery, conflict and corruption' or 'nobility, hospitality, natural beauty and severity', but also by 'diaspora, migration, conquest and cohabitation', 'mobilities and crossings'. One pluralism that they appear to have forgotten in this list, though it is somehow part of political and cultural pluralism, is legal pluralism and the pluralism of orders. The present volume addresses especially the legal complexities of the Caucasus and how the local population deals with this situation.

Jean and John Comaroff (2006) discuss the interrelation between plural legal practices in former colonies and transnational legal processes. They write that one could suppose for postcolonies that they strive toward 'single, vertically integrated sovereignties' but that the opposite appears to be the case; they become, rather, a 'tapestry of partial sovereignties' (2006, p.35), that is, territories, groups of people, networks, faiths, properties, or a mixture of them all. With Hannah Arendt's dictum that sovereignty is 'contradictory to the very condition of plurality' Comaroff and Comaroff write that plurality is, then, 'the endemic condition of the postcolony' (2006, p.35). If we push Grant's and Yalçın-Heckmann's approach of presenting the mentioned pluralisms as Caucasus paradigms a little further and combine it with the Comaroffs' argument, one might state that pluralism – and more concretely, legal pluralism – could be presented as the 'endemic condition of the Caucasus'.

Is the post-Soviet space a postcolony? This would be an understandable reply, and many researchers have discussed this issue already. Some argued that there exist some semblances of the postcolonial in post-Soviet processes (see Suny and Martin, 2001; Beissinger and Young, 2001), but upon a closer look it is difficult to make any comparisons. It becomes problematic when comparing what happened before the so-called 'posts' because Soviet Communism and European Colonialism were very different by reason of the specific nature of the Soviet 'Empire'. It appeared to be more an 'empire of nations' (Hirsch, 2005) than one single entity. It developed a centralised imperial rule, but one connected with strong national cultures, a 'hyper-processed' ethno-federalism (Broers, 2009, p.100). These processes marked the Caucasus so deeply that one has to question if one should speak of a postcolony at all. Laurence Broers (2009) argues that especially the 'western' post-Soviet states have maintained in their emancipation from the centre the supra-regional imperial nature of the empire on a local level by preserving neo-colonial relations with minorities, for example in Georgia and Azerbaijan. The anthropology of postsocialism discussed if local realities could be described in terms of a clean break, in and after the political change that might warrant describing the region as a postcolony and came to the conclusion that the North Caucasus is far from being postcolonial and in the south, 'colonial-like' policies continue to be found on the national level.

The utility of describing something as very plural and complex is also questionable. In the anthropology of law many discussions of the definition of legal pluralism have been marked by ideology and political considerations. This is understandable because the recognition of multiple forms of law in one space questions the claim of one ruler to be the sole guarantor of order and their power to enforce that order (Benda-Beckmann, 1994, p.2). The theoretical discussions on legal pluralism constituted a highly specialised debate lead by anthropologists, sociologists and lawyers. There was for example a distinction made between 'weak' and 'strong' pluralism (Griffiths, 1986) or 'state law' and 'deep' pluralism (Woodman, 1999). 'Weak' in this context referred to institutions and processes inside one state: the sovereign governs its territory but it includes different forms of law for different groups of people. There is legal pluralism but all are embedded into one central governmental structure. 'Hard' or 'deep' legal pluralism describes a state of affairs in which legal frameworks exist side by side, no matter if connected to a state or not. For Franz von Benda-Beckmann, this differentiation in types of pluralism was not very useful. His definition is broader: 'Pluralism, if we wish, can thus be viewed analytically as the coexistence of two or more sets of normative conceptions within the same process, or in aggregates of processes ... ;

but also as the coexistence of simultaneous, but different reproduction of the same normative element in more than one context' (1988, p.899). All other questions concerning the exact configuration of simultaneously existing legal frameworks, their interrelations, and their social, economic or political importance are empirical (Benda-Beckmann, 1994, p.12).

When the Comaroffs write that legal pluralism is the 'endemic condition of the postcolony' (and not of the colony, that is the time before) this sounds as if pluralism is only present in a specific period of time. The legal scholar, Jacques Vanderlinden (1971), also argues that there is a time without pluralism. 'If the political, economic, cultural or physical differences that cause legal pluralism would disappear', he writes; if a 'psychological homogenisation' of social groups into one unity takes place, or if one sovereign imposes by force the unity of the group, legal pluralism might come to an end (1971, pp.53–6). But anthropologists of law no longer argue that there is anything like a society without legal pluralism. On the contrary: Sally F. Merry, for example, writes that 'virtually every society is legally plural whether or not it has a colonial past' (1988, p.869). Legal pluralism is, then, nothing special and a characteristic feature of every society. How this pluralism is specifically defined and how people act and make sense of their life in pluralism becomes an empirical question.

But now it appears that it is no longer very useful to proclaim that pluralism, and in our case specifically, legal pluralism, is an 'endemic condition of the Caucasus' since legal pluralism is the endemic condition of basically every society. While analytically speaking it makes no sense to describe the Caucasus as a place full of different legal frameworks and different conceptions of order, one can still argue that the Caucasus is a site of condensed pluralism. It can be considered an anthropological fact that in the small region of the Caucasus one finds a vast mosaic of ethnic categories, religious diversity and multifarious or different languages (see for example, Comrie, 2008). Legal pluralism in the Caucasus or, more generally, coexistence side by side of different forms of orders has since the nineteenth century been a predominant topic of research (namely Dirr, 1925; Günther, 1931; Kovalevsky, 1886; Ladyshenskij, 1930; Luzbetak, 1951). The existing ethnic pluralism was recreated and petrified in political–administrative structures (Slezkine, 1994). On the local level, pluralism is experienced in day to day reality in multi-ethnic regions in Dagestan (Matsuzato and Ibragimov, 2005), Kabardino-Balkaria (Yemelianova, 2005), Samtskhe-Javakheti or Kvemo Kartli (Wheatley, 2009), where ethnic and religious categories are used in everyday life. So, one can say that pluralism is in fact an 'endemic condition of the Caucasus', even if this postulate can only be the start of the research and not its result. The question now is how the people in the Caucasus effectively deal with the pluralism and make sense of it. This is the main question of this volume.

'One' Caucasus

This volume includes contributions that touch both sides of Great Caucasus, that is, two regions often considered as being two distinct entities. Thomas de Waal writes that the 'South Caucasus presents a paradox in that it can be plausibly described both as a region and as not a region' (2012, p.1709). Could this be said for the whole Caucasus?

The argument that the North and the South Caucasus are two different entities is completely understandable: the 'Greater Caucasus' mountain range appears like a 1,100 kilometre long and 160 kilometre wide stone wall extending from the Caspian Sea between Baku and Derbent to the Black Sea between Sochi and Sokhumi. Certainly, there are a few openings, like those along the Black Sea or the Caspian coastline, along the Georgian Military Road from Vladikavkaz to Tbilisi, through the Terek Valley and the Jvari Pass, along the Transcaucasian Highway (Transkam) from Alagir to Tskhinvali through the Roki Tunnel, rarely used passes like the Ossetian Military Road from Kutaisi to Alagir over Mamison Pass, and some other minor passes that locals might be able to show the interested adventurer. But still, the Greater Caucasus gives the impression of a 5,000 metre high wall separating the north (ciscaucasus) and the south (transcaucasus).

De Waal sees the South Caucasus as a distinct region delimited by geography, some 'shared culture', and economics. He writes that the 'the mountains make the distinction between the North and South Caucasus much sharper than that between, for example, European and Asian Russia' (2012, pp.1710–12). There are many understandable reasons to be found in the historic development and contemporary state of the South Caucasus to conceive of it as an interconnected and able to be seized region. But we do not want to put these these two regions, the north and the south, into opposition with each other.

Richard Sakwa does not speak of one Caucasus, but of 'Caucasian Regionalisms' (Sakwa, 2011) that define the Caucasus as 'part of several superimposed regions, each with its own intraregional dynamics and extra-regional concerns, and in which political projects collide' (2011, p.467). He sees four different levels of regions. The first is the so-called 'micro-region', referring to sub-national regions like Chechnya or to Nagorno-Karabakh. The second level is the 'meso-region', that is 'the' Caucasus with its inter-state relations. The 'macro-region' on the third level makes the interdependence of the north and south even clearer: it interrelates the Caucasus with the Caspian Sea, the Black Sea and other post-Soviet states in Eurasia and the Near East. The fourth level refers to the mega-region (Western Europe, post-Soviet Eurasia and the greater Middle East).

Sakwa continues and writes that the Georgian–Russian War (2008) clearly shows that the analytical division of the area into the North and South Caucasus does not reflect the 'ontological truth'. Saying the Caucasus is one region or not is not a question of playing with words; it is a way of apprehending research questions in general. Dynamics on the level of the micro-region have to be studied in relation to the context of the mega-region, that is, the broader geopolitical framework, which makes local dynamics not look like distant and individual developments.

We have two reasons for conceiving the Caucasus in superimposed regions like Sakwa does. First, it is necessary for analytical reasons. Anthropologically informed research, which is more often than not located on the level of the micro-region, needs always to be thought of in relation to, meso- and macro-regional influences. In turn, macro-political studies are of limited use only when they do not consider the local dimension. Conflicts in the Caucasus, for example, are often discussed on the basis of clear-cut borders between states or ethnic groups, but anthropological research reveals the complexity on the level of the micro-region (see, for example, Voell and Khutsishvili, 2013).

Secondly, there is the necessity to think of the Caucasus as superimposed regions to justify the need to bring together scholars working on both 'halves' of the Caucasus. That anthropology often appears to be trapped in the study of the micro-region is also based on the fact that one only knows people working in neighbouring regions superficially and that results are only rarely compared or discussed together. This volume, which assembles papers presented at a conference in November 2011 in Batumi, Georgia (see Preface) with the explicit goal of bringing together researchers working in the North and the South Caucasus should be seen as a contribution to this process. Which is not to say that we have achieved an equal balance between texts focussing on the North and the South. This has numerous reasons, as noted in the Preface.

Tradition and Pluralism

It is difficult to say anything new about 'tradition'. Many have written extensively about this topic (see, for example, Ben-Amos, 1984; Boyer, 1990; Cohen, 1989; Finnegan, 1991; Shils, 1981). But 'tradition' is also one of those words one finds in academic texts that are not (or are no longer) defined. The same could be said about the notion 'identity', for which Rogers Brubaker and Frederick Cooper (2000) showed a wide range of uses – from instrumental to non-instrumental – and concluded that it would be better to drop the word altogether. 'Identity' is overburdened, indefinite and has contradictory significations. Brubaker and Cooper reject the use of 'identity' for the purpose of analysis because many different ideas are connected to it, making the term virtually useless. One could probably say the same for 'tradition'. But why overlook a word that everybody uses constantly? References to tradition are omnipresent in the Caucasus, both in day to day speech and in scholarship. 'Tradition' is often referred to in relation to 'law', 'identity' or 'ethnicity', the latter another over-discussed topic in anthropology.

In post-Soviet states, 'tradition' appears to be crucial in the sciences focussed on culture. There seem to be a constant necessity to carve out what is 'traditional' in one's society in the sense of what is 'genuine'. In the Caucasus, where many territories were and are contested, to have 'tradition' means to have lived in an area for a long time, basically to be 'autochthonous'. In Georgia, for example, 'tradition' is closely related to ethnic identity. During the Georgian national awaking in the nineteenth century, leading writers, scholars and public figures like Ilia Chavchavadze (1837–1907), Alexander Kazbegi (1843–1893) or Vazha-Pshavela (1861–1915) directed their attention to Georgian mountaineers, who were considered to have lived in a very traditional Georgian way for centuries. The people from the mountain regions of Khevsureti or Svaneti provided these leading Georgian intellectuals with 'a glimpse into the past of a historically hardy and enduring Georgian identity' (Jersild, 2002, pp.8–9). Georgian traditional law is considered by historians of law to be one of the most important parts of national legal culture and one of the most significant sources for the study of the history of law. Georgian traditional or customary law, like the 'Law Book of Vakhtang VI' codified by King Vakhtang VI of Kartli (1675–1737), is often presented as the foundation underlying official legal practice in Georgia. Lavrenti Janiashvili (2012, p.5) argues that the core idea behind this approach is to show that Georgia, despite being subject to decades of invasion and foreign rule, managed to uphold a 'traditional core' throughout its turbulent history.

In constructivist approaches to tradition, the usual point of departure is Eric Hobsbawm's 'invented tradition', which he defines as 'a set of practices, normally governed by overtly or tacitly accepted rules and of a ritual or symbolic nature, which seek to inculcate certain values and norms of behaviour by repetition, which automatically implies continuity with the past' (1983, p.1). More concretely, to say that something is 'traditional' – like traditional law, for example – does not mean that it emerged in ancient times but that it is a recent product and an intentional reaction to a contemporary situation. Uses of tradition are, according to Hobsbawm, a phenomenon of modernity. Today's social life in the complex 'modern world' is often structured by reference to tradition and often today's practices acquire an invented continuity with the 'suitable historic past'.

For Franz von Benda-Beckmann et al. (2003), the use of tradition in law is not a form of 'traditionalism', a somehow conservative or fundamentalist return to pristine roots. References to tradition in law are generally made as part of a political struggle for power and in rejection of state legal structures. Consequently, Benda-Beckmann et al. see that the contemporary use of traditional law consists in 'present- and future-oriented strategies for (re)asserting collective identities and for dealing with competing political and economic claims' (2003, p.297). Traditions are in this legal context invented or revitalised to provide justifications for political and economic claims. Leading actors, in actively constructing traditional law, take recourse to tradition in order to create convincing collective identities and communities. By labelling something as 'traditional', a kind of authenticity is created (Bräuchler and Widlok, 2007) through the insertion of the practice described as traditional into a supposedly ancient practice.

An example for this could be the recent controversies over landed property in Upper Svaneti (see Voell, et al., 2014). A part of this region, around the small regional capital of Mestia and the village of Ushguli, was called 'Free Svaneti' because it could maintain a certain political and cultural autonomy from all invaders until it was finally incorporated into the Czarist Russian administration in the 1870s. Law and order was based in this period on lineage structures and traditional law (Gabliani, 1925; Kharadze, 1939). The region, known for its more than two hundred stone towers (*koshki*), was for President Mikheil Saakashvili (2004–2013) a focal point for the development of tourism in Georgia. In a top-down approach directed from the centre in Tbilisi, the government invested massively in the development of a ski resort and invited foreign investors to Mestia. One of them wanted to build a hotel with the help of the regional administration, and bought a piece of land from the local owner. The investor from Canada claimed to have bought the land in accordance with the law. But there were protests from a Svan family, who said that they had used this area as a hayfield for several generations. They claimed that it was part of their traditional legal property, handed down from generation to generation within the family. The conflict, which was accompanied by mutual accusations, arrests of the leading Svan family member, accusations of bribery and the blocking of a road to Svaneti, was widely discussed in the Georgian media. It included aspects of local politics between the opposition (the leader of the Svan family) and the regional government (Saakashvili's Party). In this case, tradition was brought forward by the Svan family in the form Benda-Beckmann et al. (2003) describe. Tradition was used to claim property but also – on another level – in references to a joint Svan tradition that should unite a lineage and the Svans of Mestia, in general to ensure participation in investments and to prevent the reduction of Svaneti to cultural artefacts like the Svan towers.

But is it correct to say that 'tradition' is always only a tool in political struggles? The example from Svaneti shows that this can be the case. But does this mean that tradition is always invented? Hobsbawm himself is not clear: in his text he focuses on those traditions that were constructed over a few years or established in a short period of time, for example on the neo-Gothic architecture of the British Parliament. And, he differentiates between 'invented traditions' and 'custom'. The object and character of tradition is in his perspective on invariance, which is not the case for custom. Custom, Hobsbawm writes, 'cannot afford to be invariant, because even in 'traditional' societies life is not so. Customary and common law still shows this combination of flexibility in substance and formal adherence to precedent' (1983, p.2). This means that taking Hobsbawm to describe the inventedness of tradition, in general is to narrow his approach. Tradition is here a deliberate reconstruction, which creates links to the past and behaviour by repetition, which gives an impression of historic continuity. This is the case for the Svan example in the theoretical approach of Benda-Beckmann et al. (2003). But Hobsbawm's concept of 'custom' – and this is how tradition is often understood, especially in relation to traditional law – is, rather, a process of keeping up some continuity while constantly negotiating with the present.

While for Hobsbawm, tradition is something tangible, created almost solely to be visible, for Barry McDonald (1997), tradition has a 'virtual existence'. Like Anthony Giddens' (1979, p.63) structures, tradition is 'instantiated in social action' (McDonald 1997, p.58). Tradition does not have 'determining action', and its properties can only be described very broadly as, 'any precise description being preserved for its relative expression' (1997, p.58). Tradition, however, has a 'core character'. First, it refers to 'a shared, repeatable activity or complex of activities' and second, it creates among those people who are taking part in activities called traditional or (re)creating tradition some form of 'spiritual/emotional power'. Thirdly, these activities both activate and are activated by this emotional involvement. This emotional component in the bringing to life of activities can be called tradition. It is the link between the past and the future, reproducing traditional activities that reproduce the emotional attachment to them.

Both perspectives, Hobsbawm's and McDonald's, have much in common, but Hobsbawm has a more instrumental view of tradition. Approaches referring to Hobsbawm generally most want to describe social agency in the construction of tradition. McDonald, on the other hand, emphasises some emotional power or, for those who might see this as too esoteric, the importance of the collective performance in producing tradition. Both perspectives appear to be important and useful, depending on what one looks to explain. But one of these perspectives alone only partly reflects the uses of tradition.

In this sense, Voell et al. (2014) show with their research on Svans who have been resettled in lowland Georgia since the end of the 1980s, the instrumental and non-instrumental dimension of traditional law. The above-mentioned approach of Benda-Beckmann et al. (2003) refers to an instrumental use of traditional law to '(re)assert collective identities'. But in order to fully grasp the phenomenon of the contemporary practice of traditional law Voell et al. argue with Brubaker and Cooper. They show that there are not only instrumental uses of identity, but also dimensions of identity better described as 'self-understanding' and 'social location', that is a rather non-instrumental component of identity. Voell et al.'s research shows that the instrumental use of tradition in law is very present. But the multitudes of narratives on traditional law and on ideal type cases that would be mediated using traditional law, but are never realised when the opportunity appears reveals another dimension of traditional law, where law is used more broadly as 'one's sense of who one is'.

In Free Svaneti, the solidarity of the Svan lineages in concordance with traditional law was sealed with an oath of unity. Oaths were an important instrument in Svan legal practice. For example, one swore on an icon of a saint that a particular statement in a mediation process was the complete truth or that one would honour the agreements made during a meeting. The annual oath of unity in Free Svaneti made in the tenth century church of St Kvirike near Kala was such a binding promise. Today these oaths of unity continue to be sworn in some of the Svan villages of lowland Kvemo Kartli. The Svans were resettled to the multi-ethnic south of Georgia because many villages in Svaneti had been destroyed in massive snowfalls in the late 1980s. Though similar in form to the oath of unity in Free Svaneti, today's vow on an icon does not bind anyone to anything anymore. This important part of Svan traditional law is not used by political actors in the villages to impose some form of order. Instead, it is more like a commemoration of Svan 'traditions'. The oath here is not a politically binding oath of unity but rather an 'oath of memory' (Voell, 2013).

With McDonald's 'emotional power' in the production of tradition and 'one's sense of who one is', Brubaker and Cooper can help to explain another dimension of traditional law. The Caucasus has a long history of anthropological research by local specialists (see Mühlfried and Sokolovskiy, 2011). These local scholars mostly conducted their research in their own country, that is, they were more often than not studying their own culture. Many anthropologists do so, but these local scholars, even today in post-Soviet times are – simply speaking – active participants in constructing the very 'traditions' that they (and foreign scholars) are studying. There is a greater tendency to see ethnicity as something real, than to see it as something which is being constructed.

Local researchers are thus often labelled 'primordialists' and 'essentialists'. This has a variety of consequences. Many Western scholars simply ignore their local colleagues, or simply 'use' them for organising their research on the ground. Caucasian scholars with long experiences in the field and vital knowledge are in this case demoted to field assistants. Local concepts of tradition can be understood both from an instrumental and non-instrumental point of view. On the one hand, local researchers can take part in political struggles to enforce the right of a group to (re)settle a territory (see, for example, the 'war of memories', Shnirelman, 2003). Here, researchers apply their research to underline the truth of the claims in question. On the other hand, less political, but still important, many colleagues have been personally and emotionally involved in post-Soviet national movements; they often took part in the process of carving out national/regional traits in post-Soviet dissolution processes. Working here on tradition, means contributing to a form of local identity which in Brubaker and Cooper's terms is better described as 'social location'.

The participants in the Batumi conference differed strongly about concepts such as 'mentality' and 'ethno-psychology', which some colleagues considered a vital explanatory basis for understanding the contemporary practice of – for example – blood feud in the Caucasus. These discussions made us understand better some profound divergences between regional scientific traditions. The 'Western' team members had to learn that their social science approach had no priority over the more historical science tradition of local colleagues. In a certain way, local scholarship echoes the Boasian consideration of the impact of history, which cannot be overcome easily. The Western and the more so-called 'modern' approach is, in fact, the Malinowskian neglect of history and the inclination to explain historically grown collective traditions with their functional utility. This confrontation of these two points of view became an important part of the conference. We do not want to overcome or silence the difference, but consider it an important result of our 'intercultural' encounter (in this case between two scientific 'cultures').[1]

Pluralisms in the Caucasus

To claim that something is plural or that legal pluralism can be found in the Caucasus does mean that two or more legal systems might be present in the same social field (Merry, 1988). Legal pluralism is not a theory but an acknowledgement of a perspective that accepts the simultaneous relevance of more than one legal system. And in order to grasp this 'complexity', in this volume, we want to speak of *traditional pluralism* and *pluralism of traditions*.

With *traditional pluralism* we refer to a diachronic perspective, the historical 'fact' of pluralism in the Caucasus, that is, the superimposition of *adat* and *sharia* alongside state legal systems in history. In his historical essay, **Sergey Arutiunov** draws a picture of the importance of, and attachment to, the state by the populations of the Caucasus, caught since centuries between northern Eurasia, Asia Minor and Iran. In the Georgian Golden Age, even though the Georgian kings and queens were respected by a large part of the population, there was no real identification with the kingdom. The people on the local level continued to be organised in small feudal structures. This situation only changed superficially after the Caucasus was integrated into the Russian Empire. In the north, *adat* and *sharia* continued to be relevant, despite strong state structures. In the south, the local educated aristocrats identified with Czarist Russia but not the large part of the population. According to Arutiunov, Armenia was always different, however, and he describes it as 'the least Caucasian state' where the rule of state law was more present than elsewhere. After the fall of the Soviet Union the situation remains the same. The new Islamic movements in the North Caucasus brought new power and importance to Islamic law, which he qualifies, is more an artificial proto-*sharia.* Arutiunov concludes that there always was some form of ambiguity towards the state in the Caucasus: which will probably not change in the years to come.

Yuri Karpov describes the construction of nations in the northern Caucasus in early Soviet times. During the 1920s–30s, the (re)construction of administrative borders in the region was a central political issue. For the Bolsheviks inter-ethnic relations were part of the class struggle, and justice for the oppressed peoples of the Caucasus was a priority. But the relations between the local groups were different than perceived from the centre, and the borders drawn by the Soviet rulers different from local realities. Moreover, not all 'nations' were equally supported, like the Ossetians, who agitated to see their homeland unified in vain. From the mid-1930s a new trend appeared in the political reconfiguration of the Caucasus. Together with industrialisation and forced collectivisation, the emphasis changed

1 This interpretation is based on a conversation with Mark Münzel, former director of the Department of Cultural and Social Anthropology of the Philipps-Universität Marburg.

again and nationalities lost importance as the importance of regional autonomy increased. This policy was part of a movement that would result in the creation of a 'Soviet people' for whom ethnicity was no longer important. Karpov concludes by arguing that politics in the contemporary Russian Federation show parallels to those of the Soviet Union in the 1920s–30s.

Svan traditional law is often discussed in historical accounts of the Caucasus. But only rarely have researchers investigated the importance of traditional law during Soviet times and after. **Natia Jalabadze** and **Lavrenti Janiashvili** address this *desideratum* based on oral accounts by people who used to practice traditional law in Soviet Georgia and on specialised literature unknown outside Georgia. The authors show that traditional law continued to be relevant at the local level for so-called 'private cases' and that the Soviet administration, to a certain extent, even supported local legal practice. In a next step, the authors present their own research on the contemporary practice of Svan traditional law. Moreover, they show how traditional law is used in Kvemo Kartli in the Georgian lowlands. They describe how – like in Soviet times – traditional law is relevant at the local level. Jalabadze and Janiashvili use the example of blood feud, which, despite its importance in narratives and ideal-type representations, remains only a very small, marginal phenomenon today.

Makka Albogachieva writes about blood feud in the Republic of Ingushetia, especially about the differences between blood feud in traditional (*adat*) and religious law (*sharia*). Both legal conceptions continue to be relevant alongside state regulations even today. Blood feud as a direct reaction to murder is not simply the killing of the culprit. It has to be understood within the local system of values and the need to find a new balance. Since revenge leads to an equal and direct response, a 'counter-revenge', the feuds can continue infinitely. Albogachieva argues that this infinity of feuds might be conceived as a social norm. Most interestingly, in *adat* and *sharia*, blood feud has different consequences. Whereas in *adat*, revenge entails a collective responsibility of the extended family to respond to the initial murder, in *sharia* a more limited responsibility can be found, which is confined to individuals or a nuclear family. Albogachieva shows that legal pluralism is not only the coexistence of formal (state) and informal legal practice but of multiple non-state legal frameworks.

With *pluralism of traditions* we adopt, in turn, a synchronic perspective of contemporary pluralism as 'fact'. Whereas *traditional pluralism* describes the emergence of today's social field, with *pluralism of traditions* we want to highlight how people act in the plural social field. But with 'pluralism' we do not mean that we have only side by side systems or super-positioning of easily separable legal systems. In practice, legal concepts blur, they might be used simultaneously and local populations do not make the same distinctions that researchers do.

Ekatarina Kapustina describes how municipal elections reflect the power relations in a contemporary highland village in the Republic of Dagestan. The municipal elections – although inscribed in a wider federal context – are usually a very local procedure highly affected by family and kin relations. In the first part of her text, Kapustina shows how elections might be manipulated. It is common to buy votes or invite people, who do not live in the village to quickly register for the election. One could presume that in the Dagestani highland villages, religious authorities and imams especially, are important actors in elections. But Kapustina shows that their role should not be overestimated, especially if the imam is not a local, which is a frequent phenomenon in the highlands. In the second part of her text, Kapustina depicts how the traditional council of elders counterbalances arbitrary influences on the election process (like vote buying, registering of new villagers, etc.). As the municipal election is potentially harmful to the village community, the role of the council is to control eventual problems. To do so, they arrange informal pre-elections in which the village selects the candidates before the official vote.

Evgenia Zakharova describes an important facet of urban life in Tbilisi. In various parts of the city, neighbourhood communities of young men (*birzha*) are a prominent sub-culture until today. Before the Georgian 'Rose Revolution' (2003), the *birzha* were an independent social system with their own legal framework and codes of conduct, reflected in conceptions of honour. Their *kanonieri kurdi* (thief-in-law) culture was rooted in the neighbourhood community. But the situation changed with the election of Mikheil Saakashvili in 2004. His reforms of the police and the administration also included massive actions against the thieves-in-law, which pushed them out of public life. Zakharova notes that while previously *kanonieri kurdi* culture was the main point of reference for the *birzha*, after the Saakashvili reforms, a shift took place to conceptions of honour and manliness. But Zakharova also shows the interrelation of politics and neighbourhood communities in Tbilisi. There are important interrelations between individual political careers and the urban street culture or the brotherhood networks dominating specific neighbourhood communities. The latter support the political aspirations of young politicians and help organise political rallies. The *birzha* are still relevant in this context today. While the *kanonieri kurdi* ideology no longer appears to be very important for the *birzha*, the politicians from these neighbourhood communities continue to have some influence on them.

Conceptions of honour underlay many different forms of relationships in Georgia, but most often it is the male dimension of honour that attracts attention. **Elke Kamm** examines the female aspect of honour in family relations and its interrelation to the phenomena of bride kidnapping and virginity. Kamm opens her text by asking what is considered to be proper conduct for women and then goes on to describe the importance of honour in bride kidnapping. When a woman is kidnapped, her family loses control over her status as a virgin and over her honour. This can result in the family agreeing to a marriage they would otherwise have been against. Kamm also describes 'voluntary' bride kidnappings in which women agree to be kidnapped so as to force their parents to accept their choice of partner. The result is the same in both cases: the simple possibility that the honour of the woman was affected – and with it the honour of the entire family – makes the parents agree to a relationship. Kamm convincingly shows how bride kidnapping, female honour and virginity before marriage remain important issues in Georgia, from its discussion in talk shows to the widespread desire for medical certificates of virginity.

Stéphane Voell takes the example of a fatal car accident in a small town in southern Georgia to demonstrate how informal mechanisms of justice regulate the relationship between the Svan families involved, parallel to the state legal procedure. The possibility of an act of revenge was there; elders were even sent to mediation. The problem for Voell was that he could not find a 'functioning' Svan traditional law but only processes with elements of it. Voell describes the car accident as a 'moral breakdown' (Zigon, 2011); an intense situation in which concepts of morality rise to the surface, in this case a deep feeling of injustice. For Voell, the accident was not followed by a conflict resolution process based in traditional law. The Svans voiced their own conceptions of morality, which did not conform to state juridical process. The events that took place beside the official trial were thus processes to restore a kind of moral balance based on a Svan legal imaginary.

Besides the ideas of traditional pluralism and pluralism of tradition, namely the acknowledgement of the historic and contemporary presence of multitudes of tradition, a third dimension has to be added, namely, an *imagined traditional pluralism*, that is reconstructions or imaginaries of a history of pluralism. With this we mean, for example, the Soviet idea of the 'friendship of peoples', the staged peaceful living side by side of nations, ethnic groups, religions, cultures and traditions. Today, people recreate the good old times as a time of peaceful coexistence between groups that today are in conflict, as described by Jalabadze and Janiashvili. In Azerbaijan this peaceful coexistence is enacted at the highest political levels even today (Abbassov, 2013). Even if the so-called 'fifth column' of the Soviet passport is no longer in the Azerbaijani document, ethnic categories continue to be used in administration (in birth certificates) and in public life. Members of the government, but also scientists 'saved' the importance of ethnic relations and perpetuate the Soviet 'friendship of peoples' as the 'tolerance of the Azerbaijani people', in which non-Azerbaijani appear to be mere guests in the Azerbaijani state.

The Plurality of State Practices in the Caucasus

In this edited volume, we remain for the most part within the domain of political anthropology. This is not the place to engage in lengthy debates over the details of this sub-discipline of anthropology and it has been better done elsewhere (for example Aretxaga, 2003; Sharma and Gupta, 2006; Lewellen, 2003) so we will only present some theoretical points that frame our approach. The main focus of contemporary political anthropology is state and politics – however vaguely defined these notions are. Aradhana Sharma and Akhil Gupta (2006) even argue that we should speak of an anthropology of the state as a sub-discipline of political anthropology (2006) while others doubted if it makes sense at all to speak about an anthropology of politics at all because everything is somehow political (Herzfeld, 1997).

The Caucasus, as demonstrated in the first part of this introduction, is a region defined more through its plurality than in its unity. The chapters included in this volume, document, however, that the state has in this complex configuration a striking position. Here, the fact that the whole Caucasus shares seventy years of a common Soviet rule. Even though this period is typically referred to in terms of an ‘occupation’ or ‘colonisation’, these seventy years were the most peaceful ever in the history of the region and it is also remembered as such.

It may thus seem surprising how persistent are the local perceptions of state obligations or omnipresent state power. Although more than twenty years have passed, with new flags and new anthems, local thinking about the state as an actor capable of (but unwilling to) changing the situation persists. Most interestingly, as Iwona Kaliszewska shows in this volume, references to the ‘good old’ socialist past are even to be found in the narratives of Islamic reformers in Dagestan, the Salafis. More often than not they praise the communist times – which they barely experienced – for the supposed unity of the people and the common goal of society that today can only be achieved through Islamic brotherhood and solidarity.

This is not to say that local forms of governance or perceptions and state practices in the Caucasus are all shaped by the USSR past. It would be naïve to look for too much continuity and interpret all local state perceptions or practices in reference to the Soviet experience. The ‘micro-region’ Caucasus cannot be separated from the ‘macro-region’ Caucasus: the geopolitical situation has changed considerably, power relations altered and international actors have entered the stage, to list but a few changes that affect both thinking about the state and state officials’ actions. There are a plurality of ways in which the state is played out in the Caucasus and a plurality of ways in which state practices are experienced in the everyday lives of the region’s inhabitants. We address but some of them here.

One way of conceptualising the interrelationship of the people with ‘their’ state is the concept of citizenship, recently introduced in the anthropology of the Caucasus by Lale Yalçın-Heckmann (2012) or Florian Mühlfried (2014). They introduced the concept of citizenship as a formal category of belonging in an attempt to find a new approach to grasping the relevance of the state for the local population, especially in the South Caucasus. Mühlfried explores citizenship in the eastern Georgian region of Tusheti among shepherd nomads wandering between the highlands and the lowlands. Citizenship refers here to ‘notions of belonging’ and describes what kind of relationship one has to the state and how the state is assuming its responsibilities. Citizenship is a ‘membership category’, of both fate and potential.

Citizenship in the North Caucasus is possibly even more complex. Many of the inhabitants of the region (especially in its eastern part) do not feel themselves to be part of the ‘nation’, even if the latter is defined in political and not ethnic terms as *rossiane* (a term used to describe all inhabitants of the Russian Federation) and not *russkie* ('ethnic' Russians). Ethnic movements fighting or striving for local autonomy in the 1990s lost their importance with the rise of Islamic ideals. Suddenly, a sense of belonging to Muslim community became more important than belonging to a particular ethnic group and even more to the vaguely defined notion of *rossiane*. In the South Caucasus the nation-state link seems unbreakable, at least for the 'titular' ethnic groups. National narratives, histories, traditions and 'old–new' towns are being constructed. Therefore, regardless of the real power national governments have, the essentialised state is hardly questioned or threatened and the meta- and social-capital (Bourdieu, 1999) it holds can hardly be ignored.

In anthropological thought the state has been seen as an 'idea' (Abrams, 1988), a 'discourse' (Mitchell, 1991), a 'fetish' (Taussig, 1992) or a 'mask' disguising political practice (Abrams, 1988), to list but a few conceptualisations. The state and its workings have been a point of departure and an object of analysis for many anthropologists exploring how the state can be played out in everyday practices, discourses, rituals and celebrations, encounters with bureaucrats, monuments, spatial arrangements or even in resistance and irony (Herzfeld, 1997).

Anthropological approaches to the state focus specifically on its cultural construction. They investigate how people perceive the state and how the state manifests itself in their lives (Sharma and Gupta, 2006). While most anthropologists seem to share the assumption about the cultural constituent of state actions, the question arises regarding how to approach the state and state practices. How to research them; what to focus on? One important question that Begona Aretxaga (2003) suggests asking is how the state becomes the social subject in everyday life. We should explore daily representations, discourses, the desires of state officials and fantasies to examine the link between an elusive state form and the dynamics of peoples and movements. Sharma and Gupta (2006) call for examining the relations between daily practices and their representations. Abrams (1988) is interested in relation between the state system and the state idea while Krohn-Hansen and Nustad (2005) suggest looking at social relations and symbolic imaginings.

There has been a considerable critique of the naturalisation of the state and the reification of the state as an 'it', as an agent with a life of its own, capable of acting upon society (namely Abrams, 1988; Mitchell, 1999; Hansen and Stepputat, 2001; Sharma and Gupta, 2006; Taussig, 1997). We can speak of a state as a fiction, and we can even agree that the state is a kind of a collective illusion, though a powerful one, holding the mystifying power exemplified by media in TV series featuring state agents and secret service activities (Aretxaga, 2003, p.401). But what we should also take into account is that despite all the academic deconstruction, the state is usually perceived by the people as a unified entity, as a single and compact actor who should provide for, care and deliver and who is held responsible for misery and violence. 'If a state acts and appears as having a life on its own then we are in the presence of a fetish and must ask for the powerful ways in which this fetish works' (Aretxaga, 2003, p.401 after Nelson, 1999; Taussig, 1992, 1997).

Consequently, the topic of the role and the perception of the state in Caucasus pluralisms is one of how the different states in the Caucasus become the social subject in everyday life (Aretxaga, 2003). How the state is experienced south and north of the Great Caucasus is very different. 'The state is here' – this is the message we receive from the new glass-fronted police stations and ministries in Georgia, while in the North Caucasus the message is closer to 'Beware – keep off the state.' Here these buildings are blockhouses secured with high fences and sandbags, gun barrels sticking out from behind of them. State officials travel in armoured cars with private guards or security forces in black masks.

One way in which state is played out in the Caucasus is certainly through violence and the constant production of insecurity. States all over the world can no longer claim full monopoly over violence (though they may pretend to), being challenged by militants and other groups involved in anti-state violence. Nevertheless, state violence is still comparably greater in scope than terrorism or other kinds of anti-state activities (Sluka, Chomsky and Price, 2002). 'The state is like a sideshow and has two faces: one legitimate, the other criminal, corrupt and murderous; one rational, the other irrational and magical', writes Diane Nelson (2004, p.135). In the North Caucasus, the legitimate face is pale and distant, embodied in Putin's promises and dealings. The violent face is more tangible and visible, an excess of violent practices, of 'anti–terrorist operations' and 'security controls'. They are perceived by most inhabitants of the region as unjustified and unfair activities conducted for the sake of individual profit. The violent face of the state overlaps with the legitimate one in bureaucratic dealings. While recourse to informal practices is prolific, paperwork is done, procedures followed, law is executed and court sessions conducted – an image of order is sustained.

Iwona Kaliszewska asks how the people in Dagestan experience state practices in times of a 'war against terrorism'. Why do the same people who think of the state as a source of violence and support the introduction of the *sharia*, hang Vladimir Putin's poster from the wall and praise the old times in the USSR? In peripheral and conflict-prone places like Dagestan, the people's experience of the state can be conceptualised in terms of simultaneous lack and simultaneous excess of the state. On the one hand, the state is experienced as a source of violence and local state practices are very often silently or openly resisted with the help of the *sharia*. On the other hand, regulatory state practices are longed for and the state is still invested with some hope. Lack of the state is made up for, and an excess disdained and sometimes resisted.

Rail Safiyev reveals the informal dealings of the state representatives in his narrative of the case of Agil Khalid, a journalist attacked by 'some criminals' in Baku. The evidence – a chance video taken on the spot featuring state officials instead of the alleged 'simple criminals' turned out not to aid but to obstruct the course of the investigation. The latter was dominated by faked evidence fabricated by state officials soon after the incident. The whole process of investigation took place 'according to the law' – at least from the outside. An image of order was being carefully produced and transmitted. Informality was inscribed in mundane activities and social practices, compliant, as Rail Safiyev shows, with a neopatrimonial form of rule. 'Neopatrimonialism constitutes a superstructure of authoritarian domination whereas informality ties citizens into this superstructure', writes Safiyev. The practice of faking evidence in Azerbaijan as shown in Safiyev's chapter or extracting testimonies through torture in Chechnya (Raubisko, 2011) or Dagestan (Kaliszewska in this volume) are everyday bureaucratic practices in the region. They are inscribed in neopatrimonial systems of dependencies which state officials are forced to participate in if they do not want to lose their jobs.

The first post-Soviet elections in Armenia were a festive event. **Levon Abrahamian** and **Gayane Shagoyan** describe them as being part of a performative 'carnival' civil society that emerged during the Karabakh Movement in 1988. These first elections in Armenia were more or less free and democratic, but from election to election the process became less free and fair. From the mid-1990s on, there were decreasing possibilities to register properly to vote, and falsifications in election processes became institutionalised. In November 2005, a referendum was held in which President Robert Kocharian (1998–2008) asked for consent for constitutional reforms. The official results, which recalled Soviet-era elections, were so improbable that there were discussions in the population not about the falsification as such but about a possible message the president intended to express with such unbelievable results. On the local level, the population is well aware that so-called 'open elections' are illegal, and not free and fair. Abrahamian and Shagoyan were told that there is nothing the villagers could do because the candidates and the voters were all related to each other.

Numerous anthropologists and social scientists have engaged in debates over the state and its nature, arguing for the decline of the modern state, in particular the nation-state (Ong, 1999; Tsing, 2000). Neoliberal, transnational corporations challenge state borders and economies, and transnational flows of migrants and refugees with a tapestry of identities and loyalties. They challenge national identities once considered eternal. National governments are no longer capable of controlling or steering their economies, though they may pretend to be doing so especially in times of economic growth. Despite the seemingly inevitable decline or demise of the nation-state 'the desire for statehood continues to be intense in many parts of the world despite or perhaps because of the hollowed-out character of the state' (Arexaga, 2003, p.394). And it is not only because of the state's meta-capital (Bourdieu, 1999), its power to define and its ability to rule over different forms of power, but also globalization that fuels the desire for statehood as a guarantor of group identity and a sense of belonging to both a place and an ethnic group (see Aretxaga, 2003).

The interrelationship between transnational actors and local states in the Caucasus is described by **Elizabeth Cullen Dunn** and **Austin Cowley** using the example of humanitarian aid in Georgia after the Georgian–Russian War of August 2008. Western donors provided Georgia with money for post-war reconstruction, but ninety percent of the money was invested in 'securitising' the country. Is it possible that the main goal of the so called humanitarian intervention was not the provision of services for the direct victims of the conflict but the transformation of the nation-state? Dunn and Cowley argue that instead of providing for citizens or even promoting democracy, humanitarian funding has been used by the Georgian government to consolidate authoritarian power. This raises the question of how it reshaped the citizen-state relationship and what kinds of new dependencies and power relations emerged.

International aid in times of crisis is not the only kind of support provided by Western donors to the South Caucasus. Georgia, Armenia and Azerbaijan were recipients of different kinds of aid throughout the last two decades, from projects promoting democracy and supporting the building of a civil society to development projects intended to support so called 'community-based tourism' (CBT). **Gayane Shagoyan** discusses tourism projects in northeastern Armenia and sheds light on the influence of CBT on traditional relations in the villages, or, in other words, how tourism leads to an adaptation of local traditions. Tourism became, in the post-Soviet period, an indicator of a country's economic growth and with it the degree of integration into the Western world. CBT, however, is considered to be a soft tourism, which is adapted to local circumstances and takes regional traditions into consideration. Shagoyan shows that in relation to traditional configurations in the villages, CBT projects in her field of study are not significantly different from other forms of commercial tourism.

Corruption is one of the most popular issues when discussing the region's problems. How can we approach corruption and at the same time avoid eurocentric, simplistic treatments of it as a dysfunction or a failure of the state? **Barbara Christophe** argues against the prevailing image of failed states using the example of Georgia under President Eduard Shevardnadze (1995–2003). She describes how corruption, which is often brought forward as an indicator of the weakness of the state, may be seen as the opposite, as a tool of the Georgian government to contribute to the stabilisation of the state. Christophe shows how corruption was institutionalised and how state officials more or less chose by whom they could be bribed. Corruption was introduced to create insecurity: it installed a legal framework which nobody could follow. To do business in Georgia necessitated transgressing the rules, and these infractions had to be bought. Corruption was therefore installed through law on purpose and is not, as Christophe underlines, a specifically Georgian cultural trait. Over the years, bribery has become for all parts of society a social process that is difficult to escape. If one did not want to play the game, the risk was even to be publically accused as corrupt. Corruption is for Christophe not a cultural practice but a cultural norm, like honour, a morally justified pattern of behaviour.

While Shevardnadze's times were marked by 'corruption', regardless what was understood by it, Saakashvili's times were those of 'success'. It is instructive to take a closer look at what was popularly labelled as 'success'. **Lili Di Puppo** suggests looking at 'success' as an 'interpretation' in order to study the mechanisms through which the Georgian government engaged in the production of an image of successful reforms, especially anti-corruption reforms. After the Rose Revolution in Georgia in 2003, President Mikheil Saakashvili (2004–2013) proceeded to make radical changes in the state administration and the institutions of law enforcement. For many, Georgia became a model for successfully overcoming post-Soviet legacies. Di Puppo reviews this period and analyses the transformation from a corrupt to an uncorrupted state. She looks behind Saakashvili's anti-corruption policies and asks how the Georgian government managed to write this 'narrative of success'. She starts from the point that anti-corruption policies are not neutral activities but are a form of constructed narrative. In other words, success is not an objective state, but an interpretation. For Saakashvili it was important that the changes were implemented rapidly and visibly. He chose radical reforms rather than a long-term strategy. Saakashvili's aim was, according to Di Puppo, to emancipate the new government from the post-Soviet transition towards a neoliberal and investor-friendly state. Di Puppo describes how the government created this narrative of success and the problems related to it. An interesting example is the state audit institution, 'Chamber of Control'. During the presidency of Eduard Shevardnaze the chamber produced narratives of corruption in order to generate bribes from people accused of corruption and then withdrew the charges. But under Saakashvili the chamber was a central part of the anti-corruption campaign against practices of which the institution was itself an important part.

Order and Caucasian Pluralisms

All the contributions to this volume touch upon law, legal pluralism and 'politics'. Consequently, they all focus on conceptions of order. Order may refer to the existence of common rules and to conceptions of predictability and security. Order can also mean the absence or the restriction of violence. Order can be understood objectively, as a quality of a society, or subjectively, as an image of how order has to be (Benda-Beckmann and Pirie, 2007). This volume discusses how conceptions of order are enforced, used, followed and staged in social networks and legal practice.

The order that the state and its legal institutions prescribe, however, is far from clear. State law has changed frequently since 1990, and may still be confronted by legal residues from Soviet times. Transnational actors or non-governmental organisations may enforce their own procedures, backed by their financial or political power. Religious groups may, more or less successfully, strive to impose their own conceptions of legal order. Especially in the Caucasian highlands, a legal practice can be found which is often staged as traditional, supposedly handed down from 'ancient times'.

All of these legal conceptions are used in a historically defined social field, often in relation to political interests. People may arbitrarily opt for one law or another, mix them, create something new or simply ignore the law and act as they want to. In most cases, however, people are not free to make their own choices, and a concrete legal framework is forced upon them by existing power relations.

References

Abbasov, I., 2013. From 'Friendship of Peoples' to a Discourse of 'Tolerance': Constructing Ethnic Boundaries in Post-Soviet Azerbaijan. In: S. Voell, and K. Khutsishvili, eds, 2013. *Caucasus, Conflict, Culture: Anthropological Perspectives on Times of Crisis.* Marburg: Curupira. pp.147–68.

Abrams, P., 1988. Notes on the Difficulty of Studying the State. *Journal of Historical Sociology*, 1, pp.58–89.

Aretxaga, B., 2003. Maddening States. *Annual Review of Anthropology*, 32, pp.393–410.

Beissinger, M. R. and Young, M. C., eds, 2001. *Beyond State Crisis? Post-colonial Africa and Post-Soviet Eurasia in Comparative Perspective.* Washington: Woodrow Wilson Center Press.

Ben-Amos, D., 1984. The Seven Strands of Tradition: Varieties in its Meaning in American Folklore Scholarship. *Journal of Folklore Research*, 21, pp.97–131.

Benda-Beckmann, F., 1988. Comment on Merry. *Law and Society Review*, 22, pp.897–901.

Benda-Beckmann, F., 1994. Rechtspluralismus: Analytische Begriffsbildung oder politisch-ideologisches Programm? *Zeitschrift für Ethnologie*, 119(1), pp.1–16.

Benda-Beckmann, F., Benda-Beckmann K., Eckert J., Pirie F. and Turner, B., 2003. Vitality and Revitalisation of Tradition in Law: Going Back into the Past or Future-oriented Development? *Max Planck Institute for Social Anthropology Report*, 2002–2003, pp.129–65.

Benda-Beckmann, K. and Pirie, F., eds, 2007. *Order and Disorder: Anthropological Perspectives*. New York and Oxford: Berghahn.

Bourdieu, P., 1999. Rethinking the State: Genesis and Structure of the Bureaucratic Field. In: G. Steinmetz, ed., 1999. *State/Culture: State Formation after the Cultural Turn.* Ithaca: Cornell University Press. pp.53–72.

Boyer, P., 1990. *Tradition as Truth and Communication: A Cognitive Description of Traditional Discourse.* Cambridge: Cambridge University Press.

Bräuchler, B. and Widlok, T., 2007. Die Revitalisierung von Tradition: Im (Ver-) Handlungsfeld zwischen staatlichem und lokalem Recht. *Zeitschrift für Ethnologie*, 132, 1, pp.5–14.

Broers, L., 2009. 'David and Goliath' and 'Georgians in the Kremlin': A Post-colonial Perspective on Conflict in Post–Soviet Georgia. *Central Asian Survey*, 28(2), pp.99–118.

Brubaker, R. and Cooper, F., 2000. Beyond 'Identity'. *Theory and Society*, 29(1), pp.1–47.

Cohen, D. W., 1989. The Undefining of Oral Tradition. *Ethnohistory*, 36, pp.9–18.

Comaroff, J. L. and Comaroff, J., 2006. Law and Disorder in the Postcolony: An Introduction. In: J. Comaroff and Comaroff, J. L. eds, 2006. *Law and Disorder in the Postcolony*. Chicago and London: The University of Chicago Press. pp.1–56.

Comrie, B., 2008. Linguistic Diversity in the Caucasus. *Annual Review of Anthropology*, 37, pp.131–43.

De Waal, T., 2012. A Broken Region: The Persistent Failure of Integration Projects in the South Caucasus. *Europe-Asia Studies*, 64(9), pp.1709–23.

Dirr, A., 1925. Aus dem Gewohnheitsrecht der kaukasischen Bergvölker. *Zeitschrift für vergleichende Rechtswissenschaft*, 41, 1–2, pp.1–128.

Engle, M. S., 1988. Legal Pluralism. *Law and Society Review*, 22(5), pp.869–901.

Finnegan, R., 1991. Tradition, but What Tradition, and Tradition for Whom? *Oral Tradition*, 6, pp.104–125.

Gabliani, E., 1925. *Dzveli da akhali svaneti* [Old and New Svaneti]. Tbilisi: S.S.S.R. Sakhelmtsipo Gamomtsemloba.

Giddens, A., 1979. *Central Problems in Social Theory.* London: Macmillan.

Grant, B. and Yalçın-Heckmann, L., 2007. Introduction. In: B. Grant and L. Yalçın-Heckmann, L. eds, 2007. *Caucasus Paradigms: Anthropologies, Histories and the Making of a World Area.* Berlin: Lit., pp.1–19.

Griffiths, J., 1986. What is Legal Pluralism? *Journal of Legal Pluralism and Unofficial Law*, 24, pp.1–50.

Günther, A. H., 1931. Zusammenstöße zwischen Gesetz und Gewohnheitsrecht im Kaukasus. *Zeitschrift für vergleichende Rechtswissenschaft*, 46, pp.317–59.

Hansen, T. B. and Stepputat, F., 2001. *States of Imagination: Ethnographic Explorations of the Postcolonial State.* Durham and London: Duke University Press.

Herzfeld, M., 1997. *Cultural Intimacy: Social Poetics in the Nation-State.* New York: Routledge.

Hirsch, F., 2005. *Empire of Nations: Ethnographic Knowledge and the Making of the Soviet Union.* Ithaca: Cornell University Press.

Hobsbawm, E., 1983. Introduction: The Invention of Tradition. In: E. Hobsbawm and T. Ranger, eds, 1983. *The Invention of Tradition.* Cambridge: Cambridge University Press, pp.1–14.

Janiashvili, L., 2012. Traditional Law in Soviet Times. *Caucasus Analytical Digest*, 42, pp.5–7.

Jersild, A., 2002. *Orientalism and Empire: North Caucasus Mountain People and the Georgian Frontier, 1845–1917.* Montreal: McGill-Queen's University Press.

Kharadze, R., 1939. *Didi ojakhis gardmonashtebi svanetshi* [The Survival of Extended Families in Svaneti]. Tbilisi: SSRK Metsnierebata Akademiis Sakartvelos Pilialis Gamomtsemloba.

Kovalevsky, M., 1886. *Sovremenniy obichay i dryevniy zakon: obichnoye pravo Osetin Vistoriko-sravnitelnom Osveshtenii* [Contemporary Customs and Ancient Laws: Customary Law of Ossetians in Historical and Comparative Perspective], 2 vols. Moscow: Gatzuk.

Krohn-Hansen, C. and Nustad, K. G., 2005. *State Formation: Anthropological Perspectives.* London: Pluto Press.

Ladyshenskij, A. M., 1930. Zur Erforschung der Rechtsgewohnheiten der Bergvölker des Kaukasus. *Zeitschrift für Ethnologie* 62, pp.227–44.
Lewellen, T. C., 2003. *Political Anthropology: An Introduction.* Westport: Praeger.
Luzbetak, L. J., 1951. *Marriage and the Family in Caucasus: A Contribution to the Study on North Caucasian Ethnology and Customary Law*. Vienna: St. Gabriel Mission Press.
Matsuzato, K. and Ibragimov, M. R., 2005. Islamic Politics at the Sub-regional Level in Dagestan: Tariqa Brotherhoods, Ethnicities, Localism and the Spiritual Bond. *Europe-Asia Studies*, 57, 5, pp.753–79.
McDonald, B., 1997. Tradition as Personal Relationship. *The Journal of American Folklore*, 110, pp.47–67.
Mitchell, T., 1991. The Limits of the State: Beyond Statist Approaches and Their Critics. *American Political Science Review*, 85, pp.77–96.
Mitchell, T., 1999. Society, Economy, and the State Effect. In: G. Steinmetz, ed. 1999. *State/Culture: State Formation after the Cultural Turn.* Ithaca, London: Cornell University Press. pp.76–97.
Mühlfried, F., 2014. *Being a State and States of Being in Highland Georgia.* Oxford and New York: Berghahn.
Mühlfried, F. and Sokolovskiy, S., eds, 2011. *Exploring the Edge of Empire: Soviet Era Anthropology in the Caucasus and Central Asia.* Munster and Zurich: Lit.
Nelson, D. M., 1999. *A Finger in the Wound: Body Politics in Quincentennial Guatemala.* Berkeley: University of California Press.
Nelson, D. M., 2004. Anthropologist Discovers Legendary Two-Faced Indian! Margins, the State, and Duplicity in Postwar Guatemala. In: V. Das and D. Poole, eds. 2004. *Anthropology in the Margins of the State: Comparative Ethnographies.* Santa Fe and Oxford: James Currey.
Ong, A., 1999. *Flexible Citizenship: The Cultural Logics of Transnationality.* Durham: Duke University Press.
Raubisko, I., 2011. Life in a Negative – Positive Space: Moral Transformations in Post-War Chechnya. PhD thesis. University of Oxford.
Sakwa, R., 2011. The Clash of Regionalisms and Caucasian Conflicts. *Europe-Asia Studies*, 63(3), pp.467–91.
Sharma, A. and Gupta, A., 2006. Introduction: Rethinking Theories of the State in an Age of Globalization. In: A. Sharma and A. Gupta, eds, 2006. *The Anthropology of the State: A Reader*. Oxford and Malden: Blackwell. pp.1–41.
Shils, E., 1981. *Tradition.* Chicago: University of Chicago Press.
Shnirelman, V. A., 2003. *Voiny pamiati: mify, identichnost i politika v Zakavkazie* [Memory Wars: Myths, Identity and Politics in Transcaucasia]. Moscow: Akademkniga.
Slezkine, Y., 1994. The USSR as a Communal Apartment, or How a Socialist State Promoted Ethnic Particularism. *Slavic Review*, 53(2), pp.414–52.
Sluka, J., Chomsky N. and Price, D., 2002. What Anthropologists Should Know about the Concept of Terrorism: A Response to David Price. *Anthropology Today*, 18(2), pp.22–3.

Suny, R. G. and Martin, T., eds, 2001. *A State of Nations: Empire and Nation-making in the Age of Lenin and Stalin.* Oxford University Press.

Taussig, M., 1992. *The Nervous System.* New York: Routledge.

Taussig, M., 1997. *The Magic of the State.* New York: Routledge.

Tsing, A., 2000. The Global Situation. *Cultural Anthropology*, 15, pp.327–60.

Vanderlinden, J., 1971. Le Pluralisme Juridique: Essai de Synthèse. In: J. Gillissen, ed., *Le Pluralisme Juridique.* Brussels: Éditions de l'Université de Bruxelles. pp.19–56.

Voell, S., 2013. Oath of Memory: The Taking of Oaths on Icons in Svan Villages of Southern Georgia. *Iran and the Caucasus*, 17(2), pp.29–45.

Voell, S. and Khutsishvili, K., eds, 2013. *Caucasus, Conflict, Culture: Anthropological Perspectives on Times of Crisis.* Marburg: Curupira.

Voell, S., Jalabadze, N., Janiashvili, L. and Kamm, E., 2014. Identity and Traditional Law: Local Legal Conceptions in Svan Villages (Georgia). *Anthropological Journal of European Cultures* 23(2), pp. 98–118.

Wheatley, J., 2009. The Integration of National Minorities in the Samtskhe-Javakheti and Kvemo Kartli provinces of Georgia: Five Years into the Presidency of Mikheil Saakashvili. *ECMI Working Paper*, 44, pp.1–57.

Woodman, G. R., 1999. The Idea of Legal Pluralism. In: B. Dupret, M. Berger and L. al-Zwaini, eds, 1999. *Legal Pluralism in the Arab World.* The Hague: Kluwer Law International. pp.3–19.

Yalçın-Heckmann, L., 2012. Re-thinking Citizenship in the South Caucasus. *Europe-Asia Studies* 64(9), pp.1724–38.

Yemelianova, G. M., 2005. Kinship, Ethnicity and Religion in Post-Communist Societies: Russia's Autonomous Republic of Kabardino-Balkariya. *Ethnicities*, 5(1), pp.51–82.

Zigon, J., 2011. Multiple Moralities: Discourses, Practices, and Breakdowns in Post-Soviet Russia. In: J. Zigon, ed. 2011. *Multiple Moralities and Religions in Post-Soviet Russia.* New York and Oxford: Berghahn. pp.3–15.

Chapter 2
Triple Laws and Quasi-states in the Caucasus

Sergey Arutiunov

In the last two millennia of antiquity, the rise of more or less centralised feudal states (between third and thirteenth centuries), feudal dismemberment after the Mongol invasion (thirteenth century) and the Russian conquest since the early eighteenth century the Caucasus was an area of constant clashes between three larger worlds – those of the northern Eurasian plains (later known as Russia), of Asia Minor (the Ottoman Empire since 1453), and of Iran (or Persia). It is against this backdrop that the relations between the state and its citizens (or subjects) in the Caucasus should be considered.

Today, the Caucasus area consists of three formally independent and internationally recognised states (Armenia, Azerbaijan and Georgia), three unrecognised quasi-states utterly dependent on their patrons (Abkhazia, South Ossetia and Nagorno-Karabakh), seven republics of the Russian Federation (from west to east, Adygea, Karachay-Cherkessia, Kabardino-Balkaria, North Ossetia-Alania, Ingushetia, Chechnya and Dagestan), whose practical dependency on Russia and conformity with the all-Russian legal system, despite their ardently verbalised loyalty, practically diminishes more or less in the same west-to-east order, and the districts of Krasnodar and Stavropol, which can be considered ethnic, social and economic enclaves of Russia proper.

The Golden Age of all-Caucasian statehood at the turn of the thirteenth century coincided with the reign of Queen Tamar (1160–1213) and her son George IV (1191–1223), when the Georgian Kingdom incorporated into a complex empire nearly all of the Caucasus in a multiplex system of vassal, allied and protected states where the more or less thorough rule of law, relative peace and economic prosperity was basically available to all its subjects, irrespective of ethnicity or creed. But this period was too short to generate anything like a parliamentary system or any likeness of a Magna Carta, despite some embryonic trends towards both. Royal power was respected by many, if not all of the subjects, but the feeling of belonging to the state was as yet nearly absent. The Georgian highlanders admired and adored the queen and the king and respected them as semi-gods, but did not feel themselves to be subjects. Their social lives followed not any royal decrees but their own customary *adat* laws alone. In the plains, the state laws were more rigidly enforced, although mainly in the sphere of taxation, while in day to day life, religious norms and *adat* definitely prevailed. The rules and decrees of local feudal lords had necessarily to be obeyed, although grudgingly.

The period of feudal dismemberment could add nothing to the development of a feeling of belonging to a state. All the following petty kingdoms, princedoms, khanates, arch-bishoprics, and other feudal holdings could not pretend to any role as political actors, balancing between mighty conquerors and patrons, the Ottoman Empire, Persia and Russia. Their borders were unstable, their ability to maintain any social order oscillated between weak and nil, and the local population could rely only on their own means and the forces of their own communes or *djamaat* to safeguard their existence.

The situation changed only with the advent of the Czarist Russian rule, which arrived in the various parts of Caucasus in a long period of wars between the 1760s and the 1880s. Russian rule meant a relatively stable rule of law and a relative freedom of economic activity. Still, a good number of Muslims (from twenty to eighty percent, depending on the region), especially from Circassia, preferred to emigrate, and the rest by no means considered the White Czar their legal sovereign. *Sharia* and *adat* laws continued to be valued much more than the *kanon* of the government. True, a number of aristocratic Circassians and other Caucasian highlanders faithfully served as officers in the army of the Czar, but this was more a case of personal honour, the loyalty of honest knight-mercenaries, like that of the Circassians in Syria and Jordan who are loyal to their rulers while the Israeli Circassians are loyal to Eretz Israel (Land of Israel).

As concerns the Christian population, we can learn from the memoirs and novels of nineteenth century authors that only the highly Russified Georgian aristocracy considered the Russian Empire as 'their' genuine state. The peasant masses felt completely alienated from the 'big men' (*didkatsebi*) of power, while the Georgian Orthodox Church was deprived of its autocephaly. For Armenians, a lot depended on the personality of the viceroy (*namestnik*), whose position could range from the overt Armenophobia of Prince Grigory Sergeyevich Golitsyn (1838–1907) to the strongly Armenophilic position of Count Illarion Ivanovich Vorontsov-Dashkov (1837–1916). The memory of the latter is gratefully cherished by many Armenians even today, while the discrimination of the Armenian Apostolic Church by Golitsyn is still remembered with anger. Still it must be mentioned that the Armenians are the least 'Caucasian' of the peoples of Caucasus, possessing no aristocratic estates, preserving very little of their *adat* heritage. They are the most bourgeois in their development and thus more interested in the rule of law, economic liberties and government protection.

The ideology of the state and state–citizen relations among Armenians was elaborated by Shahamir Shahamirian (1723–1797) and his Madras circle in exile already in the 1770s, and was obviously strongly influenced by the British political system. It remained a project, but Armenian society in the nineteenth and twentieth centuries continued to demonstrate a readiness to obey state law in general. It only wanted and wants the laws and the government to be more efficient and just than they actually are. The role of *adat* and religious norms are seen as demonstrating a tendency to the opposite.

This reduction in legal security can be observed throughout the Caucasus, albeit to varying degrees. But what takes its place is not a loyalty to the state, nor a confidence in state law, but something else, new in apparition and archaic in essence. These are the pseudo-*sharia* laws imposed by the Salafites (Wahhabites) upon their followers and entire rural communities (*djamaat*), and the 'street law' and 'life according concepts' (*zhizn po poniatiam*), more or less characteristic for the lower strata of urban life throughout the Russian Federation. The proliferation of bourgeois–capitalist relations does not automatically make citizens out of bandits; in fact often the opposite takes place. When the legal system is weak and courts are corrupt, business is more and more oriented towards the grey and even the completely black economy, where *poniatia* more than the law are the things that matter. The old *sharia* law and traditional *adat* are being replaced by a quasi-*sharia* and pseudo-*adat* law, and old sheikhs and elders are being pushed aside by criminal and semi-criminal *avtoritet*. Sheikhs and elders may maintain their hold as social actors, but they are inevitably being linked more and more to these new *avtoritet*. Otherwise they perish, if not physically, then at least socially.

These processes are unevenly distributed in the social and geographic space. Their intensity is increasing along a northwest-southeast-axis. The influence of both traditional Tarikatist and Salafite Islam increases along the same basic axis as well, together with the increasing aridity of the climate, the degree of rural overpopulation and hidden unemployment, decreasing fertility of soils, Slavic population and the level of general modernisation in the total population.

This does not mean that the level of crime and corruption throughout the Krasnodar territory in the northwest is particularly low. As the case of the Kushchevskaya Massacre (4 November 2010) has demonstrated, it is still quite high. But what is a public scandal in Krasnodar, is perceived, more or less as a matter of fact, as daily life in Dagestan and Chechnya. The level of arbitrariness is especially high in the unrecognised quasi-states, notwithstanding a certain counterweight in the thinking of the local people and their shared feeling of being residents of a besieged and endangered fortress. No such feeling is present in the consciousness of the inhabitants of seven North Caucasian republics, which in a way also demonstrate some features of quasi-states. It is definitely present in the consciousness of Georgia and Armenia.

To summarise, the attitudes of citizens towards the state in all the countries of the Caucasus is, to say the least, ambiguous. People do not trust in the state and they do not identify themselves with it. Nation is one thing, the state quite another. A person perceives him or herself not as a citizen, nor as a subject but only as a member of a society on which the power of the state is artificially superimposed. The official law is obeyed in as much as it is enforced, *adat* is obeyed because disobedience results in shame, and for the Caucasians shame is a sanction more effective than any other. The attitude towards the state authorities is most explicitly formulated by many Chechens – 'it's better to stay as far from them as possible'.

As has been brilliantly demonstrated by Barasbi Bgazhnokov, the people of the Caucasus, especially the Kabardins and other Circassians, but Chechens and other highlanders as well, do not overly value the concept of private or personal property. Yes, it may be immoral to steal from one's own kin, from members of the same clan or tribe, or from close neighbours, but if the owner of the stolen goods, be it cattle, money, or any other valuable, is 'an alien', is of a different ethnicity, and most certainly when the owner is the state or a depersonalised corporation, stealing is considered less a sin than a virtue, a macho act to be admired rather than disapproved of.

A certain person or a family may be engaged in stealing, robbery, banditry, slavery, kidnapping, and so on. Neighbours and relatives may silently disapprove of such actions as being 'un-Islamic' (against *sharia* norms, unless they are committed under a *fatwa*), or out of fear that the sanctions of the authorities may fall upon not only the immediate culprits but upon the whole community or village. But publicly they will always pretend that they know nothing, have seen nothing and have heard nothing. Any public discussion of anybody's crime or misdemeanour, let alone any reporting of it to the police or other state authorities, is considered grave misbehaviour in itself. The famous Adyghean poem Azepsh Goudaberd tells of a knight who accidentally became a witness of the murder of the prince whose vassal he had been. Concealing this knowledge would be committing treachery against the family of the prince, disclosing it would bring shame upon him. Both lines of behaviour would be immoral according to the national and aristocratic codes of honour, the so-called *adyghe habze* and *worke habze*. To resolve this dilemma the knight chose voluntary exile and stayed away from his family and household for many years.

Reporting crimes and misdemeanours today is considered immoral by many ethnic Russians too (it is contemptuously labelled *stukachestvo*) but this is a comparatively recent phenomenon: mainly the result of the experience of the Stalinist purges. Public morale was quite different in Czarist Russia, where the slogan *gosudarevo slovo i delo* was not an empty phrase. However, in the Caucasus, *stukachestvo* was considered the most shameful of crimes since times immemorial. This makes the work of the police, of investigators and security forces especially difficult.

It must be mentioned that any prohibition against reporting crimes constituted a certain adaptive and defensive mechanism against social self-destruction. In an atmosphere of incessant raiding and feuding so typical to social life in the Caucasus, reporting other people's felonies would not diminish either the number of such felonies or the total violent death toll caused by them. On the contrary, it would augment them, being yet another reason for carrying out a raid or beginning a feud.

For many centuries, if not millennia, the interrelationship of the social situation and respect for the law continued to oscillate in a cyclic pattern, similar to the rise and fall of *asabiyyah* ('social solidarity') described by Ibn Khaldun in the fourteenth century. It reflected the differences between the lowland/urbanised and the highland/rural segments of the general populations. In the (usually quite short) periods of relative peace and prosperity, the lowland/urban population grew and began to interiorise the values and modes of behaviour more or less typical for Western societies developing along bourgeois lines. Periodically, a foreign invasion, an internecine war, or another crisis or disaster would destroy and ruin the cities, decimate their populations, and force them into exile or emigration. The surplus highland/rural population would then settle in the devastated and depopulated ruins of the cities, bringing with them their 'uncivilised mentality'. This continues to take place today, although under different conditions, throughout all of the Caucasus. As the modern Chechnyan proverb goes: 'It happens that a rural Chechen leaves his *aul* [a highland village] to settle in a city. But the *aul* will never leave the rural Chechen's heart.' And this is true not only for Chechens. In fact, it is happening throughout the Caucasus. This ancient 'highland vs lowland' paradigm is reproduced under modern conditions. Thousands of the best-educated Georgians, Armenians, Dagestanis, Chechens, and so on, let alone cosmopolitan Russian, Jewish and Greek populations, have left their places of origin and have left for Russia or the West, with hopes of finding a place that would better correspond to their ideas of a state with a rule of law and a market economy. The vacated niches are filled with yesterday's highlanders, peasants and their descendants.

Chapter 3

The Dialectics of Nation-state Construction in the North Caucasus in the 1920s–30s

Yuri Karpov

I would first like to clarify what I mean by dialectics and nation-state construction in this chapter. I am guided by the academic definition of dialectics, that is, a description of a phenomenon or process in its entirety, of development and of a contradicting inconsistency. 'Construction' is a process and a phenomenon at the same time. It is extended through time and not necessarily straightforward, because in the case of any constructions there are almost always circumstances that will lead to corrections. At the same time, inconsistency and contradiction can be traced here as well because in this case there are quite legitimate questions as to who is constructing what. Is it the 'greater' state constructing 'nations' and its own structure and system through them? Or the other way around: are the 'nations' self-organising and create the state in the form of a mosaic? The contradictions and the integrity are clear, as is the developmental process, since it cannot be a momentary and one-time act.

The key point in assessing these processes is to analyse how the politicians at any point in time understood the 'essence' of 'nation', or of 'people'. In this regard it should be noted that by the beginning of the twentieth century, Russian academia had followed the European norm and begun to define 'nation' and 'people' as an objective reality and a subject of politics. Russian social-democrats, represented here by their left wing – the Bolsheviks – discussed inter-ethnic relations as the driving mechanism of historical processes – the class struggle. On this basis, relations between nations were interpreted as a struggle between the oppressors and the oppressed, and were going to be subject to appropriate transformations in the construction of a 'just' society.

Justice for previously 'oppressed' peoples was from the very beginning a proclaimed goal of the Soviet authorities. In the North Caucasus, the mountaineers were promised the return of territories lost to the Cossack settlements in exchange for their support in the civil war. The proclamation of the Republic of Dagestan (1921) and the Mountain Republic of the Northern Caucasus (1917) went hand in hand with the return of rights taken away from the mountaineers by the Czars and generals. This became the main political thesis of the Bolshevik Party and the state in the region.

Political declarations did not always comply with the realities on the ground. The Mountain Republic formed by the Bolsheviks was an ambitious project for solving the national question in the region. Despite the ethnic and cultural diversity of the North Caucasus and the internal contradictions between the local peoples, for the 'big' government, 'mountaineers' were essentially similar. It is noteworthy that Moscow's policy was originally to combine the Mountain Republic and Dagestan. However, the leadership of the latter strongly disagreed. The first plans for economic decentralisation were very abstract. Moscow wanted to create a common economic region in the Caucasus between the Black and Caspian Seas, from the Manych River to the mountain of Ararat. It was only the lack of railway communication between the North and the South Caucasus that forced them to abandon the plan (CSA RNOA № 44). This area corresponded almost completely to what the Soviet ethnographers referred to as a common cultural–historical area.

Other plans for economic development of the country and the Caucasus were more realistic and were soon implemented. However, their discussion was also based in 'ethnographic' realities or pseudo-realities and the political ambitions of the newly created national autonomies. The plan for the North Caucasus was based on the principle of economic rationality for each of its administrative–territorial entities, but was burdened by the economic failure of national entities, which, however, could not as a matter of proletarian solidarity be left to their fate. The choice was deliberate: 'the development of national autonomies' is what the planners said. This was to be echoed by the politicians, who said that it 'will for a long time be powered by resources that will be formed' in the newly formed Southeast region (later the North Caucasus region), by 'Russian' regions. After some debate, during which the national autonomies raised the question of the formation of their own economic areas without the 'Russian' regions, or proposed to combine them with the Transcaucasian Democratic Federative Republic (1918), the issue was resolved in favour of the unification of the North Caucasus. In addition to the national autonomies, the provinces of Terek, Kuban, Stavropol and Don were also included within the new unit. The only region that managed to stay independent was Dagestan. Local leaders emphasised the importance of their republic for the proliferation of the global revolution and their country's special role in Caucasian politics. The claims of the North Caucasus region to take from Dagestan its lowland areas in 1922–1923 (Achikulak and Kizlyar districts), nearly half of the total territory of Dagestan, almost ended in a new Caucasian war. Dagestan's leadership was unwilling to obey the 'intermediate' power of the regional centre – Rostov. 'Only the centre [Moscow]' – read their appeal to the Kremlin – 'with its global scale and significance can understand that by helping Dagestan at the cost of other areas, it pays the costs of the world revolution spreading it in the Middle East. Don, Kuban and Terek with their largely peasant economies, their populations imbued with Russian nationalism and chauvinism, will not be able to rise to such levels of consciousness' (CSA RD № 490). The central government made concessions.

In respect to national autonomies and their relationships with one another, the country's leadership chose the principle of parity. However, it worked poorly. The neighbours' claims to territories in Kabarda provoked protests, and after a year and a half Kabarda seceded from the Mountain Autonomous Soviet Socialist Republic (Mountain ASSR), resulting in the collapse of the whole republic and, in turn, the model of a multinational federal region. Land disputes between the autonomous regions persisted throughout the first half of the 1920s and would have continued if Moscow had not made efforts to pacify them. In the last days of the Mountain ASSR, when only the North Ossetian, Ingush and Sunzha (Cossack) districts remained, the leaders of the first two districts were involved in disputes over the rights to industrial enterprises located in Vladikavkaz. North Ossetia was more active. Authorities from Moscow refused these claims since they did not want to see Ossetian economic domination over Ingushetia (CSA RD, № 25. Fol. 66–68).

Contradictions in the Karachay-Cherkessia region were expressed in the power struggle between the Karachays and Cherkess (CSA RD, № 25. Fol. 128–137). It was finally decided to divide the autonomous region into 'national' halves in order to 'keep the mountaineers from disputes and to direct them towards working on cultural development and creativity' (CD MF RR. F. 7, Inv. 1, № 95, Fol. 21). Moscow and Rostov (the centre of the North Caucasian region) sought to maintain a 'balance … of the national forces' in the region. In the decision made in 1926–1927 to extend the application of the law on compulsory military service to mountaineer peoples and in order 'to avoid antagonism between national regions' it was stipulated that the implementation of the law in all areas of the region be carried out simultaneously (CD MF RR. F. 7, Inv. 1, № 607, Fol. 60).

In general, the inclusion of national regions within the North Caucasus region, their subsidised economic and social stability did not infringe on the autonomous social and cultural rights granted to them previously. In the 1920s the central government felt 'obliged' by 'global'-scale issues to maintain them.

There is good reason to call these years a period of 'flourishing national identities' (Kadio, 2010, p.148). However, the central government saw that it was necessary to support all the demands of the various 'peoples' indiscriminately. Claims made by Ossetian politicians to unite North and South Ossetia were discussed from economic and political standpoints. In the first case, a merger was considered possible as part of the Russian Soviet Federative Socialist Republic, in the second within Georgia (CD MF RR. F. 7, Inv. 1, № 95, Fol. 21–22). However, it was decided that the implementation of this plan would cause problems with other national autonomous regions of the Northern Caucasus and the RSFSR as a whole (Gatagova, 2005, pp. 283, 286, 297–98, 310). As a result, the requests of the Ossetian side were ignored.

The 1920s and the first half of the 1930s was marked by a large-scale indigenisation campaign, which was, in general, a result of good intentions and objective needs, but in practice extremely formalised and excessively ideological. The decision of the Party Congress to implement 'indigenisation' had to be put into practice locally, unconditionally and in a short time. 'Nationalisation' was 'structured' by replacing responsible workers, specialists and technical staff with local nationals. The replacement of workers was not problematic, but things went less smoothly with the specialists, since there were almost no accountants, doctors or engineers among the locals. Therefore it was recommended to keep the old specialists, even if they were not members of the Party. 'The nationalisation of the technical staff' – so the minutes of a meeting devoted to this problem reported – 'should be postponed for now, so that, on the one hand, it does not spoil the relationship between the mountaineers and others, and, on the other hand it does not provoke [or rather, discredit] the Party bodies because large masses of people say that all this is done at the order of the Regional Committee'. And further: 'We must take into account that the salaries of technical employees will not satisfy the mountaineers. Gradually, as non-mountaineers leave their jobs in due course, mountaineers should be provided with benefits when applying for these vacancies without violating labor laws' (Ibid. № 42. Fol. 81). In the early 1930s indigenisation continued to be a priority. In North Ossetia 'extraordinary groups of three members for Ossetianisation' were created (Ibid. № 666. Fol. 4), and in Chechnya, which had received the Grozny oil fields and refining companies, they demanded the translation of relevant technical documentation into the Chechen language (Letifov, 1972, p.204, p.209).

However, in the early to mid-1930s, during the period of active industrialisation, collectivisation, and transformation of the entire complex of the socio-economic and political life of the country, the special focus on the national factor was perceived to be excessive. After a meeting of the Communist Party of the Soviet Union (CPSU) in 1934 on the introduction of a course on 'civil history' and the creation of appropriate textbooks, a number of issues began to be expressed more clearly: the notion of the Soviet state as successor to the Russian state, the role of the Russian people in bringing the state together, the need to introduce general education and university courses on the history of the USSR, instead of on the history of the peoples of the USSR (which, in fact, was not 'Russian history' either) (Litvin, 2009, pp.503–07; Stalin, 2006, p.203). These years were also marked by arguments that the words of the anthem 'Unbreakable union of freeborn Republics, Great Russia has welded forever to stand', refute the thesis of a collective nation (belonging to Stalin), because the union was not a continuation but a negation of 'one indivisible Russia'. The unity of the peoples within the new state was a result of the destruction of Czarist Russia – the prison of nations. These arguments were ignored by the political leadership (Ganelin, 1998, p.112).

At the same time, there appeared in the centre a political trend towards the unification of local ethnic diversity. As a result, Ingushetia was attached to Chechnya and justified not as 'an assimilation of ethnic groups, but rather as their harmonious fusion. The merging of nations … is atrophying national peculiarities, and later leads towards their complete disappearance' (Dimanstein, 1935, p.62). The lists prepared for the next census included 'Chechen-Ingush' and 'Karachay-Balkar'. At the same time, the small peoples of Dagestan preserved their 'independence', since, according to official versions, ethno-cultural processes had not yet been studied there (Grande, 1936, pp.74–80). This only took place in the 1950s, and they lost their 'independence' in due course.

The trend quickly became more and more clear – the status of national units was increasing, transforming them from regions into republics, but the 'national' was clearly absorbed by the 'socio-political' content 'of the new formation'. The documents of these years did not provide the names of settlements. Instead there were names of collective farms. The nationality of the inhabitants of villages was not mentioned in any way (except for limited cases in the Autonomous Regions and the Autonomous Soviet Socialist Republics). Just as, according to the Constitution of 1936, the severity of the class conflict within the country was put in the past (the Cossacks and the clergy had their rights reinstated), so was the national question pushed aside – because originally it correlated almost directly with class antagonisms. Henceforth, the national question could be 'solved' much more 'easily'.

In the second half of the 1930s, the local leaders who in the preceding ten to fifteen years had called for the inclusion of lowland territories into their republics (regions) and the relocation of their fellow mountaineers, were accused of not having faith in the possibility of building socialism in the mountains. The inclusion of the Kizlyar district within Dagestan was now viewed as a wasteful measure based on the need for a more successful development of a socialist economy. The district was therefore given to the Ordjonikidze (Stavropol) region. The ethnic map, which during the revolutionary and post-revolutionary periods was an effective tool in the hands of the Bolsheviks, had lost its value. But the notion of the 'national' remained and occupied the social niche of culture – 'national in form and socialist in content'.

The change in the political line on the 'national question' needs to be regarded as a move from an 'ethnic' interpretation of 'nation' and the 'national' to a 'civic' model. Many years later it resulted in the emergence of 'the Soviet people'. It generally proved to be consistent with the concept of 'ethnicity' as 'citizenship' – 'French citizens being French', 'American citizens being Americans'. The 'national' issue as an ethnic question emerged again in 1943–1944 when deportations were organised based on national and not on social criteria. Further settlement of peoples in liberated territories was also implemented on an ethnic basis.

Generally, the activities of the Soviet state as a whole in the North Caucasus region in the 1920–1930s, was not a 'triumph of Leninist (or Leninist-Stalinist) national policy' but a dialectical political phenomenon or process. Underlining the national aspect of politics, which was claimed necessary at one stage in the construction of a state political system, turned out to be unnecessary in an established state system. The national (ethnic) aspect gained in importance during critical periods, as illustrated again in late 1980s–90s. It is remarkable that the modern history of the Russian Federation began largely as a repetition of the history of the Soviet state of the 1920s–30s. But that is a topic for another discussion.

References

Central State Archive of the Republic of Dagestan, CSA RD. F. p-1, Inv. 1, № 490. Fol. 7.

Central State Archive of the Republic of North Ossetia – Alania, CSA RNOA. F. r-41, Inv. 1, № 44, Fol. 200 et seq.

Centre for Documentation of Modern History of the Rostov Region, CD MF RR. F. 7, Inv. 1, № 95.

Dimanstein, S., 1935. Otnoshenie Marksizma–Leninizma k voprosu ob assimilyatsii natsionalnostey [Attitude of Marxism–Leninism to the Issue of Ethnic Assimilation]. *Revolution and Nationalities*, 7.

Ganelin, R. S., 1998. Stalin i Sovetskaya istoriografiya predvoennykh let [Stalin and the Soviet Historiography of the pre-War Years]. *Novy Chasovoi, Russian Military Historic Magazine*, 6–7.

Gatagova, L. S., Lugovaya and Rogovaya, eds, 2005. *CK RKP (b) – VKP (b) i natsionalny vopros* [The RCP (b) – CPSU (b) and National Issue]. *Moscow.*

Grande, B., 1936. Spisok narodnostey SSSR [List of Nationalities of the USSR]. *Revolution and Nationalities*, 1936(4).

Kadio, Z., 2010. *Laboratoriya Imperii: Rossiya/SSSR, 1890–1940* [Laboratory of Empire: Russia / USSR, 1890–1940]. Moscow.

Letifov, A. L., 1972. *Istoricheskiy opyt natsionalno-gosudarstvennogo stroitelstva na Severnom Kavkaze* [The Historical Experience of Nation-building in the Northern Caucasus]. Makhachkala.

Litvin, A. L., ed., 2009. *Dnevnik istorika S. A. Piontkovskogo (1927–1934)* [The Diary of the Historian S. A. Piontkovsky (1927–1934)]. Kazan.

Stalin, I. V., 2006. *Istoricheskaya ideologiya v SSSR v 1920–1950 gg.: Perepiska s istorikami, statyi i zametki po istorii, stenogrammy vistupleniy. Sb. Dok. i Mat. 1, 1920–1930 gg.* [The Historic Ideology of the Soviet Union in 1920s–50s: Correspondence with Historians, Articles and Notes on the History, Transcripts of Speeches. Documents and Materials, Part 1. 1920–1930s]. St Petersburg.

Chapter 4

Traditional Law and Blood Feud: Svan Legal Practice in Soviet Times and in Contemporary Southern Georgia

Natia Jalabadze and Lavrenti Janiashvili

We conducted research in Svan villages in the region of Kvemo Kartli in southern Georgia and asked if traditional law continues to be practised.[1] Svans have been migrating from their homeland in the highlands of Svaneti to Kvemo Kartli since the end of the 1980s (see Stéphane Voell in this volume). They were first resettled there following the long and hard winter of 1987 when villages and infrastructure in the mountains was destroyed because of heavy snowfalls and avalanches. In the last ten years, however, more new migrants have arrived from Svaneti. This time they came for economic reasons: the Svans no longer saw any possibilities for leading decent lives in their home villages. The question in our research project was to find out whether Svan traditional law continued to be practised in Kvemo Kartli, and especially if the blood feud was still relevant. We then wanted to answer the question if the use of traditional law in Kvemo Kartli might be described as some form of revitalisation of a tradition forgotten in the years of socialism or if existing practice showed some form of continuity. The latter would mean that traditional law was also practised in Soviet times.

This chapter traces the questions we pursued in our research project: first we will show that traditional law was present in effect, in Soviet Georgia. We describe how local legal practice was part of the legal culture in Svaneti even if officially, traditional law was not tolerated. Second, we will discuss the relevance of traditional law in Svan villages in contemporary Kvemo Kartli. Our emphasis lies here on the practice of blood feud, which was severely sanctioned in Soviet times and is equally prohibited today, but remains vivid through occasional cases of revenge and narrations about Svan ideals among the Svan population.

---

1 The fieldwork took place within the framework of the research project 'The Revitalisation of Traditional Law in the Republic of Georgia' (2009–2011, project leaders: Stéphane Voell and Mark Münzel, financed by the Volkswagen Foundation) at the Institute for Comparative Cultural Research, Department of Cultural and Social Anthropology of the Philipps-University Marburg (Germany) and the Ivane Javakhishvili Institute for History and Ethnology, Tbilisi.

Our research on contemporary references to the blood feud in Kvemo Kartli enters uncharted territory. Blood feud has always aroused the special interest of Georgian researchers, both historians and legal scholars. Their studies, however, were focused on the highland regions of eastern and western Georgia (basically in Svaneti and Khevsureti). Researchers have never studied this institution in the lowlands, like in Kvemo Kartli. They did not even think it possible that it existed there because of the established opinion that this tradition could only be found in the highlands. Blood feuding, however, was not only a phenomenon in the remote highlands; its practice has also been observed in the lowland regions in different historical periods. Incidents related to blood feuds sometimes occur in Georgia's lowland regions even today. From time to time one will hear rumours that certain incidents of homicide have blood revenge motives. But what actions lead to a blood feud? What kind of society is this, in which a practice regarded as barbarian (though modified over time) is still found in the lowlands? What are the reasons for its existence and sustainability? These were the main questions behind our research. During our work it became clear that even though the Svans engaged in considerable conversation about the blood feud and its importance, only a few cases of blood feud could be identified today. The topos of blood feud, however, remains astonishingly important among the Georgian highlanders settled in Kvemo Kartli.

The Place of Traditional Law in Soviet Legislation

Georgian legal culture is much influenced by traditional law, as well as by the state and religious laws of neighbouring countries (Janiashvili, 2012). Throughout the centuries, different legal systems have co-existed side by side in all regions of Georgia. Svan traditional law is here only one example among others. The relationships and regulations predominating in the mountains were mainly based upon traditional law, while in the lowlands, state and religious law were of utmost significance.

Feudal legislation in Georgia was so viable that some of these norms continued to be used even after the country's annexation by Russia in the nineteenth century. The legal code of Vakhtang VI (1675–1735) continued to have relevance, as witnessed in the decree 'On the Establishment of Internal Administration in Georgia' of Alexander I (1877–1825), in which the civil courts in Georgia were ordered to follow Vakhtang's code. This legal code was widely accepted by the population, because its rules were not foreign to the people. It emerged in part out of traditional practice, which was not the case for the Czarist legal framework.

The situation changed radically during the Soviet period. The totalitarian communist regime looked to reform all parts of social life, overcoming traditional law and subsuming everything to its interests. From the first days of the establishment of the communist regime, the Soviet authorities tried to include the entire population of Georgia into a single Soviet legal frame. A decree was issued regarding the abolishment of the old courts and the establishment of the Courts of Workers and Peasants. In addition, special courts were introduced, like the Revolutionary Tribunals. In 1923, a system of common courts was installed and organised as follows: the Supreme Court (highest level of jurisdiction), Provincial Court (one in western and one in eastern Georgia), District People's Court and Red Cross Military Tribunal. By 1926, 91 judges worked in 73 districts (Kacharava, 1926, p.2).

In scholarly literature published between 1920 and 1940 (Andronikashvili, 1939; Japaridze, 1925, 1930; Kvirkvelia, 1922, 1935; Saradjishvili, 1921; Vacheishvili, 1939), the disintegration of the old legal system and the ensuing difficulties faced by state authorities and the local population in regulating legal issues in the 1920s is described. The situation changed drastically in the 1930s, when collectivisation and industrialisation began to take hold and the proprietary and ideological interests of the communist state were declared as the first priority. The justice system was oriented appropriately towards these goals. Political and socio-economic changes also had their impact on the legal literature. Publications in the legal field issued in Georgian were full of Marxist-Leninist ideology and did not reflect the complex legal situation of that period. The authors avoided expressing their true opinion, restricting themselves to the ideological framework (Japaridze, 1930, p.457). This is not surprising since the voicing of any opinion different from the official one was punished ruthlessly. It is noteworthy that the publication of special legal periodicals in Georgian ended in this period. Soviet legal literature acknowledged the role of socialist customs and traditions in the establishment of socialist legal norms. Traditional legal norms were entirely disregarded in legislation. On the practical level, the Soviet legislator tried to eliminate traditional norms by making the official law more severe. Capital punishment by firing squad, for example, was foreseen for murder in the name of blood feud (article 104, Criminal Code of Georgia SSR).

The communist leaders, however, were soon compelled to consider local social specifics. Locally, traditional legal norms continued to function, representing an active social phenomenon, amended according to a specific time and situation. In the first years of the establishment of the Soviet regime, the practice of the use of traditional institutions was virtually unrestricted. The great majority of disputes, especially family disputes, were solved according to tradition and people seldom addressed official authorities. The practice of penal law was different: these proceedings were taken over by the state entirely (Beselia, 1928, p.436). However, significant space was left for the use of traditional law in penal law as well, specifically, the regulation of so-called 'private crimes'. These were 'any action or inaction threatening the Soviet order or the rule of law established by the authorities of workers and peasants for the transitional period to communist rule of order'. Private crimes were crimes not prosecuted by the state but by a private person (the damaged party) (Erkomaishvili, 1928, p.531). This practice was justified as a means to ease the pressure on overworked courts. Ivane Surguladze (1928, p.436) describes a significant number of precedents labelled 'private crimes' that were treated without any involvement of the state, simply because the injured party did not appeal to a court.

Traditional norms played an important role in social relationships and everyday life during the communist period and determined the rights and obligations of an individual towards society. Traditional law decided what actions were to be considered crimes that needed to be punished or at least condemned, and what actions deserved approval and praise. Despite the fact that asserting legal obligations on the basis of traditional law was limited in that period, the attitude of the majority of people in society towards the violators of traditional norms remained negative. Influenced by socio-cultural and psychological factors, people maintained a loyalty to their traditions (spiritual life, respect of the elderly, hospitality, keeping one's word, family relationships, rules of property division, exogamy, gender relationships, and so on), which is still reflected in everyday life today (Kekelia, 1989).

Svan Traditional Law in Soviet Georgia

Civil legal conflicts between Svans were settled almost entirely on the basis of traditional law during the Soviet period, according to the statements of our respondents. The influence of traditional law on penal prosecution was also significant. They explained that all issues had once been regulated by tradition in Svan communities and that this situation has been preserved to the present day (although exceptions were also named). Scientific literature confirms these claims: according to Gegeshidze (1975), traditional relationships continued to be practised in Svaneti in the 1960s. The members of a lineage (*gvari*) went through good and bad together. For example, not only family members, but all the members of a lineage mourned a deceased member of the community together.

In the 1960s, very few legal conflicts were brought to court. Gegeshidze himself was an employee of the local court. He also confirmed the moral unity of the family and the members of a lineage. In the period 1964–1979, there were no cases of divorce or other family conflicts treated in court, although they did happen. The head of the people's court confirmed that such cases were not brought to the state courts since elders and mediators helped in the resolution of these conflicts. Their verdict was considered final. Gegeshidze outlines that the head of the court was 'officially content' with this situation because such conflict resolution procedures always resulted in correct decisions (1975, pp.115–16).

As mentioned above, one aspect of Svan traditional law was especially critical for Soviet legislators: blood feud was condemned. Traditionally, the institution of blood feud among Georgian highlanders (among others, the Svans) took place in several stages: the act of murder, the act of vengeance and the act of reconciliation. Each of these stages was based on different legal norms, norms of behaviour and restrictions that the representatives of both parties (the offending and the injured family) were to consider. These norms varied in the different districts and communities. For a long time (specifically: until the 1940s), blood feud in highland Svaneti had a rather intense character. According to Egnate Gabliani, 'the killing of a Svan is an insult inflicted on the whole lineage (community) and they try to be courteous and not too loud until they wash off the shame; a man might be reproached as a son of an "unavenged man" and that is a great infamy. In cases where the son did not avenge the crime, the obligation was passed on to the grandson and it might continue for centuries. There were cases in Svaneti, when a wife remained with a child after her husband's death; if she gave birth to a boy, when he grew up he "took blood" for his murdered father' (1925, p.134).

The practising of the blood feud in Soviet times was punishable by death. But according to Mikhako Kekelia, this legislation led to strange inconsistencies. If, for example, a man in Tbilisi killed the murderer of his son, it probably would not have been categorised as blood feud and he would have been punished less severely than a Svan committing exactly the same act in Svaneti. There, this killing would have been automatically labelled a blood feud (1990, p.17).

Traditional Legal Practice under Soviet Rule

The main institutions in the implementation of traditional law among the Svans were the people's assembly and the mediatory court. The crimes heard by these bodies can be divided into two categories. First, crimes against the interests of the community, for example, betrayal of the community or violation of the exogamy rule and second, crimes against individuals, for example, the murder or wounding/crippling of another, damage to property and moral failings.

The people's assembly was the highest instance of Svan justice. It was headed by a *makhvshi* (elected elder) elected by the assembly. The assembly could expel a family from the village, burn their house and even impose capital punishment. The death penalty was applied to the traitors (Kharadze and Surguladze, 1962, p.42). The assembly did not report to any higher authority. It was entitled to discuss and settle internal and external issues. The issue of the election of the head of the community or village was decided by the assembly of all the residents of the village or community – men and women – of more than twenty years of age (Charkviani, 1967, p.67).

A good example for the functioning of this institution is a case recorded in the 1930s in the village of Kala. Several people (one of them a resident of Kala) stole sacred items from the church of St Kvirike, the most sacred site in Svaneti. The thieves fled, roamed the mountains and got lost. They eventually managed to return to the village. The people captured them, called the assembly together and decided to punish the criminals by stoning. The villager was not punished with the other thieves. Instead, his entire lineage was expelled from the village and banned from entering the church of St Kvirike. The people of Kala reconciled with the banned lineage only recently. The decision to do so was made by the entire community. It was fairly difficult because large parts of the community had resettled elsewhere in Georgia. They elders made a list, visited all the families from Kala and made them sign that they agreed to the reconciliation. Then they went to Kala, called an assembly, sacrificed a bull, apologised to the people and begged St Kvirike for forgiveness.

Fieldwork data shows that mediatory courts were very popular during the communist period. The Svan population did not trust state institutions and tried to involve them as little as possible in their local legal relationships. Although some individuals eagerly consented to work in state institutions, were employed by the Party or served in civil posts, in the village they still remained loyal to their old traditions. If a theft occurred and the culprit was punished by the police (at the time called the *militia*), the injured party would not be content and made sure the culprit paid some form of fine, too. If the culprit did not admit to the theft, the injured party would make them swear an oath.

An oath was used when a person was accused of having violated a norm, that is, of having committed a crime, having betrayed an individual or of having had sexual intercourse with a married woman. In this case, the suspect would be asked by their accuser or the mediators to swear an oath on an icon (Voell, 2013). He would swear on the icon in the presence of witnesses that he did not commit the deed he was accused of. In serious cases the oath was made in the above-mentioned church of St Kvirike in Kala. In less important cases the oath taker did not go to the church. The touching of a corner of a church or its door was sufficient to prove that the oath taker did not commit the alleged act and knew nothing about it. The suspect was considered innocent after that.

It is noteworthy that according to traditional law, all participants in this process should swear an oath, including the accusing parties and the mediators. The disputing parties swear that they agree to reconcile, will not change their mind and speak the truth. They also make an 'oath of loyalty', that is, they swear to respect the decision and implement it without any delay. They also swear to be loyal to each other and that there will be no hostility between them.

Blood Feud in Kvemo Kartli

The Kvemo Kartli region is marked by its ethnic and religious diversity. Apart from the small number of indigenous Georgians, the population of Kvemo Kartli includes, among others, Azerbaijanis,[2] Armenians, and Greeks as well as Georgian migrants from Imereti, Lechkhumi, Svaneti, Khevsureti, Ratcha, and Adjara (see Jalabadze and Janiashvili, 2013). The Svans and Adjarians were resettled in Kvemo Kartli after natural disasters in their home regions at the end of the 1980s. In the last ten years, many more Svans have relocated to Kvemo Kartli for economic reasons (see Stéphane Voell in this volume).

2 'Azerbaijanis' and 'Azeris' are words used synonymously in the literature.

The administrative region of Kvemo Kartli is ideal for carrying out the research on the degree of and reasons for the preservation of traditional legal practices. Our fieldwork shows that today, blood feuding is no longer practiced among non-Georgian groups such as the Azerbaijanis or Adjarians, where this was once a tradition. Neither can blood feuding be observed among indigenous Georgians. This does not exclude that a murder might be avenged, but in this case it is not inspired by blood feud ideology. Generally, murders that occur in the region among the above-mentioned groups come under the jurisdiction of the law enforcement agencies and are the objects of state legal proceedings. Though not frequently observed in the region, the practice of blood feuding among migrant Georgian groups is preserved among the Svans and to a lesser degree among the Khevsurs.

Transformed, less intense, and somewhat concealed practices of blood feud can still be observed today in Svaneti (Jalabadze, 2012). There are mediators (*morval*) who still regulate cases of blood feud according to traditional legal norms, making reconciliation arrangements, setting penalties, organising feasts, and so on. However, in the course of time the norms and rules have changed. The circle of those responsible for blood has been narrowed from all-male lineage members to close male relatives of the culprit. Compensation for blood is no longer paid in cattle and land but in money. Finally, the ostentatious celebrations have become more modest.

Interviews with Svan respondents gave evidence that blood feuding among Svans is practised mainly with other Svans. A feud that was begun in Svaneti will be continued in the lowlands. Although these cases are rare today in Kvemo Kartli, the stories of these feuds can be heard in every district populated by Svan migrants: 'One Svan man killed another Svan. The murderer was arrested. The offended party first burned the culprit's house and then killed his innocent cousin. They are now in prison, but imprisonment means nothing. They are still responsible for blood. I can't predict what will happen after, but as there were equal number of deaths on both sides, negotiations for reconciliation could start. During negotiations, everything will be considered; the burning of the house will also be taken into consideration' (field material, Dmanisi, 2009).

Another case of a burnt house was confirmed in the municipality of Dmanisi. After committing a murder, the culprit left his village and the family who had been offended burned his house. Traditionally, this was not considered a mitigating factor by the elders when mediating. However, according to informants, now such matters are taken into consideration. Neither is the imprisonment of the culprit a mitigating factor. Imprisonment does not always keep the avengers from fulfilling their intentions.

Migrant Svans consider it shameful 'when the blood is not avenged' (*siskhlis sherchena*). A respondent from Dmanisi recollects: 'During the Abkhazian–Georgian conflict, there was an authoritative man, a driver in Chuberi, who was highly respected by the Svans. He was killed. I don't know for what reason exactly. He had three brothers. I wonder why they hadn't avenged his death yet! Such cases among migrant Svans are rare. It is shameful, when someone kills your relative and you do not "take" blood. Different men have different tactics, some do it very slyly, some do it immediately, and some wait for several years. It is shameful to hire someone to do it' (field material, Dmanisi, 2009).

Several years ago a sixteen year old girl was killed accidentally in Gardabani in the Svan community of Lemshvaniera (see Stéphane Voell in this volume for another case involving a car accident). She was on her way to the school graduation banquet. Three girls were waiting for their friends outside. The boys decided to take them away by car. The day was rainy and the roads were wet. Three people were in the car, two neighbours and a brother of one of the girls. When they were approaching the gate, the driver lost control and crashed into one of the girls. This was a terrible tragedy. Forty days after the young girl's death the whole village was still grieving. The families of the girl and the driver were neighbours and good friends. By Svan tradition, the fact that the death was an accident would not have mattered, but among the lowland Svans this is considered in the mediation process and also when discussing the issue of compensation. The mediator decided it was possible to reconcile the families. The male members of the girl's family were for reconciliation but the women were against it. They were especially aggressive because the rumour was that the driver's family had not behaved appropriately. The girl's family demanded that they leave the village and move elsewhere (as would have been the case traditionally). However, the boy's family has no other place to live; they had migrated from Svaneti and had begun a new life in Gardabani. Now they would have to leave their new house and everything they had acquired after living for decades in the lowlands. The problem has not yet been resolved; mediation is continuing. They still live in the same village but nobody knows what will happen.

In order to prevent a blood feud, women sometimes claim responsibility for the crimes of their men. There was such a case in Dmanisi, where a woman took the blame for a killing to protect the real culprit, her husband. Women, were free from retaliatory blood vengeance, although lately, they too have come to be included in the phenomenon (such as in the North Caucasus, where this has become especially intense). We were told the story of a Svan woman from Kodori (Abkhazia), who took the revenge meant for her husband. Today this woman lives in a village near Mtskheta (near Tbilisi).

Respondents said that sometimes, when a man is murdered on both sides, a blood feud can end. In cases where the parties consider both of them guilty, the feud is ended. No traditional official reconciliation procedures are then necessary. One respondent from Dmanisi told us: 'In case the man killed has brothers, I will not ignore them. I will see what they intend to do, and if they are passive, then I will also be quiet'.

The traditional ostentatious ceremony of reconciliation is no longer practised. The compensation has changed as well. Blood money is now real money, paid to the family that has been offended. Feuding might end if the party that has been offended has no male relatives, who usually are responsible for blood. It is also possible to hear discontent among some Svans (although they are not against blood feuding as such) regarding the killing of a culprit's innocent relatives.

For Svans, blood feuding is a traditional norm that all men are held to maintain. Each Svan community has its own authorities on the traditional norms concerning blood feud. They are involved in the process of reconciliation as mediators. According to the information of a Svan man from Dmanisi provided: 'For us, the sanctuary is the most sacred thing. They have great importance for the reconciliation. When we arrived here [in Dmanisi], first we did not have any churches but then we constructed them on the places of old ruined sanctuaries and built new ones. If the mediators so decide, we might go to Svaneti to make an oath on the icon there. Sometimes mediators are invited from Svaneti to settle the problem but generally, cases of blood feuding are rare in the lowlands' (field material, Dmanisi, 2009).

Though cases of blood feuding have apparently become rare in Svan communities in Kvemo Kartli, no one will blame a man who finds and kills his father's killer, even many years after the incident, or will blame him if he kills the descendant of the culprit. The disposition of the Svan population towards the custom is positive. According to the majority of male (and even some female respondents), 'blood feud is a good tradition' as one informant put it, 'because it adjusts human relations and makes a man control his behaviour in order to avoid possible offence' (field material, Gardabani, 2010).

The attitude towards blood feud is well manifested in the interviews with Svan respondents. According to the information of a Svan migrant in Dmanisi: 'Svans have the tradition of blood feud, they practise it, though in Dmanisi I never heard of a case; but if it occurs, then who could forgive it, no Svan would forgive it' (field material, Dmanisi, 2009). Another said: 'I have heard about cases where vengeance was not taken, but I wonder, how I could not avenge the murder of my kinsman! Blood feud is everywhere in the world, not only in Svaneti. Just imagine – someone kills your sibling! What would you do then? And you speak as if only Svans practise it! Why only Svans?' (field material, Gardabani, 2010).

Apparently, the younger generation of Svans, who have not been brought up in Svaneti know Svan traditions and try to observe them: 'We listen to our parents and learn from them, we always try to maintain the rules of behaviour, the relationship between the elder and the young. We attend the family [lineage] meetings. There all the representatives of our lineage from different parts of Georgia gather. We listen to their talks and decisions and then try to follow them' (field material, Dmanisi, 2009).

Conflicts between Svans and their Neighbours in Kvemo Kartli

As was mentioned above, the study of the Kvemo Kartli region has shown a higher frequency of feuding among Svans than between Svans and members of other ethnic groups. When they first arrived in Kvemo Kartli, bloody confrontations took place between Svans and locals (Azerbaijanis, Armenians and non-Svan Georgians). Local respondents spoke about these confrontations. The most sensational incident was between young Svan and Azerbaijani men in Marneuli, which grew in 1989 into a serious intergroup conflict in which the Azerbaijanis from four districts were involved (Trier and Turashvili, 2007, p.42).

These conflicts between Svans and ethnic minority groups took place all over the region but mainly in the municipalities of Marneuli, Gardabani, Bolnisi and Dmanisi. They were between Svans and Azerbaijanis, and between Svans, Armenians and Greeks in Tsalka. In 1992, for example, a serious incident took place between a Svan and a local Georgian[3] in the village of Gantiadi in the municipality of Dmanisi. In 1991, seven Svan families arrived to live in Dmanisi. However, all of them had to leave the village soon as a result of the following terrible accident. In 1992, a group of drunken Svan youths killed a young Georgian from the village. The villagers took gruesome revenge by killing an innocent Svan migrant. In the shortest possible time the Svan migrants either abandoned their houses (which were then occupied by families belonging to the local population), or exchanged houses in order to move away from the village (Trier and Turashvili, 2007, p.33).

In 2006, in Tsalka, a fight between drunken groups of Svans and Armenians outside a restaurant ended in a fatal knifing. A twenty-four year old Armenian was killed and another twenty-five year old man was wounded. The Georgian police arrested some Svans involved in the case. Local Armenians held a protest rally outside the Tsalka police station and demanded the lynching of the suspects (field material, Tsalka, 2008). Another incident occurred in the Gardabani district: 'About five years ago, there was an incident between Svans and Azerbaijanis in the village of Lemshvaniera. The Svans from the village hired a young Azerbaijani herdsman who was staying near the village. Then, a dissolute young Svan from Tskaltubo (West Georgia, near Kutaisi) came to Lemshvaniera. One day, he took some schoolboys with him and went to the herdsman. A fight took place and one of the Svan boys shot the herdsman. Azerbaijanis from the nearby villages met and decided to attack the offender's family. But there were three boys there and the Azerbaijanis did not know exactly who the murderer was. The police were informed and they arrived and forced the Azerbaijanis to leave. Shavlokhashvili was the chief of the police at the time and he remembers saying: 'I will not let any Azerbaijani kill a Georgian'. He called a special task force to ease the tension (field material, Gardabani, 2010). A respondent from Gardabani recollected: 'An Azerbaijani man killed a Svan from Lemshvaniera. The Svans killed not only the murderer, but also his protector. The Azerbaijanis were afraid and did not react' (field material, Gardabani, 2010).

Many cases of murders between Svans and non-Svans did not escalate into blood feud. Svans have their arguments in regard to this: 'Azerbaijanis also practised blood feud in the past. They rarely practise it now. Actually, they are

3 Svans are also Georgians, but in order to differentiate between Svans and non-Svan Georgians we write of Svans and Georgians.

afraid of Svans. They know that the Svans will never let the Azerbaijanis oppress them' (field material, Gardabani, 2010).

Conclusion

We have shown that traditional law is still vital among Svans in Kvemo Kartli and continues to play a significant role in social relationships and everyday life. Moreover, Svan legal practice in southern Georgia is not a new practice or some form of revitalisation of practices thought to be forgotten. Despite the efforts of the Soviet regime, both community meetings and mediatory courts have been preserved. It could be argued that despite attempts to change the legal system by the Soviet regime, the traditional legal system remains a core source of historically developed moral values and ethnic identity.

In Svan villages in Kvemo Kartli today, traditional law and especially the topos of the blood feud remains vivid. But how can the preservation of this topos and the custom of blood-feuding on the one hand and the virtual disappearance of blood feuding as a practice among the Svans of Kvemo Kartli, be explained? First, this might be an after-effect of the migration process. In Kvemo Kartli, the Svan population lives together in compact settlements. The first migration wave to Kvemo Kartli was unexpected, unplanned, and, in turn, rather painful. The Svan population happens to have been settled in proximity to other ethnic groups that also had very clear identities (national identity, name, mother tongue, religion, and cultural traditions). The difficult process of acculturation that they had to undergo was accompanied by a no-less complex process of adaptation to a different climatic–geographical environment. All this favoured the Svan inclination to establish a firm footing among these groups in reference to their specific ethnic identity. This resulted in the preservation of traditional norms of everyday life and traditional behavioural stereotypes.

Another reason for the preservation of traditional law among the lowland Svans, and especially the topos of blood feud, might be family and kinship ties, which are still an important source of authority. Most Svans residing in Kvemo Kartli have retained close ties to their home region. Some of them have relatives there, some have built new houses or repaired the old ones, and some of them have started businesses there. They maintain continuity with their traditional Svan environment. While the tradition has undergone certain changes, its use and interpretation in Svaneti and Kvemo Kartli differs only slightly. The ties that the Kvemo Kartli migrants have maintained or re-established with their home region provide for the preservation of, among other things, the blood feud topos.

References

Andronikashvili, L. ed., 1939. *Samokalako samartali* [Civil Law], vol. 1. Tbilisi: Sakhelmtsipo universiteti.

Beselia, K., 1928. Gamoklevis shedegebi (tsalkis sakhalkho sasamartlos gamokvlevis mokhsenebidan) [From the Reports of Investigations of the Tsalka Public Court]. *Sabchota Samartali* 19, pp.464–67.

Charkviani, A., 1967. *Svaneti (XIX saukunis meore naxevari da XX saukunis dasatsqishi)* [Svaneti (Second Half of the 19th Century and Beginning of the 20th Century]. Tbilisi: Metsniereba.

Erkomaishvili, A., 1928. Kerdzo danashaulis shesakheb [On Private Crime]. *Sabchota Samartali* 23, pp.529–32.

Gabliani, E., 1925. *Dzveli da akhali svaneti* [Old and New Svaneti]. Tbilisi: Sakhelmtsipo Gamomtsemloba.

Gegeshidze, M., ed., 1975. *Sakartvelos mtis zonis mosakhleobis ekonomikuri da sotsialuri aktivizatsiis sakitkhebi* [Questions on Economic and Social Activities in the Georgian Mountain Zones], vol. 1. Tbilisi: Ivane Javakhishvilis Sakhelobis Istoriisa Etnograpiis Instituti.

Jalabadze, N., 2012. The Resurgence of Blood Feud in the Georgian Lowlands. *Caucasus Analytical Digest* 42, pp.7–9.

Jalabadze, N. and Janiashvili, L., 2013. Perspectives for the Integration of Ethnic Minorities in a Multicultural Region: The Example of Kvemo Kartli. In: S. Voell and K. Khutsishvili, eds, *Caucasus Conflict Culture: Anthropological Perspectives on Times of Crisis*. Marburg: Curupira. pp.281–89.

Janiashvili, L., 2012. Traditional Law in Soviet Times. *Caucasus Analytical Digest* 42, pp.5–7.

Japaridze, S., 1925. *Savachro samartali* [Commercial Law]. Tbilisi: Tbilisis saxelmtcipo universitetis studentta gamocema.

Japaridze, S., 1930. *Sameurneo-administratsiuli samartali* [Economic-administrative Law]. Tbilisi: Samretsvelo-ekonomikuri (komerciuli) ganatlebis damkhmare komiteti.

Kacharava, A., 1926. Sabchota sasamartlo sakartvelos gasabjoebis khuti tslis tavse [The Soviet Court Five Years after Sovietization]. *Sabchota Samartali* 1, pp.2–5.

Kekelia, M., 1989. *Erovnuli tradiciebis sotsialuri punktsia* [The Social Function of National Traditions]. Tbilisi: Metcniereba.

Kekelia, M., 1990. Zogierti ram siskl-mesiskhleobis shemonakhulobastan dakavshirebit [Some of the Issues Regarding the Persistancy of Blood Feuding]. *Kartuli chveulebiti samartali* 2, pp.11–22.

Kharadze, R. and Surguladze, I., 1962. Shesavali cerili [Introduction]. In: B. Nizharadze, *Istoriul-etnograpiuli tserilebi* [Historic-ethnographic Writings], vol. 1. Tbilisi: Tbilisi Universitetis Gamomtsemloba, pp.4–47.

Kvirkvelia, B., 1922. Aplikacia tu kasatsia? [Aplication or Cassation?]. *Moambe* 30, pp.28–31.

Kvirkvelia, B., ed., 1935. *Sakhelmtsipo da samartali* [State and Law]. Tbilisi: Sakhelgamis me-2 stamba.
Saradjishvili, I., 1921: Sakhalkho sasamartlota daarsebi [On the Establishment of Peoples' Courts]. *Moambe* 18, pp.23–5.
Surguladze, I., 1928. Kerdzo danashauli shesakheb [On Private Crime]. *Sabchota Samartali* 18, pp.432–42.
Trier, T. and Turashvili, M., 2007. *The Resettlement of Ecologically Displaced Persons, Solution of a Problem or Creation of a New One? Eco-Migration in Georgia 1981–2006*. Flensburg: ECMI.
Vacheishvili, A., ed., 1939. *Siskhlis samartali* [Penal Law]. Tbilisi: Stalinis sakhelobis sakh. un-tis iurdiuli fakulteti da iurdiuli daustsrebeli institutis tbilisis piliali.
Voell, S., 2013. Oath of Memory: The Taking of Oaths on Icons in Svan Villages of Southern Georgia. *Iran and the Caucasus* 17(2), pp.29–45.

Chapter 5
Blood Feud in Ingushetia: Differences in *adat* and *sharia*

Makka Albogachieva

The Ingush custom of blood feud (Ingush: *chir*, *pkha*, *dov*) continues to exist, at least in part, in modern society. Scottish missionaries travelling among the Ingush in 1822 noted that 'Among them there is almost no one that has come to full age and who would not have been guilty of shedding blood, or did not seek revenge for a family member or a friend' (RHSA, 8809). A murder, even committed accidentally, certainly led to another, since the relatives of the murdered person avenged the death by killing his murderer. The people involved in these blood feuds are called *dovkhoy* (those who are seeking revenge) in Ingush. At the beginning of the nineteenth century the Ingush became Russian subjects. The reform of local law and the introduction of a state court system closer to *adat* (traditional law) and *sharia*[1] began, and the time that followed was characterised by the simultaneous practice of several legal systems. The system was constantly changed and amended until 1917, when the Soviet legal regime was introduced. This latter system, to some extent, took into account the 'remnants' of the previous social order such as the blood feud, polygamy, abduction of girls, tribal solidarity, etc.

Societal Dimension of the Blood Feud

A blood feud was originally a mechanism for responding to violations within social establishments; it prevented many incidents because a person is not considered an individual but part of a 'whole'. The subject shifted from the individual to the tribal context within which the individual was integrated. This custom played the role of the state, regulating relationships between community members – preventing crimes and punishing criminals (see Lavrenti Janiashvili and Natia Jalabadze in this volume). It maintained a certain degree of public order, social justice and equality, preventing the spread of arbitrariness and anarchy in society.

Common consciousness safeguarded the interests of the group by mobilising its members to defend each other. It demanded common action, to the point of

1 The Ingush people adopted Islam in the 18th/19th centuries. They are Sunni Muslims following the views and school of Abu al-Hasan al-Ash'ari and the Shafi'i laws. *Sharia* is Muslim religious law that spread among the Ingush in that period.

the complete destruction of the enemy, or recognition of defeat at the hands of the latter, and their subjugation (Dmitriev, 2003, p.113). The point of the blood feud is not the physical extermination of the enemy but the compulsion to value and respect human lives. Revenge is imperative because it is a response to crimes already committed. Revenge is a 'double-sided exchange', resulting in the return of insults, and changes in the roles of the offender and the offended. Resentment causes counter-resentment and the initial relationship in inverted: the offended becomes the offender and vice versa. Revenge is no longer a desire that is suppressed and curbed by the law; it is the social norm (Verdier, 1980).

Not every kind of offence ends in a blood feud, only those that, according to folk customs are punishable through a deadly feud. Each nation may have its own traditional law, and the causes of blood feud may be different. For example, among the Ingush, in addition to murders, blood feuds could be caused by activities such as violence, personal offences, cutting a pear tree (generally considered sacred in Ingushetia during the pagan period), violence against women or guests, mutilation, abduction of women, rape, adultery, seduction of an unmarried woman or kidnapping a girl without her consent in order to bring about a marriage. Leontovich wrote that such crimes called forth the passion of the Ingush and resulted in the most desperate and bloody of crimes (1883, p.148). 'The Ingush believe verbal abuse is the most sensitive offence and avenge it to the death of the person who uttered the insult. They can get angry for no tangible reason during a conversation, but they are easy to calm down. Their enthusiasm is manifested openly, without the slightest pretence. Contempt for life is seen as a virtue, and the slightest sign of fear is the greatest disgrace. They prefer death to captivity' (Blaramberg, 1992, p.342). The word of the Ingush is considered the most dangerous weapon: 'a bullet hits one, but the tongue nine', they say.

One more very important detail characteristic for blood feuds should be noted: it applies only to those nations that have a similar rule. After expeditions to Ingushetia in 1919–1921, Yakovlev devoted two large chapters to blood feuds in his work, 'The Ingush' (SPb BAAS no. 574). He notes that 'an Ingush is deeply indoctrinated with the view that another Ingush like himself cannot force or impose anything on him that would hamper his freedom or would cause damage to him. Otherwise, the violator would be held responsible by the offended side .... The Ingush rule of blood feud did not apply to the Russians. On the contrary, it applied to the kin and friends (*kunak*) of the Ingush and in some cases they could even enter into a blood feud with their old highlander neighbours, the Ossetians, Chechens and even Kabardins' (Yakovlev, 1925, p.116). This leads to the assumption that blood feud applies only to societies for which this practice has been known before.

Divergent Liabilities for Blood Feud in *adat* and *sharia*

Blood feud has its own rules and over the years they have changed, been supplemented or radically reformed. Thus, for malicious killing of elders in Ingushetia in the 1880s, both the known and the anonymous criminals were publicly cursed. In most regions of Chechnya and Ingushetia this was done by using copper basins, pots and trays like drums and hitting them with sticks, and by firing guns and shouting loud curses against the offender. In some cases, an effigy of the criminal was built on the roadside. It was constructed as a big pile (*karlag*) of stones, lumps of earth or wood chips. Every passer-by had to curse the perpetrator of a crime and throw any of those things onto the pile. But this custom has disappeared.

Despite the fact that the modern Ingush are Sunni Muslim, in their daily lives, references to *adat* are quite important. A constant switching between *adat* rules and *sharia* rules takes place. It is important to bear in mind that the convergence of *sharia* with *adat* was conditioned by the fact that the elders are the guardians of *adat* while the guardians of *sharia* are the *kadi*, the experts on Islamic law. It should also be noted that common positions exist in Ingush *adat* and *sharia* regarding revenge. At the same time, there are fundamental differences, which will be discussed below.

'The basic principle of *adat* was the principle of responsibility not in respect to the individual, but to the collective to which one belongs' (Dmitriev, 2003, p.111). Revenge was undertaken as a special form of self-defence so as not to disrupt the pre-existing balance between clans. In order not to become weaker than the offender, the clan of the offended should either cause an equivalent offence towards the hostile clan or kill an equivalent member of it. Avengers were not interested in whether it was an intentional or accidental murder, or whether a wealthy or poor mountaineer was killed. Therefore, sometimes the poor had to risk their lives to avenge the death of their wealthy compatriot, even if he was the one who exploited them on a daily basis (Zhupikova, 2007, p.127).

Unlike *adat*, Islam recognises personal responsibility for any kind of crime. According to the Ingush, *adat*, blood revenge, was carried out by any member of the family, or clan to whom the murdered individual belonged. It could be his nephews from both paternal and maternal sides. If necessary, any member of the *teip* could avenge (Dalgat, 2008, p.108) a crime.[2] According to *sharia*, the obligation to seek revenge applied only to sons, unless the deceased was childless, in which case his brothers or nephews were called upon to do so (Kardavi, 2004, p.305). If a tragedy occurs between close relatives, the collective responsibility is reduced – the representative of the victim cannot execute a close relative in the male line, who has murdered another relative of the same male line (father, son, brother).

2 A *teip* is a kin-based group in Chechnya and Ingushetia. Its members believe in a common (often mythological) descent and (or) a territorial location.

The blood feud is a principle according to which if someone commits a murder, he or someone from his family, clan or tribe, must be deprived of his life in retaliation. For example, in Saxon custom, a blood feud was extended only to the killer and his sons, while in Burgundy revenge could only be exacted upon the actual murderer. Ancient Russian customs allowed revenge to be exacted upon brothers for a brother, sons for fathers, etc. (Kosven, 1925). According to the Ingush *adat*, relatives of the murdered can choose any man from the offender's clan if it is not possible to identify the killer. If a group committs a murder, then in Ingush *adat*, revenge can be exacted upon all participants. However, this *adat* rule is supplemented in modern times by *sharia* law. According to *sharia*, it is only the direct perpetrator of a murder who is considered an object of revenge; any partners who did not contribute actively to the crime do not become targets of revenge.

Oaths and the Reconciliation of Blood Feuds

If someone is suspected of murder, he must take a cleansing oath (*duv baa*). An oath for the Ingush was and still is of great importance. In all controversial issues, in order to prove his innocence, an Ingush must be ready to appear before the people's court or, if necessary, the *sharia* court, where he takes an oath on the Quran. Even if it is a false oath, he is relieved of responsibility for the crime. The Ingush believe that the person will receive his sentence, either in this life or in a future life.

Despite the fact that the Ingush are devout Muslims, some rules of *adat* are important in everyday life and are applied in some cases. According to *sharia*, an oath is taken only by the accused, while according to the local *adat*, witnesses may be present during the oath to confirm its validity. The witnesses, however, are not required to take an oath. Those who refuse to take an oath are considered guilty.

If a crime is solved and the perpetrator known, his family and friends will make attempts at reconciliation with the offended party, and this continues as long as it is thought that a positive result is possible – over months, years or even decades. However, it should be noted that there is a category of people who will never forgive a crime, although they will not take revenge either. Their purpose is to make the target of revenge live in perpetual fear. It is also a kind of revenge, since the offender will continue to be a target until official reconciliation.

It should be noted that relatives from the paternal side of an offender's family may not be among the envoys of reconciliation. These can be either relatives from the maternal side or any respectable people from the community. With the consent of the offended party, the offender's side may pay compensation.

In *sharia*, forgiving a murderer a the most charitable act. Relatives of a murder victim may opt out of revenge, having received a ransom (equivalent to the value of one hundred camels), or agree to forgive without compensation (Albogachieva, 2011a, p.482). It should be noted, that the best thing for the relatives of a murder victim to do, according to *sharia*, is to forgive without compensation. Forgiveness accompanied by financial compensation is the second-best option.

If no truce has been concluded, the relatives of the murderer observe a kind of etiquette prescribed for such a category of people. They do not attend weddings and funerals where close relatives of the victim may be present, and women wear dark clothing. They avoid not only intentional, but also accidental meetings. The closest relatives of a killer will be forced to resign from work or they can no longer go to school; they do not appear in public places and live a secluded life until reconciliation has been achieved. This has significant economic consequences. In these families women are forced to work, the men sit at home or leave the country so as to avoid being tracked down by the avengers. They may find a new job in exile and send money home. All this time, close relatives have been sending representatives to the side that has been offended with the hope of agreeing to some terms. This continues until reconciliation is achieved or until the murder is avenged.

The avenger also has to comply with prescribed behavioural standards. According to Ingush *adat*, blood feud cannot be carried out when a person is sleeping or defenceless, that is, unarmed, naked, bathing or unconscious. Murder committed from a hiding place, from behind or in an ambush, or without any warning is condemned and considered treacherous.

It should be noted that imprisonment and natural death did not automatically put an end to a blood feud. About the debt of honour and blood, the Ingush say: 'Do not rush, but do not forget!' In cases where the avenger dies, the duty of vengeance is passed on to his son or brother. Cases have been recorded where the great-grandsons became the victims of blood feuds for what their ancestors had done. In all cases, it was not permitted to kill women and children.

It is believed that it is better to resolve all issues related to blood feuds as soon as possible so that the descendants may live in peace. This applies both to the object of vengeance and to its subject. When an offender dies a natural death without revenge or forgiveness, his closest family members become objects of revenge, be it his father, brother, son, grandson, or, if there are no other direct male relatives, his nephews.

Society may ostracise a killer's family for deliberate and brutal murder. In some cases the elders of the clan force an offender and his family to leave their houses for the sake of their own safety. Most often, this option is given those who by fate have become the rivals of a powerful clan known to be 'cruel, bad people'. The latter should not be taken literally as it is generally used to describe a clan that does not easily forgive an offence. An Ingush proverb says: 'Let me be at feud with good people instead of a relative of bad ones.' Such families are often inflexible, and negotiating with them is quite difficult. It is necessary to wait for some time for the pain and passions to subside.

Sometimes parties prefer to simply end the relationship temporarily, while the perpetrator of a crime is in custody. During this time, relatives and members of the conciliation commission will do everything possible to resolve the conflict, and if by the end of the prison term hopes for a truce are not realised, the murderer will not be able to return home. In cases where it is not possible to reconcile the rival clans, the family of the offender moves to another residence, temporarily or permanently.

The forms of reconciliation have undergone various changes after the adoption of Islam. Modern reconciliation occurs in the vicinity of the mosque. But, since only prayers are allowed in a prayer house and the courtyard of a mosque, forgiveness needs to be arranged outside. A reconciliation procedure is usually scheduled after the Friday prayers because there are a large number of people at the mosque on these days. In Ingush tradition, a woman does not attend a mosque, so, there is usually no traditional division into male and female sections. Women do not appear as witnesses or as participants of the reconciliation ceremony either, only men are present. The head of the victim's family announces that from now on he has no claims or complaints. He forgives the offender and embraces him. He takes an oath and gives an assurance that if ever anyone from among his relatives breaks the current agreement his family bears no responsibility for that murderer. This is a deviation from the norm, and it happens very rarely. Society rejects such people; they become outcasts because they are perjurers.

After the declaration of forgiveness, a group of men led by the elders of the family and members of the conciliation commission appear. They walk slowly towards the victim's family, with heads lowered in silence. The men line up and the avengers approach each of them, shake hands, embrace them and say, 'I forgive you for the sake of Allah' (*Az pkha bitar khiona d'la dukh*) before walking away peacefully (field material, 2010). The direct participation of the murderer in the reconciliation ceremony is not obligatory. In most cases, the ceremony takes place in their absence. In Chechnya it is one of the obligatory ritual details of the reconciliation process (Albogachieva, 2011, p.19). Much moral and spiritual education is conducted during the rite of reconciliation. The importance and value of forgiveness from the perspective of Islam is explained to all those who are present.

Each reconciliation brings relief to the participants of the conflict, since the participants no longer need to hide, while others do not need to search endlessly for the killer. In accordance with *sharia*, it is a most virtuous and charitable act. Therefore, the most significant, time-consuming and demanding part of the work is undertaken by the Ingush clergy. To achieve positive results in matters of blood feuds, conciliatory commissions are set up in the republic's *muftiat* to keep records of all cases and deal with these complex issues in cooperation with society. These commissions constantly interact with the state justice system, and if there was a car accident they return a verdict based on the judgments of the traffic police. The existence of the conciliation commission in the Republic of Ingushetia may be a sign of the need for civil society to reach reconciliation and harmony.

References

Albogachieva, M., 2011. Iz istorii borby s krovnoy mestyu [Stories of Struggle against Vendettas]. *Forum for Anthropology and Culture*, 14. Available at <http://anthropologie.kunstkamera.ru/07/ 14online/albogachieva_1/> [Accessed 5 March 2014]

Blaramberg, I., 1992. *Caucasian Manuscript*. Stavropol: Stavropol Publishing House.

Dalgat, B. K., 2008. *Rodovoy byt i obychnoe pravo Chechentsev i Ingushey. Issledovania i materialy 1892–1894* [Tribal Life and Customary Law of the Chechens and the Ingush. Research and Materials]. Moscow: IMLI RAN.

Dmitriev, V. A., 2003. Adaty i shariat u Kavkazskikh gortsev [Customary Law and Sharia of Highlanders in the Caucasus]. *Russia and the Caucasus*. St Petersburg.

Kardavi, S. Y., 2004. *Dozvolennoe i zapretnoe v Islame* [Allowed and Prohibited in Islam]. Moscow.

Kosven, M. O., 1925. *Prestuplenie i nakazanie v dogosudarstvennom obshestve* [Crime and Punishment in Pre-state Societies]. Moscow and Leningrad.

Leontovich, F. I., 1883. *Adaty Kavkazskikh gortsev. Materialy po obychnomu pravu severnogo i vostochnogo Kavkaza* [*Adats* of the Caucasian Highlanders. Materials on the Customary Law of the Northern and Eastern Caucasus], vol. 2. Odessa.

Russian State Historical Archive, RSHA. F. 797, Inv. 2. 8809. 19. SPb BAAS. F. 800. Inv. 6. no. 574. Fol. 16. St Petersburg: Branch of the Archive of Academy of Sciences.

Verdier, R., 1980. *Le Systeme Vindicatoire: La Vengeance*. Paris: Editions Cujas.

Yakovlev, N. F., 1925. *Ingushi* [The Ingush]. Moscow.

Zhupikova, E. F., 2007. *Povstancheskoe dvijenie na Severnom Kavkaze v 1920–1925 godakh* [Insurgency in the North Caucasus in 1920–1925]. Moscow: Academy of Historical Sciences.

Chapter 6
Municipal Elections in Dagestan: Political Events in a Village Community

Ekaterina Kapustina

It is not rare for elections to serve as an object of scientific research. Elections are not only significant as political events. They are also important social events that reveal structural specifics of the community where elections take place (see Levon Abrahamian and Gayane Shagoyan in this volume). Elections can be considered an 'issue' of a kind that a community being studied must 'respond to', and react to with the available means and in conformity with the rules that operate within it. A number of studies describe and analyse elections in the context of democratisation of society (see Caldeira and Holston, 1999; Pastor, 1998). Some scholars look at elections as a technological process and find cultural peculiarities and meanings in the analysis of their execution (Coles, 2004). This chapter, however, is devoted not to the study of the election process but uses the event as a foil to reveal the workings of a modern village community in rural mountain Dagestan.

Dagestan is one of the most multi-ethnic republics of the Russian Federation. More than thirty indigenous ethnic groups live there and the issue of the ethnic self-perception of local groups remains urgent. Linguistic diversity makes Dagestan not only a 'land of mountains' (as per the Turkic origin of the name) but also a 'mountain of languages'. The majority of languages spoken in Dagestan belong to the Northeast Caucasian family of languages (Avar, Lak, Dargin, Lezgic, and others), although Turkish languages (for example, Kumyk, Nogai, Azerbaijani),Iranian (Tat) and others are also spoken. All large ethnic groups have written languages based on the Cyrillic alphabet. Scores of unwritten ones are used mostly in the mountainous districts of the republic. The vast majority of the population is Muslim; exceptions include the Russians and Armenians living in cities and in the north of Dagestan.

The variety of cultures in Dagestan has many common elements. Dagestan was in the past, and continues to be, a specific, integrated cultural space, which allows for the analysis of a variety of research questions based on material from all parts of Dagestan, keeping in mind the specifics of this or that local community.

In the course of migration processes that have taken place in the last hundred years in which many mountain dwellers left their home villages and moved to the plains or cities of the republic and beyond, the social and cultural image of the republic has changed (Karpov and Kapustina, 2011). Nevertheless, all mountain areas in Dagestan are still largely inhabited.

The modernisation of traditional village social institutions began around 150 years ago and continues to date. A key feature of Dagestani society is thus a combination of traditional and modern social elements. This is more evident for mountain villages because the populations of many settlements on the plain changed considerably after taking in migrants from mountain districts of the republic. The material and interviews used in this chapter are from fieldwork done in the period 2008 to 2011 in the mountain villages of western and central Dagestan.

The village community remains a popular research subject today as in the past. First, I must explain the nature of the village society in the Dagestani context. To do so, it is first necessary to define the meaning of term *djamaat*, mentioned in many citations: 'According to the socio-cultural character of a traditional mountain settlement, a village community was organised into the form of a so-called village commune or what local dwellers using Arabic, term *djamaat*. (Karpov, 2007, p.6, emphasis added).

The character, context and origins of *djamaat* are the subject of an ongoing discussion (Bobrovnikov, 2004; Karpov, 2007). Today, the term is used by the informants in various contexts – to describe the village community, the religious community, or the village population including all migrants from the village that maintain contact with it (see Iwona Kaliszewska in this volume). Sometimes, *djamaat* is used to indicate a group of selected, respected people, analogous to *dvatsatka* (a group of twenty) for the council of elders (Magomedkhanov, 2008, p.174). In mass media and contemporary political discourse, the term *djamaat* is also used in reference to illegal military groups of Muslim radicals fighting against the federal state. I will use *djamaat* here as meaning a village community, and moreover in every case I will try to explain the precise meaning of the term. It is interesting for me to understand how political events common between all federal subjects fit into the specific social structure of a Dagestani village community.

The elections of the head of the village administration and members of the district assembly often emerge as a high point in the political life of a Dagestani village. The last two decades have shown that these events are usually painful, both for individual villagers and the village community as a social organism. Here, I will limit myself to the election of the head of the village administration, rural deputies and – to a lesser extent – with the election of the head of the district and the district deputies. I will deliberately avoid discussing elections at higher levels since the rural community has shown little interest in them in recent years and has little influence on results.

First, I want to focus on the head of the municipality. The head of the village is elected for four years by direct secret ballot. It is the highest administrative position in the village. Even though the salary of the head of the village is higher than that of most villagers working in the administration, it is still relatively low and cannot be compared with the income of businessmen or with successful cattle-breeders. The head of the village, though, has significant influence on the course of developments in the village and is in a position to influence the distribution of monies (often in his own favour and in favour of his own inner circle). It is, additionally, an undoubtedly prestigious position. The role of the village deputies in the political and economic life of the village is less pronounced, they do not have direct access to the village budget and much less attention is paid to their elections.

To study an election as a significant social event for the village community, it is necessary to identify the main characteristics of the event, the agents involved, the resources villagers use in reaching their goals, and the terms and conditions under which they operate. The first part of the chapter deals with these questions. In the second part, I will look at different conflicts that arise in the course of the election campaign and mechanisms used to resolve them.

Rural Political Technologies and Resources

Let us define the main agents involved in the electoral process and the resources they use to achieve their goals, as well as the terms and conditions under which they operate. While every rural community has its own specifics, a number of details common to most mountain villages can be identified. At the time, it is usually the villagers themselves, or, in extreme cases, people from the village, but living in urban areas of Dagestan and beyond, who take part in municipal elections. The vast majority of the villagers are almost always old-timers and, due to the predominance of endogamy strategies, they can be related in kinship with each other. In principle, the following methods can be pointed out for producing the desired rural votes in municipal elections, used in Dagestani society today. There is little doubt that kinship is essential when it comes to elections, particularly at the level of the municipality: 'Those with the most relatives become deputies' (field material, 2007, male, aged 30).

The vote for one or other candidate for the position of head of administration is thus determined directly by kinship. But, in such a close-knit community where everyone is related in varying degree to everyone else, it is not uncommon that the voter is related to two or more candidates. This is true to a lesser extent for regional centres as well, but small mountain villages are more affected. In this case, other factors and actions become relevant.

Each candidate has his own campaign headquarters manned by relatives and close friends, who divide responsibilities between themselves. Ideally, the staff is made up both of respected elders able to prevent conflicts and those who are ready to attack the opponent, both through argument as well as through the use of physical force.

Vote buying is an extremely common tactic and is used in all elections. The price of a vote varies greatly from village to village, and often depends on the candidates' and/or their patrons' ability to pay. In 2011, it varied from 1,000 to 5,000 roubles or more per vote/family. The votes of close relatives need not be purchased since these voters are expected to vote for their relative anyway. Money, goods or even services can serve as payment: 'According to a story told by a member of the electoral commission, a few days before the election, the candidate for the Kaspiysk city council asked one of the voters who would decide who his family would support directly, '"Who gives more [money]?" People were demanding a bag of flour for the votes of a whole family, asking for intervention in legal proceedings or asking for work for their children' (Lazarev, 2010, p.12).

Sometimes, candidates invest pre-election campaign money in the village infrastructure in an attempt to win the villagers' confidence and support. For instance, in the village of Karata, one of the most powerful villagers, in an attempt to ensure that the entire village vote for him in the district election, financed the construction of a road to the upper part of the village. One of my informants characterised these kinds of activities in clearly positive terms, even though it was an improper use of funds allocated by the state.

Another popular method to increase the number of votes is that people, who support a specific candidate (their relatives, friends or clients), register as residents in a village for the period of the election so as to vote there: 'In villages where there should be a maximum of 600 people there were 800 people. Everywhere you found one hundred to two hundred more people than there were [supposed to be]. Anyone from any other district can be registered. Let's assume I'm running for election. I would say to someone, 'Are you my friend? Then go, register and vote for me!' 'I would register everyone in my family for you if you like!' 'Now, register them all!' And he registers all the *tukhum* [lineage], all his kin, and they come in vans for the election and vote' (field material, 2010, male, aged 40). Generally, on election day, the candidates will ensure that all their relatives with the right to vote in the village come from all over the country to do so.

Villagers in the cities will actively influence the election in their native village, support desired candidates and go to vote, since many of them are still registered in the village. For example, the members of the expatriate organisation from Karata in the capital will actively discuss who is best suited to be village head, or who is best suited to represent the village in district elections. Many 'residents' of Karata (about half of them) are merely registered 'in the mountains'. They live in the city, and often have done so for a long time. Thus, urban resources and decisions made by the expatriate community may have a significant impact on the results of elections.

Athletics associations play an important role in Dagestani politics (Solonenko, 2011). Their resources are used to intimidate rivals, maintain order or cause disorder at polling stations, etc. At the village level they play only a limited role, if any at all, since their active presence would be viewed by the community as a form of alien interference in local affairs. According to one informant, once, a group of young athletes allegedly connected to the famous Dagestani and federal politician Gadzhi Makhachev came to support one of the candidates for the position of village head in his village: 'Fighters came, their cars were pushed into the ravine and there their Mercedes' remain. They were lucky not to suffer the same fate' (field material, 2011, male, aged 38).

During the election, when all kinds of conflicts escalate, the social status of a person becomes more relevant than in 'peaceful' times. For example, the division of villagers in Karata into a 'lower group' and an 'upper group' becomes important during elections. The people of the lower group are the descendants of freemen (*uzden*), those of the upper group are the descendants of the *lak* ('slaves'). *Uzden* and *lak* are the social estates that existed in Dagestan long before the republic was incorporated into the Russian Empire. They were officially abolished in the 1860s, but the memory of a family's social origin is still vital and relevant. According to one informant, the upper group in Karata usually put forward one candidate. This is, according to the villager, due to the greater cohesion of the upper group; while the lower group in this village is not as unanimous. Thus, often they put up several candidates for election.

The Role of the Imam in Elections

At a time when the role of Islam in Dagestani villages is clearly growing, it is not surprising that in villages where religiosity and the authority of a given imam is high, the latter can influence the course and results of an election. The imam can act as a mediator, can support the candidacy of one or other villager and can persuade members of a community to vote for that candidate. There are cases where the imam is himself a candidate for office. For example, in the village of Aknada, the imam announced his candidacy but did not receive the support of villagers who suggested that he devotes himself to spiritual rather than political matters.

Imams can also maintain a neutral position. In the village of Khushtada, for example, an imam who was born in another *djamaat*, and had only lived in the village for a few years, left the village during the elections so as to avoid giving the impression of supporting any particular candidate.

The role of the imam should nevertheless not be overestimated, even in very religious communities. The imam may not play an independent political role, especially if he is an outsider (a protégé of the Spiritual Board of Muslims of Dagestan), or a young man (not unlikely in Dagestan). The authority of the imam is largely dependent on his personal qualities, as well as on how well he is informed about the problems of the village (Karpov and Kapustina, 2011, p.154).

The Council of Elders

One of the most prominent social structures in the village is the council of elders, called the *djamaat*, 'the twenty', or 'the coordinating council'. Often this body is constituted officially at the municipal level as a deliberative body or as a municipal council. Elsewhere, it exists as either a public organisation; or, it is not formalised in any way. The degree of formality does not directly affect its efficiency.

Elected by the whole community, respected and generally competent in religious matters, the council of elders plays an important role in the electoral process. In Karata, the '*djamaat* summoned the candidates for election as head of the village and asked each what he wanted, what he was going to do. Some were asked to give way to another. “To give way or not, that’s his doing, of course, but it’s no good to go against the *djamaat*, everyone will know about it’” (field material, 2011, male, aged 62). In the village of Khushtada, the role of the *djamaat* in elections is described as follows: ‘In early 2007, the coordinating council discussed the nominated candidates for the district assembly and the People’s Assembly of Dagestan. The people voted for those recommended by the *djamaat*’ (Karpov and Kapustina, 2011, p.158).

That ‘traditional’ social institutions play an important role in ‘modern’ politics is very common. It should not be forgotten that in this case, such councils are elected by all members of the community and even if they are not formalised, they almost always represent the will of the majority. In this sense it is impossible to ignore the role that the community and community structures in elections. While the individual is formally endowed by the constitution to decide alone for whom they will vote, this right does have certain limits. The decision of the *djamaat* is sometimes considered to stand above personal will. This situation is typical for the Dagestani village community in the past: ‘The community either directly or via created institutions formed and quite closely regulated relations in certain communities and it can be assumed that it suppressed the initiative of the individuals that made up the community’ (Karpov, 2007, p.20).

A very illustrative event is the case of the village of Gergebil. There, at the request of members of the village, all candidates for the post of head of the village, including the incumbent, withdrew their candidacies and elections were postponed until the next year: ‘They were asked to withdraw their candidacies since yet another, more trusted person was desired as head of the village. The people said that none of the registered candidates qualified’ (*Vibori glavi*, 2010).

In trying to understand this case, the extent to which the *djamaat* played a role is important. In interviews, informants describe the *djamaat* in various ways, as strong, weak, ‘solid’, or as ‘no longer what it was before’. However, the balance of power between the head of the village and the *djamaat* may often shift in favour of the latter: ‘The head of the village plays a big role at the moment. He is responsible for everything .... And he is elected by the *djamaat* ... If he doesn’t cope – he can be removed ... The head of the administration must be subordinate. The *djamaat* is God and king here’ (field material, 2004, male, aged 56).

Elections as a Problem for Village Society: Preventing and Overcoming Conflicts

In the context of interactions between individuals and the rural community that dictates its will to an individual, one needs to see the electoral process as a kind of threat to peace and unity in the community. One informant, who himself campaigned for office in his village said: ‘The most harmful thing to the republic is elections’ (field material, 2010, male, aged 40).

The nightly news verifies this stance, frequently reporting fights between candidates and their supporters. Political assassinations during elections have become a norm in the republic since the 1990s and continue to this day. This has resulted in discussions in Dagestan about no longer calling elections. My informants often spoke about this, too. Some referred to the discrepancy between the idea of elections and the *sharia*, some cited the rise in violence during elections and pointed out that they destroyed families, and entire rural communities. Various rural communities have begun to search for alternatives.

In Karata, it has become customary to hold some elections in several stages. Before the officially designated election day in the village, 'mini-elections' are held. After prayer in the mosque it is announced that at a certain time all should come to the square to participate in a mini-election, the purpose of which is to select one candidate from a group of supporters (in the case of elections for village head), or from the whole village (if the head of the district is being elected). For example, in 2007, in such mini-elections villagers tried to choose a single candidate from Karata for head of the district. When a person is chosen in such a manner he receives the support of the villagers in the official election; others must withdraw their candidacies. Elections in the mosque were a variation (sometimes held before a mini-election). An odd number of voters (for example, thirteen) are chosen from among the respected pious members of the community and they in turn choose one candidate from among all applicants. The losing candidates in these pre-elections are in no way obligated to accept these decisions. The last time such elections were held, the losing party did not accept the result, claiming that many of those elected were relatives of the winner. In the end, the candidates met in the official elections.

In Gagatli, all the men gathered in the mosque (the village has a very religious community) before the election and decided to avoid possible conflicts and squabbles among the villagers by cancelling the elections and extending the mandate of the current head. All the ballots were filled out formally, but it was not a real election.

In Kharbuk, a few years ago, the influential head of the village was killed in a car accident. After the tragedy, a gathering was called in the village, where the *djamaat* decided to hand over the power to his son, a student who studied and lived in Makhachkala. This choice was made, according to informants, out of respect for his father and in an attempt to avoid the squabbles and conflicts of an election. The young man was only twenty-two years old when he was elected to this highest village post and in 2008 he was the youngest head of a village administration in Russia.

In the village of Khushtada the deputy for the district assembly was chosen by lot. This was interpreted as 'divine justice' – as the will of Allah. And again, this method of election was chosen in an attempt to avoid the inevitable conflicts of an election by ballot. The results of the draw were accepted by everyone.

Elections also provoke conflicts within the family, a problem that is actively discussed in the community. In almost every rural community examined, such conflicts could be identified. These family conflicts often ended in divorce when spouses supported different candidates. In one case, to avoid such a conflict, a women in the village of Khushtada decided that half of the eligible voters in the family would vote for one candidate and the other half for the other. The children followed this decision and took part in this 'just' resolution. Another villager left with his family right before the election because he was related to both candidates. Thus, he avoided having to make a choice between them.

When it is still not possible to avoid a conflict, attempts can be made to resolve it. This is when the practice of *masliat* – of making a truce – comes into play. The institution of *masliatchi*, of mediators called to broker a reconciliation between parties in both civil and criminal cases, is still very common in Dagestan today, according to attorney Rasul Kadiev, despite the fact that in 2010, Russia passed a law against such mediators. They continue to operate parallel to Russian legislation, sometimes deciding against state law if need be (Kadiev, 2011). The professional *masliatchi* are popular with a very wide range of people. On the village level the *masliatchi* know all the parties in a conflict personally. In Karat, for example, there can always be found a respected and pious person in each candidate's campaign headquarters who is willing to carry out *masliat* using their authority and influence.

Masliat can be used as part of a pre-election strategy – it is a means to enlist the support of potential supporters. For example, a *masliat* was held between the head of the Akhvakh district and another villager. The two families were in conflict since 2007. In 2011, a *masliat* was finally agreed upon. According to other villagers, the supporters of the head needed the *masliat* to ensure success in the next election. They wanted to resolve the conflict and thus increase their number of supporters. The *masliat* was held at a restaurant in Makhachkala with the respected villagers and representatives of the mosque taking part. A truce is made 'for the sake of Allah' – as it should be. The relatives of the district head definitely associated reconciliation with future elections.

Conclusions

Elections are acute experiences on the village level, an ambiguous, but vibrant phenomenon in rural life. They involve the entire rural community, including villagers that do not permanently live there.

The democratic basis of modern elections is the will of the individual but this ideal is modified by various social institutions such as family, kin, the council of elders and the *djamaat*. Norms such as unity and peace in the community are valued higher than individual choice and the strict execution of state law. Under these conditions a so-called 'communal consciousness' (Karpov, 2004, p.160) emerges as a relevant factor in rural Dagestan. This peculiarity of Dagestani villages make electoral strategies of this region stand out in the all-Russian context, where a common village consciousness has often been replaced by individualism.

Elections produce conflicts. At the same time they encourage villagers to look for ways to prevent or overcome them. Elections bring to light the fact that the rural community is a single organism that perceives its unity as a social value.

References

Bobrovnikov, V., 2004. Arheologia stroitelstva islamskih traditsii v dagestanskom kolhoze [Construction of Islamic Traditions in a Dagestani Collective Farm – An Archeology]. *Ab Imperio*, 3, pp.563–93.

Caldeira, T. P. R. and Holston, J., 1999. Democracy and Violence in Brazil. *Comparative Studies in Society and History*, 41(4), pp.691–729.

Coles, K. A., 2004. Election Day: The Construction of Democracy through Technique. *Cultural Anthropology*, 19(4), pp.551–80.

Kadiev, R., 2011. *Yuridicheskaya situatsiya po Dagestanu [Legal situation in Dagestan].* Available at <http://kadievrasul.livejournal.com/15890.html> [Accessed 4 November 2011].

Karpov, Y. Y., 2004. Lichnost i traditsionnie sotsialnie instituti: printsipi vzaimodeistvia [Personality and Traditional Social Institutions: The Principles of Interaction]. In: Y. Y. Karpov, ed., 2004. *Severniy Kavkaz: chelovek v sisteme sotsiokulturnih svyazei* [North Caucasus: Man in the System of Social and Cultural Ties]. St Petersburg: Peterburgskoe vostokovedenie, pp.107–67.

Karpov, Y. Y., 2007. Gornoe dagestanskoe selenie: ot traditsionnogo djamaata k nineshnemu sotsialnomu obliku [Dagestani Mountain Village: From Traditional *djamaat* to a Contemporary Social Situation]. In: S. A. Shtyrkov, ed., *Severniy Kavkaz: traditsionnoe sel'skoe soobshestvo – sotsialnie roli, obshestvennoe mnenie, vlastnie otnosheniya* [North Caucasus: A Traditional Rural Society – Social Roles, Public Opinion, Power Relations]. St Petersburg: Nauka. pp.5–74.

Karpov, Y. Y. and Kapustina, E. L., 2011. *Gortsi posle gor: Migratsionnie protsessi v Dagestane v XX – v nachale XXI vekov, ih sotsialnie i etnokulturnie posledstviya i perspektivi* [Highlanders after the Mountains: Immigration Processes in Dagestan in the 20th and at the Beginning of the 21st century, their Social and Ethno-cultural Implications and Perspectives]. St Petersburg: Peterburgskoe vostokovedenie.

Lazarev, E., 2010. Formal'nie i neformal'nie institute v elektoral'nom protsesse (na primere mestnih viborov v Respublike Dagestan) [Formal and Informal Institutes in Electoral Proccess (on the example of local elections in Dagestan)]. Available at <http://www.eu.spb.ru/images/M_center/Preprint_Lazarev_2.pdf> [Accessed 29 October 2011].

Magomedkhanov, M., 2008. *Dagestantsi: Etnoyazikovie i sotsiokulturnie aspekti samosoznaniya* [Dagestanis: Ethno-linguistic and Socio-cultural Aspects of Self-consciousness]. Moscow: Dinem.

Pastor, R. A., 1998. Mediating Elections. *Journal of Democracy*, 9(1), pp.154–63.

Solonenko, M., 2011. 'Silovoy resurs' vo vnutrenney politike Dagestana [The 'Power Factor' in the Internal Politics of Dagestan]. In: Y. K. Chistov, ed., Radlovskiy sbornik. St Petersburg: MAE RAS. pp.118–32.

Vibori glavi, 2010. *Vibori glavi dagestanskogo sela Gergebil perenesli na polgoda* [Election of the Head of a Dagestani Village, Gergebil Postponed for Six months]. Available at <http://ria.ru/politics/20101008/283432938.html> [Accessed 29 November 2011].

Chapter 7

The Tbilisi 'Street' as a Legal and Political Phenomenon in Georgia

Evgenia Zakharova

Quite recently the 'street' was one of the most important social institutions that organised youth in Georgia. One could often hear the words 'academy of the street' from those living in Georgia, emphasising the vital social role attributed to this unofficial educational institution. By 'street', I mean the specific discursive and practiced space, characteristic for Tbilisi and many other (if not for all) urban areas in Georgia, that in the conscience of Georgian urban residents signifies a whole spectrum of associations, from gunfights to the *kanonieri kurdi* (thieves-in-law), 'street ideals' and life in urban residential blocks – *ubani*.

This chapter will examine two recent chronological periods – before and after the reforms launched by the new authorities after the Rose Revolution of 2003, which became a starting point of street transformation, too. Before the reforms the 'street' played an important role in social network building, linking the young men first within their neighbourhood block, and then wider and wider, so that a web of connections emerged little by little to cover the whole city. One of the key institutions in the neighbourhood community and in Tbilisi street culture as well, is the male block-based peer groups called *birzha* which are made up of boys in their late twenties. In Georgian, *birzha* denotes a male peer group associated with a specific neighbourhood community that interacts mostly in public space, what elsewhere has been classified as a 'street-corner society'. If we turn to studies of street communities in different cultures, as well as to the history of Tbilisi *birzha* themselves, we see that depending on the social, economic and historical context, such communities may take different forms – from local leisure groups to bands with a distinct social structure and hierarchy, formal leader, budget and written statute (Jankowski, 1991; Koehler, 2000; Venkatesh and Levitt, 2000; Vigil, 1988; Whyte, 1943; Anderson, 1999; Volkov, 2002; Stivenson, 2006).

In this chapter, I will describe the Tbilisi streets as a forum of legal and political life of Georgia. I will deal with the specific attitude toward law and order among modern Georgian city dwellers as regarded and interpreted through the prism of conceptions of masculinity and honour that operate in the streets in Georgia (on conceptions of honour see Elke Kamm in this volume). The second part of the chapter will deal with the interaction between the street, and state political powers. I will shed light on the possible ways of collaboration between the street and political elites and reveal the factors, both contributing to and preventing this collaboration. The chapter is based on fieldwork data collected in Tbilisi in August 2007, November 2009 and January to February 2010, as well as an analysis of media reports over seven years and discussions on Georgian-language Internet forums.

The Street in Tbilisi as a Legal Factor in Georgia

In Soviet and post-Soviet urban Georgia (from the late 1960s to the present), official Soviet legal procedure coexisted with extra-court mediation, that is, a state of legal pluralism. Depending on the gravity of a conflict and the social position of the parties involved, the mediators were either neighbourhood leaders or criminal authorities – *kanonieri kurdi* or those standing close to them in the underworld hierarchy. The state long closed its eyes to the existence of traditional law (while actually applying it, too). With Mikheil Saakashvili's presidency (2004–2013) the existence and force of traditional law in the city was officially acknowledged and a campaign against this system of relations was declared.

Due to the existence of alternative means of conflict resolution and enforcement, negative attitudes were generally endemic in Georgian urban culture towards state institutions and towards the machinery of state justice in particular. In the years after the Rose Revolution of 2003, however, a change in public opinion has emerged: trust in state law and in state institutions has risen and faith in customary means of conflict resolution has declined. I will look at some aspects of this shift through the prism of street culture. To define the factors that led to this shift, I will begin with describing the main features of street culture, focusing on the period before the changes that the street experienced in the years following Rose Revolution.

In Tbilisi local identity, the feeling of belonging to a neighbourhood was and is extremely vital. Local belonging, defined by the answer to the question 'Where are you from?' is the major element of street culture. Among teenagers the question 'What *ubani* are you from?' is often one of the first questions to ask when meeting a new person. Representatives of the older generation state that in their younger years they could easily distinguish residents of different *ubani* based on the dialect of that specific neighbourhood. With Georgian urban street culture, I mean the culture of these urban neighbourhood communities. What is considered 'just' and 'unjust' on the street is constituted by a set of rules and norms called *kuchuri gageba* or street notions. Everything in conflict with 'street notions' could be severely sanctioned if the person whose interests were damaged decided to addresses street authorities for mediation. Street notions are identified with 'thieves' law', the code which operated and still operates in Soviet and post-Soviet prisons. This association of street notions with the thieves' code was regarded as one of the grounds for their validity.

Until not long ago, for the *birzha*, a *kanonieri kurdi* was a man who enjoyed power, money and privileges, a person they wanted to emulate. Teenagers with high status in the *birzha* who pursued a criminal career were called *dzveli bichebi* ('old boys'). The set of qualities and behavioural characteristics of the *dzveli bichebi* was called *dzvelbichoba*. Another notion of critical importance in Georgian culture is the concept of manliness which summarises ideas of masculine honour. In contrast to *dzvelbichoba*, it is relevant not only for the street, but in general defines the image of 'a real Georgian'. Thus, we are dealing with two concepts of manliness in local culture, one of which is specific for street culture (*dzvelbichoba*), and one which is relevant for Georgian culture in general. In the late Soviet and early post-Soviet periods these two concepts almost coincided in their content.

The world of thieves and the concomitant style of behaviour had prestige not only among teenagers. In a Tbilisi newspaper, the author of an article on the 'problem of the street' asks the reader: 'Probably, you often heard fathers say that they want to bring up their sons as future thieves-in-law and to respect each other?' To be a thief or to be close to the underworld was considered prestigious. The figure of the thief as a neighbourhood leader applying *kuchuri gageba* was identified with a form of justice. At the same time, this ability to ensure justice is denied by the state.

One can speak of the consistent negation of official power and legal institutions in Georgian society during the Soviet period. This becomes all the more clear if we take into account that it was considered completely natural. It went without saying that state officials always used their positions for achieving personal goals. The logic that 'the state has its laws, we have our own' is a predictable consequence of the legal situation in the Soviet years.

The corruption and the arbitrariness of the police and courts reached its peak in the early 1990s and contributed to the negative image of the state, and its law-enforcement institutions in particular. In this period, the police became one of the gangs in Tbilisi; but while the gangs obeyed their street law, the police were not bound by any code.

The attitudes towards law and order that have determined local relations with state institutions of control and enforcement can be derived largely from ideas of manliness and honour in Georgian culture. The protection of one's honour and the honour of one's family and friends is the core virtue of a man – even when it runs counter to state law.

While visiting a Tbilisi school, President Mikheil Saakashvili (2010) made a speech on the increase in criminality among adolescents and said: 'The day before yesterday an eighteen year old boy was shot before everybody's eyes right after his birthday party. Those to blame escaped, but none of the young people who were there came forward as witnesses. Not only are the killers monsters but also those who saw everything and did not say a word to the police. They think that it would mean squealing.'

It was not by chance that in this public speech the head of the state focused his attention on informing the police and used a colloquialism to denote this act. Informing the police was considered to be one of the most severe violations of *kuchuri gageba* norms. It was the unwillingness to inform that became the driving factor behind the refusal to seek help from the police.

From the local perspective, to ask police for help in solving one's problems meant to be an informer. A strong disapproval of informing was a crucial part of street culture: being an informant the gravest crime. But while this attitude is common in many cultures, in Georgia it can imply different actions. In Georgian street culture, simply reporting an incident to the police was understood as 'informing'. In comparison to the socially distant and hostile police, an offender was conceived of as socially close. The victim of a crime inevitably found himself in the same camp of resistance to the state as the perpetrator.

One should note that applying to the police was regarded as informing not only in the street norms and values of *dzvelbichoba*. Such a viewpoint was widespread in Georgian society in general. It conflicted with honour, the concept of manliness.

Being a witness was regarded as close to informing. Among young boys in the *birzha*, the word 'witness' itself was taboo, even in its meaning as an eyewitness and not a witness for the state. Instead of the word 'witness' a euphemism had to be used.

The second reason for not going to police lay in the fact that in street culture this was understood as an inability to solve one's own problems. And a person who is not able to stand up for himself is not a *vazhkatsi*, not a man of honour. At the same time, the idea of being able to solve one's problems did not conflict with the possibility of resorting to social capital gained through different kinds of connections – family, school, neighbourhood or others. On the contrary, the absence of such social capital offered grounds to suspect one's honour. Real men must have such connections.

Not going to the police was a norm. Resisting the police meant displaying particular valour. This motive appeared in many interviews. Informants emphasised their or their friends' heroic behaviour in police stations. When told about the refusal to testify by any means, they proudly spoke of cases when they managed to trick police officers. Such behaviour was socially approved and became evidence of a man's courage and enhanced his prestige.

With Saakashvili's election to president, the state started a demonstrative campaign against the 'street' and the whole system of informal rules and underground economy based on *kuchuri gageba*. It was evident to everybody in Georgia that this system embraced the whole of Georgian society and had, for many decades, ensured stability and order. The new regime argued that the 'street' represented an instrument of corruption and the interests of various criminal groups and thus proclaimed the goal of changing the mechanism for the maintenance of order, both in society as a whole and on the street in particular.

One of the main measures that were undertaken by the authorities was the passing of new legislation against organised crime and racketeering, imposing penalties not only for 'membership in the thieves' world', but even for bearing the title of thief. Criminal law was enriched with new terms – *kanonieri kurdi*, the 'thieves' world and belonging to it' and so on (*Sakartvelos siskhlis samartlis saprotseso kodeksi*, 2010). Everyone who acknowledged the authority of the thieves' world and regularly acted in it was defined as a member. Among other measures that were undertaken by the state, one should mention the broad coverage in the press of criminal trials and the sentencing of *kanonieri kurdi* and officials accused of corruption and the repeated documentation in the media of 'immoral' and ' thieves' law' behaviour. Among the undertakings aimed to reduce juvenile crime was the program of 'safe schools', which included measures directed at increasing control over students and developing their legal knowledge. The program included the attempt to establish in the school structure the position of 'speaker-policeman' who would be responsible for controlling school students' behaviour and conducting educational seminars. The school curriculum was enriched with a new subject, which aimed to educate adolescents on their relations with the law. Much emphasis was placed on the work of neighbourhood inspectors with teenagers. The state tried to enforce its claim to the monopoly on violence and sought to take control of those spheres (street life in particular) that had until then been the sole domain of the thieves' law and neighbourhood groups.

The war on the thieves' world became the subject of public discussions. The growth of street crime defined as *bespredzeli* (crime and violence that is not controlled by thieves) is attributed to this struggle. Many thought that the order offered by the thieves-in-law and the role of mediator, attributed to some local thieves, especially among teenagers, helped to restrain the level of violence in the streets. At the same time, in today's Georgian society it is widely believed that crime and corruption has been considerably reduced (see Lilli Di Puppo in this volume). But, we should not overestimate the objectivity of public opinion on the changes going on in society. It is formed largely under the influence of mass media that in recent years have caused moral panic by claiming a growth in juvenile crime that the statistics do not register.

The changes that took place on the street itself are interesting. Participant observation and interview data reveal disenchantment with the thieves' law as a source of justice. Film footage shown on Georgian television showed that acts committed by thieves were compatible with neither the *dzvelbichoba* nor with more general ideas of manliness (collaboration with police or security services, for example). Thus the *dzvelbichoba* could no longer act as a standard of manliness, even in street culture. The norms of the thieves' world are no longer being addressed; and instead of 'Let's speak like thieves!', what is now heard is 'Let's speak like men!' The suggestion of asking a thief or any other figure whose authority is based on proximity to the underworld for mediation will today call forth nothing but laughter. Informants themselves realise the change of priorities among youth, the fact that street notions are not followed consistently any more.

Nevertheless, old and new views that coexist in Georgia still clash. Once I asked an acquaintance to introduce me to her friend's son, whom I wanted to interview. This seventeen year old boy had received a suspended sentence for injuring someone with a knife in a street fight, and, as my acquaintance assured me, had substantial authority on the street. But contact was refused with the words, 'Zura's mother probably won't like if her son is interviewed on this subject –

although at heart she is proud that Zura is so manly, she realises that this has gone out of fashion' (field material, Tbilisi, 2009, woman, aged 44).

Male Neighbourhood Communities in the Political Life of Georgia

The Rose Revolution and the mass political protests of 2011 in Georgia were notable for the active participation of youth. Youth activism became one of the most important driving forces of the National Movement that was headed by Mikheil Saakashvili in the early 2000s and today represents the leading political party in Georgia. It was the youth movement *Kmara* ('enough') that gave impulse for the first 'colour revolution' in post-Soviet space. Active participation in political movements by students and youth was a characteristic of Soviet Georgia as well. In 1978, among the striking examples, is the movement for the maintenance of the official status of Georgian when Tbilisi State University students led a mass rally to maintain the rights of the native language. Youth, and the students of Tbilisi University in particular also played a considerable role in the national movement of the late 1980s.

Data from different cultural studies of youth street communities describe complex and variable relations between the street and social movements. In different historical and political contexts, the street has been dragged into nationalist, religious and revolutionary mass activities.

Taking into consideration the meaning of the street in urban Georgia as a social institution, and the extent of *birzha* involvement in street practices, it would be hard to imagine that this resource could be neglected by the Georgian political elite. Despite the large number of publications on the youth movements' involvement in the coloured revolutions and other political events in post-Soviet countries (Nikolayenko, 2007; O'Beachaina and Poleseb, 2010; Mcglinchey, 2009; Roche, 2010), the machinery of mass involvement of youth in politics in Georgia and the nature of the interests of these young people apart from the official goals of this or that movement, has yet to be examined. How did connections between the political elite and the street emerge in Georgia and what role did the street, street leaders, and street networks have in the political mobilisation of youth?

The defining factor here is the presence of both direct and indirect, often genetic, bonds between today's political elite and the street. Some of the members of the political elite began their careers as active members, sometimes as leaders of armed street gangs ('brotherhoods'). These brotherhoods appeared and operated actively in Tbilisi at the beginning of the 1990s. With the decline of Soviet authority, they were the product of the transformation of neighbourhood communities and emerged out of traditional local peer communities. These gangs (the brotherhoods like Kulinarielebi, Borotebi, Iosebidzelebi or Nutsubidzis sadzmo) were organised on a local basis. Starting with simple racketeering, they slowly expanded to gain quite a significant material base. The members of these groups started to play the political game as well, some of them managing to occupy prominent political positions. The density of networks in Georgian society does not allow for such biographical episodes to be concealed. The argument of having been 'mixed up in dubious affairs' is often used by opponents in fights for political power. For instance, one high-ranking official was accused of having 'good relations with *kulinarielebi*; it is like a minus, negative point … He had to prove that he was just an acquaintance of the *kulinarielebi*, but was never close to them, since he lived abroad at that time' (field material, Tbilisi, 2011, man, aged 53).

The representatives of the generation of the political elite who were young during the period of the brotherhood's most active years inevitably experienced the stage of socialisation prescribed by public opinion of that time, that is they were quite successful participants of these street communities: 'These, our ministers, I know them all … They were ordinary students who were in the *birzha* and so on. They were not grinds, not like those, whom we called communists, those excellent students, homebodies, who did not go outside and were interested only in books. They were not like these. They were guys who understood the *dzvelbichoba* laws and so on' (field material, Tbilisi, 2011, woman, aged 30).

Thus, today's political actors usually know the rules of the street from their own experience; they are able to talk the language of the street and know all too well what resources it can offer and how to benefit from these resources: 'These guys, who adjusted to these situations, did not break their bonds with the people with whom they were together [on the street]; when it was necessary they manipulated these boys' (field material, Tbilisi, 2011, man, aged 53).

In other cases, contact may have been established through mediators between the two worlds: 'They [politicians] come, but not themselves, but those from this *ubani* who have bonds with the street: the deputy's driver, the deputy's relative, an authority in the *ubani*' (field material, Tbilisi, 2011, man, aged 22).

When do modern Georgian political players turn to the resources of the street? Informants speak of two types of political events that may be organised with the help of the street. The first are the elections, as E. describes them: 'I worked in [name of the political party] for some time, just don't mention the name of the party, they are my friends and will be offended. When the elections were held all the parties in the *ubani* had links with these neighbourhood guys. And it is the party with connections that wins the elections. Why do they? These neighbourhood guys are the controlling force. Firstly, you learn [from them] what people think, that is, whom they vote for and so on. And then, these neighbourhood guys have power to influence the people in who to vote for. And it is always the party who has more of such neighbourhood guys that wins' (field material, Tbilisi, 2011, man, aged 30).

Their engagement in the neighbourhood community and their authority made it possible for the *birzha* to monitor the electoral mood and successfully participate in election campaigns. The 'neighbourhood guys' that E. speaks of are well-known; in the old, low-storey neighbourhoods of Tbilisi; people know them by name; they know the new ones by sight. Mainly, they are their peers or their peers' family members: 'For example, I am a cool guy [*kai tipi*] in the *ubani*, guys respect me, the neighbourhood guys, and I tell them that I am, brothers, a member of this party. Now the elections are coming, this party must win, whatever it takes. You must vote for this party; your family members must vote for this party' (field material, Tbilisi, 2011, man, aged 30).

During the presidency of Eduard Shevardnadze, the power of the street was used for the falsification of elections. Neighbourhood guys put the forged ballots into the ballot-box: 'they burst into the room, this *maqurebeli*[1] with his guys, maybe they did not used weapons but when, you know, you saw that he was a gangster, maybe he will break your head now, they burst in, threw in what they wanted, and nobody said a word' (field material, Tbilisi, 2011, woman, aged 30).

The second type of political event in which the street is involved is represented by mass protests. In this case, the role of street leaders is to provide for or, as the case may be, prevent the participation of the people that they influence in the mass protest. For instance, I was told about a neighbourhood leader who provided for the participation of the young men of his neighbourhood in a protest organised by the opposition. The well-known publicist, Dato Turashvili, in his book 'It Was and It Was not' (2009), on the role of students in the national movement in Georgia in the late 1980s in which he was himself an activist, recalls that during the well-known events of 9 April 1989, while preparing to clash with the troops that were sent to the capital, the students decided to organise resistance groups according to neighbourhood affiliations. They 'were sure that if we organise ourselves this way, we will fight better and more willingly' (Turashvili, 2009, p.136).[2] This example is significant, firstly, since it clearly shows the potential of neighbourhood local identity. Despite the fact that young activists were united primarily by their status as students and not by their belonging to this or that neighbourhood, when organising resistance groups, they consciously manipulated the feeling of local patriotism.[3] Secondly, this episode reveals the potential of the Tbilisi street as a social institution. In this case, this potential shows up in the ability of the street to mobilise the masses, which people themselves are aware of. In some social and political contexts, the *birzha* are able to transform them into militant units. Preconditions for this process can also be found in the aggressive masculinity that is characteristic of these communities. Young men that have grown up together in one neighbourhood are able to self-organise. Yuri Botyakov states of the Sokhumi that 'the high level of citizens' self-organisation is actively used by official power

1 This term is used to denote a person with special authority in the neighbourhood communities. In most cases this authority originated from the proximity to the *kanonieri kurdi*, which may be both real or proclaimed.

2 This was an anti-government protest of the Georgian National Movement that lasted many days and was suppressed on 9 April by Soviet army troops and commandos on the orders of the Politburo of the Communist Party's Central Committee.

3 This is still a factor today. In 2008, during the August war between Russia and Georgia, young men who did not wish to join the militia explained their decision saying: 'When they (Russian troops) enter Tbilisi, I will defend my *ubani*'.

structures …. Residents of Sokhumi's neighbourhoods constitute the personnel of the Abkhazian Army military units, and represent its most efficient part' (Botyakov, 2013).

While preparing political events that entail the involvement of neighbourhood leaders and human resources that they are able to provide, big political parties open so-called neighbourhood 'headquarters'. This 'office' is organised in an apartment located in the neighbourhood where the *birzha*, whose members are going to be engaged, gathers. For example, 'an apartment was rented on Shanidze, one former … this [former *birzha participant*], now well-off and with money, paid for it; and he had a direct assignment for them. He paid a certain sum, rented the apartment, gave out three hundred lari per month to these guys … and they had the direct task to gather votes, to advertise, to threaten, to do everything that they needed' (field material, Tbilisi, 2011, man, aged 53).

Communication with the street is made possible through street experience in the life of a political figure. In the cited example, the neighbourhood 'headquarters' were created during the election campaign, but informants say that the practice of using such 'offices' for the preparation of oppositional street actions is also common: 'They [neighbourhood guys] gathered there, planned everything, for example, ten people will stand here, ten people will stand there with banners' (field material, Tbilisi, 2011, man, aged 22).

The organisation of such headquarters is one of the means that political players use to motivate the 'neighbourhood guys' to collaborate. In addition to a monetary reward, they are given an alternative to the street-corner, a more comfortable meeting place, with leisure activities and the self-esteem associated with such an institution. The recruitment did not stop there: 'I remember … The Ukrainian activist girls arrived in tents: cool girls. In short, they did everything, solely to have people' (field material, Tbilisi, 2011, man, aged 22).

The members of the *birzha* are often motivated by their ambition to advance in this or that political movement. Taking into account the massive problem of unemployment in Georgia, and the low prestige of many professions and service industry jobs among especially young men, even the vaguest of perspectives for a possible political carrier may be very attractive for the young men from a *birzha*.

One should not exclude patriotic motives that may have encouraged even those young men who originally decided to collaborate with political unions for other reasons. One of my informants made the witty comment that: 'Appetite comes with eating, then you enter these *mugamebi* [Georgian slang: 'you get a taste for this situation, you understand it'], when you are there you say, "my native land". You need it at least as a screen, you need to say something; you won't say that you came to make a career. And later, maybe, you become inspired by this feeling, it becomes a part of your life. You persuade yourself that you are really a patriot, that you love your native land' (field material, Tbilisi 2011, man, aged 22).

Apart from voluntary participation in this or that political event, direct pressure from the political powers interested in street support may also be used. An example of forced collaboration is the case of providing for the participation of the *birzha* by the local community of the street leader in the street action mentioned before. It is not hard to find the means to put pressure on neighbourhood leaders – the majority of them have a personal history that makes them coercible: 'It is even psychological … they know that when the guy was imprisoned he was twelve; he came out at thirty; he spent eighteen years there. Imagine what freedom means for him, simply when he is given to understand, even if it is only insinuated, that if you refuse to do this, you will have problems again: and it is more important for him than money and whatever […] If today you can go outdoors and walk freely, have your *sostavi* [group of friends] and move from *ubani* to *ubani*, you won't be able to do this anymore' (field material, Tbilisi, 2011, man, aged 22).

As for the nature of leadership in today's neighbourhood communities, the members of the *birzha* see it as a community of equals; there is no explicit hierarchy. The leaders as a rule, have only informal authority, their status in the *ubani* is not mentioned directly. Community members do not recognise their having a right to command the *birzha* in any way. They can only apply indirect influence to provide for the participation of the people in any event: 'He knew that he couldn't ask anybody not to [participate in the action], but generally rumours were spread that he was told to do this, and there was talk that those who respect him should not' (field material, Tbilisi, 2011, man, aged 22).

One should take into consideration the taboo on any form of collaboration with the state and participation in politics, such as was adopted by the Tbilisi streets from the thieves' world. Quite recently, it was one of the most important norms of the street code. Despite the fact that the views associated with thieves' law are gradually losing status in street ideology, one can expect that street leaders, nevertheless, avoid openly breaching the norms that until quite recently were conceived as being core values of street culture and the respect for which were considered to be among the merits of being a real man.

Nevertheless, now and then, the collaboration between street leaders and the political elite is made known in street communities. It gives rise to rumours 'that the whole street is ruled from above' (field material, Tbilisi, 2011, man, aged 22).

Already in the early 2000s, in the period of creation and activity of the Kmara youth movement, participation in street actions was generally unpopular on the street. At that time, 'joining Kmara meant something … Thieves held authority, theft was prestigious. Kmara and all this graffiti for me personally [was unattractive]' (field material, Tbilisi 2011, man, aged 22).

It can be argued that youth that associated themselves with the values and norms of street culture were critical of the Kmara; there were no street youth among the official activists and leaders of the movement. At the same time, it seems that neighbourhood leaders were connected with the movement. These may well have been the most flexible and far-seeing of them. They were leaders who were able to quickly navigate the changing political situation and assess possible benefits associated with these changes. But only those who were able to manoeuvre between the need to embed their actions to the street code and to manoeuvre between practices that inevitably demanded its violation, could permit themselves to openly participate in the movement. The rest could take their stand only in the periphery of the movement, maintaining a wait and see attitude while using some advantages of being close. That is how an informant commented on the motives of such young men: 'If I make friends with him, I will be inviolable, if I need something, I will use him. Well, you keep good relations with him to have a way in there' (field material, Tbilisi, 2011, man, aged 22).

A very recent shift in street culture, caused by the fall of the prestige of the thieves' world and its code, made possible not only the participation of street youth in politics, but, according to some of my informants, even made it fashionable to be involved in this or that political movement. The peak of street involvement in mass actions was in 2006–2008. However, as I was able to conclude from interview data, by 2009 this process had begun to decline. The opposition street action, 'City of Prison Cells', which was much talked of owing to the expressiveness of its realisation, is the last outburst of this activity: 'The last bit of energy was sucked out by this 'City of Prison Cells'. People thought that the opposition could save our country, but now people don't believe in anything anymore, everyone has lost hope. And, there is no sense in joining political parties'. (field material, Tbilisi, 2011, man, aged 22).

Conclusion

In recent years the state has sought to gain control of the street, to regulate it and to make it controllable and manageable, and to eliminate it as an alternative legal sphere. The street was a competitor to the state, offering alternative means of management, regulation and control. The ideas and notions that were widespread in the street implied negative attitudes to state institutions of law and order; the state was denied trust, one of the core values of street culture.

The specificity of feelings for law and order in Georgian urban culture is to a great extent determined by the ideas of manhood, male valour and honour. Protection of personal honour and the honour of the community that a person belongs to (be it a family, neighbourhood community or group of friends) is considered the height of male responsibility and virtue, more important than one's duty as a law-abiding citizen. Cooperation with state legal institutions, and particularly the reporting of information to them was interpreted as denunciation and seen as most damaging to one's personal reputation. The victim and the persecutor in many conflicts were often on the same side: against the state. By offering its services in the sphere of control and coercion, the state laid claim to what was traditionally considered to be an issue of a man's individual honour. By doing this, the state turned a man into someone unable to stand up for himself. In the years following the Rose Revolution the rise in trust in state legal institutions, particularly the police, went hand in hand with a weakening of customary street conflict resolution practices.

The state is nevertheless compelled to take the street into consideration as a possible political instrument. In recent decades, the street was involved in two types of political events – in election campaigns and in the organisation of mass political protests. The effective use of the street in the organisation of these events is enabled by the social capital of former street actors com-politicians, by means of which they are able to mobilise considerable human resources. Solidarity built on the basis of local patriotism, at critical moments, may prevail over other solidarities, demonstrating the priority of neighbourhood pride. Aggressive practices of masculinity characterize the culture of street communities and create the potential for the formation of military units.

Establishing connections between political elites and the street is promoted by the fact that the many political actors of today have street experience themselves. Most of them are able to speak the language of the street or at least understand it. One should consider, however, also the factors that hinder the collaboration of the street with state and political elites. A taboo on collaboration with the state and participation in politics originating in the thieves' code existed in Georgian street culture until very recently. Despite the abrupt fall in the prestige of the thieves' code in recent years, this taboo still may influence the process of building relationships between the street and political institutions.

References

Anderson, E., 1999. *Code of the Street: Decency, Violence, and the Moral Life of the Inner City.* New York: Norton Publishers.

Botyakov, J. M., 2013. Proyavleniya sistemy organizatsii abkhazskogo soobshchestva v usloviyakh sovremennogo goroda (na primere Sukhuma) [Organization of the Abkhaz communities in a Modern City (an example of Sukhum)]. In: J. M. Botyakov, ed., *Kavkazskiy gorod: potentsial etnokul'turnykh svyazey v urbanisticheskoy srede* [Caucasian City: Ethnocultural Links in an Urban Environment]. St Petersburg: MAE RAN. pp.228–29.

Forum.ge, 2012. *Kai bichoba, kurduli gageba.* Available at <http://forum.ge/?f=19&showtopic=33708587&st=15> [Accessed 1 February 2012].

Jankowski, M. S., 1991. *Islands in the Street: Gangs and American Urban Society.* Berkeley and Los Angeles: University of California Press.

Koehler, J., 2000. *Die Zeit der Jungs: Zur Organisation von Gewalt und der Austragung von Konflikten in Georgien.* Münster: Lit.

McGlinchey, E. M., 2009. Searching for *Kamalot*: Political Patronage and Youth Politics in Uzbekistan. *Europe-Asia Studies* 61(7), pp.1137–50.

Nikolayenko, O., 2007. The Revolt of the Post-Soviet Generation: Youth Movements in Serbia, Georgia, and Ukraine. *Comparative Politics* 39(2), pp.169–88.

O'Beachaina, D. and Poleseb, A., 2010. 'Rocking the Vote': New Forms of Youth Organizations in Eastern Europe and the Former Soviet Union. *Journal of Youth Studies* 13(5), pp.615–30.

Presa.ge, 2009. *Kai bichebi, tsud kveqanashi* ['Cool Boys' in a Bad country]. Available at <http://presa.ge/print.php?i=3115> [Accessed 25 April 2009].

Roche, S., 2010. From Youth Bulge to Conflict: The Case of Tajikistan. *Central Asian Survey* 29(4), pp.405–19.

Saakashvili, M., 2010. *Sakartvelos prezidentma mikheil saakashvilma sakhelmtsipo teknikur universitetshi zhani kalandadzis sakhelobis auditoria gakhsna* [President of Georgia Mikheil Saakashvili Opened a Cabinet of Zhani Kalandadze in the State Technical University], Available at ≤http://president.gov.ge/print_txt.php?id=341&1=G> [Accessed 14 August 2010].

Sakartvelos siskhlis samartlis saprotseso kodeksi [Georgian Criminal Code of Practice], *2010. Tbilisi.*

Stivenson, S., 2006. Kazanskiy leviafan: molodezhnye territorialnye gruppirovki i problema sotsialnogo poryadka [The Kazan Leviathan: Russian Street Gangs as Agents of Social Order]. *Otechestvennye zapiski* 3(29). Available at <http://www.strana-oz.ru/?numid=30&article=1265> [Accessed 18 May 2010].

Turashvili, D., 2009. *Iko da ara iko ra* [It Was and It Was not]. Tbilisi: Tsignis Sakhelosno.

Venkatesh, S. and Levitt, S., 2000. 'Are We a Family or a Business?' History and Disjuncture in the Urban American Street Gang. *Theory and Society* 29(4), pp.427–62.

Vigil, D., 1988. Group Processes and Street Identity: Adolescent Chicano Gang Members. *Ethos* 16(4), pp.421–45.

Volkov, V., 2002. *Silovoe predprinimatelstvo* [Power Enterprise]. Izd-vo Evrop. un-ta v SPb. St Petersburg and Moscow.

Whyte, W., 1943. *Street Corner Society*. Chicago: University of Chicago Press.

Chapter 8

Dimensions of Honour in Kvemo Kartli, Georgia: The Importance of Virginity in the Name of Honour

Elke Kamm

> 'If a woman is not a virgin before marriage, what will happen?'
> Tina[1] (age 23): 'They will throw her out of the house.'
>
> 'For whom is virginity of such importance?'
> Natia (age 45): 'It is important for everybody; for the wife herself, for the husband and of course for the whole family.... There is a canon, which says, you have to marry a virgin.'
>
> 'Why is it so important for a woman to be a virgin?'
> Eka (age 62): 'It is like this in Georgia, especially in Georgia. It is tradition. It is the characteristic of Georgia.'

These three statements are parts of interviews from my field research diary. The research[2] was conducted in the region of Kvemo Kartli in Georgia and its surrounding villages in July and August 2009, and from March to November 2010. I recorded approximately 65 interviews, mainly with women aged between 14 and 90. The research question I was interested in was how women and men in Georgia perceive concepts of honour and shame and how these conceptions affect and influence people in their daily lives, and which strategies are developed to overcome these strict, gender-based rules and social norms? Virginity, which is considered woman's honour, will be discussed along with a case of involuntary bride kidnapping.

---

1 All names in this chapter have been anonymised.

2 The fieldwork took place within the framework of the research project 'The Revitalisation of Traditional Law in the Republic of Georgia' (2009–2011, project leaders: Stéphane Voell and Mark Münzel, financed by the Volkswagen Foundation) at the Institute for Comparative Cultural Research, Department of Cultural and Social Anthropology of the Philipps-University Marburg (Germany) and the Ivane Javakhishvili Institute for History and Ethnology, Tbilisi.

Tetritskaro, the regional centre of the municipality of the same name, is part of the administrative region of Kvemo Kartli. Located 35 kilometres south of the capital of Tbilisi, it is very multi-ethnic in character, being home to Armenians, Azerbaijanis,[3] Russians and Georgians (see Natia Jalabadze and Lavrenti Janiashvili, and also Stéphane Voell in this volume). Before the collapse of the Soviet Union, Greeks and Azerbaijanis made up the majority in this region. After Georgian independence in 1991, most of the Greek and Armenian population returned to Greece or Armenia, respectively, or they migrated to Russia. The houses they abandoned were subsequently occupied by Georgians from the mountainous regions of Racha and Svaneti who had had to leave their homes for economic and ecologic reasons (Trier and Turashvili, 2007; Wheatley 2009).

Gender-based Social Norms: Explanations and Perceptions of Honour and Shame

Being an honourable person is important in Georgian society. A person with honour is trusted and seen as a reputable member of society. In several fields, that is, in social relationships and at the economic level, honour appears to regulate the social status of men and women (Mars and Altman, 1983).

Julian Pitt-Rivers and Jean G. Peristiany (1974) were pioneers in classifying Mediterranean societies as 'honour and shame societies'. They considered honour as proper individual behaviour that corresponds to their peer group's values and in accord with a system of social norms adopted through socialisation and imitation. Every person has to adhere to these conceptions in order to maintain or to increase their honour. Individual behaviour is judged by others and permeates the entire group (Pitt-Rivers 1974, pp.19–77). In general, honour can be described as a form of social control within a society (Giordano 1994, pp.172–92). I do not share Pitt-Rivers's and Peristiany's rather essentialist view of honour and shame societies, but their core concept will be useful for the following analysis concerning gendered perceptions of honour and shame in Georgian society. Perceptions of honour and shame play an important role in decision-making, behaviour and judgment in the region of Tetritskaro and its surrounding villages which was studied.

During my field research in Tetritskaro, I was often told that a woman had to meet several requirements to be considered honourable and marriageable. The requirements focused on her behaviour. A woman is expected to be reserved and modest and to conform to moral standards. Most respondents pointed especially to the value of a woman's physical integrity, that is, her virginity. Even the tiniest rumour about an unaccompanied meeting with a man who was not her relative could hurt her and her family's integrity. Her family was expected to control her

3 The terms, 'Azerbaijanis' and 'Azeris' are used synonymously in the literature.

movements and the company she kept. *Patiosneba, ghirseba, sindisi, namusi*[4] and *sakheli* were the Georgian terms used to describe gender-based honourable behaviour in the interviews I conducted. These terms can be translated into the English terms of honour, uprightness, respect and 'name'. I was interested which ideas my respondents associated with the notions of *patiosneba, ghirseba, sindisi, namusi* and *sakheli*. Dictionaries do not make a gender-based difference in the translations suggested by Apridonidze et al. (2006). Thus, I tried to elucidate explanations and connotations from my respondents. Table 8.1 shows the distinctions made between these four terms as related to the English term honour in comparison to their formal translation.

Table 8.1

	Associations made by respondents	Georgian–English Dictionary (Apridonidze, et al., 2006)
patiosneba	loyalty towards the husband (honesty)	1) honour, uprightness, 2) having respect
ghirseba	free of mistakes, self-respect, honesty	1) worth, 2) dignity, honour, 3) self-respect, 4) quality, standard, 5) (social) title, rank, 6) gravity
sindisi	kind-heartedness, honesty, not spreading rumours	conscience
namusi	purity (connoted to female sexuality), loyalty (of a woman to her husband)	honour, conscience
sakheli	reputation, fame, 'name'	1) 'name', 2) renown, fame, glory.

The associations agree in most cases but especially for *patiosneba* and *namusi*, the associations of my respondents are more complex than the simple equivalencies made in the dictionary.[5] The definitions in the dictionary do not match those of the respondents because they are based on other associations: and because of inconsistencies and double standards between genders inherent in the construction of honour and honourable behaviour. In terms of *patiosani*, my respondent, Nunu, pointed out that if a man had an affair with another woman, he would be forgiven. But if a woman had an affair, it would be shameful and she would no longer be considered as having *patiosneba*. Nunu said that while a man might be forgiven

4 *Namus(i)* in Arabic means 'law', 'custom', or 'honour'. In Hebrew, *namus* (*nmūs* or *nūmūsā*) means 'law'. The Ancient Greek word *nómos* also refers to 'law' and 'custom' (Soyağacı, 2010)

5 Certainly, no ordinary dictionary is in a position to explain in any detail the cultural associations and codes of the country.

and still have *patiosneba*, a woman cannot be forgiven. What is valid for men is not valid for women and vice versa.

Namusi is associated with women's sexual behaviour, an association that is lacking completely in the dictionary definition. *Namusi* was rarely used to describe men's behaviour during my interviews but was used to describe women's attitudes, especially a woman's physical integrity, namely, her virginity. Before continuing to the case of a forced bride kidnapping to demonstrate gender-based behaviour concerning honour (*patiosneba*, *ghirseba*, *sindisi*, *namusi* and *sakheli*) and shame (*sirtskhvili*), it is necessary to point out that all these terms are not static or used in every place by every individual in the same way, all the time. The terms honour and shame and their associations are constructed by each society and individual, and change in how they construct gender roles and attitudes. Because they are constructs, they are to a certain extent negotiable and can easily reveal inconsistencies and double standards. Sometimes, to give the appearance of being an honourable woman or man is much more important than actually being one (Schiffauer, 2008, p.25). This complex situation will be described later on the basis of the attitudes of men and women, families and society in the concrete case of a forced bride kidnapping.

Three Concepts of Virginity

Social norms in Georgia expect different forms of behaviour from men than from women. Men have to be brave and assertive, while women are expected to be modest and reserved. These perceptions lead to the glorification of womanhood in Georgia. A Georgian woman is considered pure, and adored as sacred, if she conforms to social norms and standards. Her status as a virgin is especially important for her reputation and honour, that of her future husband, and of their respective families. This includes not only her physical integrity but how she behaves.

My research has shown that the concept of virginity in Georgia has three distinct aspects. First, virginity is seen as a woman's physical status, meaning the existence of an intact hymen (physical integrity of virginity). Second, a woman is considered a virgin if she has never had sexual intercourse with a man (sexual integrity of virginity). Third, a woman is considered virgin, if her behaviour is virgin-like, modest and reserved (behavioural virginity).

Physically, it is believed that a virgin must have an intact hymen, which will tear on the wedding night. Notwithstanding, Anke Bernau (2007) has demonstrated that already in the seventeenth century, physicians discovered that some women do not even have a hymen and others have one that is so elastic that it does not tear. Women who are physically active, some athletes, for example, often tear their hymen in the course of athletic activity. Therefore an intact hymen or bleeding upon first intercourse is in no way conclusive evidence of a woman's status as a virgin (Bernau, 2007; Wild, et al., 2009). Traditional concepts and views, such as blood on the bed-sheet, or the physical integrity of virginity cannot apply to all women.

The second aspect to be discussed is the sexual integrity of virginity. As an objective fact, this seems to be the most important but the least independently verifiable aspect. For the future husband, its importance stems from the desire to ensure the purity of the blood line. He has to ensure that his descendants are his own flesh and blood. Otherwise he would risk being excluded from his inheritance. Therefore, he needs to know or believe that he will marry a virgin. For a Georgian man it is considered shameful to marry a woman who is not a virgin. He would be mocked by his friends.

The third aspect emphasises behavioural virginity. Before marriage, a woman must be modest, reserved, and to conform to moral standards, if she is to be marriageable. This behaviour is also an indicator of her status as a virgin. After marriage, she is supposed to continue to behave in this manner as it reflects on her own and her husband's reputation. This third aspect obviously differs from the first and the second ones, as it applies to a woman's life both before and after marriage. For her husband and his role in society, it is important to demonstrate his dominance in the household. By marrying a woman with the prescribed virginal behaviour, he can ensure his position in society. Rumours – based on truth or not – may easily destroy the belief about a woman's virginity and make it very difficult for her to prove otherwise.

The Case of a Forced Bride Kidnapping in Tetritskaro

Tsiala, a sixteen year old respondent, told me the story of her close friend Tea, who was kidnapped in 2009 in Tetritskaro at the age of fifteen. Tea was on her way to private piano lessons, and was walking along the edge of the park along the main road in Tetritskaro when the following occurred:

> Tsiala: 'And there was a man waiting in his car with his friends and they dragged her [Tea] into the car and fled. ... She cried. But she could not help herself by crying.'
>
> — 'Did her parents report the case to the police?'
>
> Tsiala: 'No, her stepfather himself was working for the police and he managed it alone. When her parents found out where she was and went to pick her up, she did not want to come with them. She was afraid that the people could think badly of her. That's why she stayed in [the neighbouring city of] Rustavi.' ...
>
> — 'Why didn't she go home with her parents?'
>
> Tsiala: 'She was ashamed to return to Tetritskaro.'

> — 'Why was she ashamed? She had been kidnapped. Couldn't she return home afterwards?'
>
> Tsiala: 'She was also ashamed to go back to school.'

The kidnapped girl did not want to return home because of her fear of social stigmatisation. Therefore, she decided to stay with her kidnapper to save herself and her family from being subjected to rumours and disgrace. My respondent, Tsiala, often mentioned shame in reference to the feelings of her kidnapped friend Tea. In other interviews, the concepts of shame were also used to describe the feelings of the kidnapped person in this type of situation. The abductee is ashamed because she stayed some hours or days alone with a strange man or men and no relative can corroborate that nothing happened. The women feel ashamed and often agree to marry their kidnapper to avoid the unavoidable rumours. Despite the fact that they are innocent victims, they still feel guilty about the whole situation and try to do everything to undo the situation (Hilgers, 2006, pp.13–15). Shame is at work in decision-making after a bride kidnapping because shame goes along with feelings of guilt (Hilgers, 2006, p.15). In most cases, the kidnapped girl marries her kidnapper to overcome her shame, and to restore her own and her family's reputation.

Such kidnappings are rare but not unknown. Some respondents told me that in the past they happened more often. Today (as in the past), voluntary kidnappings (elopements) are more frequent. Marriage in the past was, as a rule, arranged. A couple that wanted to marry against the will of the parents thus staged a kidnapping. Today, many young people stage such a kidnapping – they elope – so as to live together with their lovers and experience sexual relations within an accepted norm. Tatia and her boyfriend eloped when she was sixteen years old:

> Tatia (age 23): 'We [she and her boyfriend] planned the kidnapping. ... My uncle wanted to take me to his village. ... He did not want me to meet this man again [her boyfriend]. ... We called a taxi from Tbilisi and the taxi came. We have a garden behind the house and I left through the rear gate because my boyfriend was waiting there for me in the taxi. We then left in this taxi.

Tatia's parents were working in Greece at the time and when they received the news of her elopement, they were worried and tried to resolve the situation with Tatia's uncle by phone. Tatia and her boyfriend were staying with relatives in Tbilisi and both of them were afraid of the trouble back home. Tatia's family was displeased about the elopement; Tatia's father, especially, was angry.

> — 'When did your parents make up with you?'
>
> Tatia: 'After two months they made up with me. [...] They did not like it [even] when a woman stays away for one or two days.

The police tried to find them after the elopement but they were not successful. A few months later, Tatia and her boyfriend were officially married in a registry office (they had no church wedding).

Today it is 'modern' to use bride kidnapping as a form of marriage, especially among youth, not just to avoid problems with parents and have sexual relations but also as an expression of and response to the lack of prospects in today's Georgia. Marriage and family are still a way to position oneself in society.

Perceptions of gendered behaviour play a role in these cases. In most of the cases where women were literally kidnapped, they did not return to their families because they feared social degradation. That is, that the kidnapper and/or other people might spread rumours about the kidnapping and say that the woman was no longer a virgin. If her virginity is questioned, there is no way for a woman to prove her integrity. This is an enormous form of social pressure for the girl and her family. She will agree to a marriage to maintain her individual honour, but also the honour of the family, that is the integrity of its reputation and its social status.

Involuntary bride kidnapping is still considered a socially acceptable form of marriage in lieu of a formally arranged marriage. As mentioned above, these kidnappings are seen, if they happen, as peccadillos and not as crimes. This makes it difficult to get information on these cases and it makes it all the more difficult for the kidnapped girl to report the case to the police and return home without fear of social stigmatisation and disgrace.

Involuntary bride kidnapping is thus one possibility for a man or his family to force a girl or another family into accepting marriage. The kidnapping follows the same pattern in most cases; the kidnapper and his friends will hire a car or a taxi and stake out the places the girl frequents. She will be dragged into the car and they will bring the girl to a relative's or a friend's house, preferably in another city or village. They will confiscate the girl's mobile phone so that she will be unable to contact her family or friends. If the girl's parents have an idea, about where to find her and get in touch with the kidnapper, the latter might tell the parents under what conditions he would return the girl. But, as a rule, he will dictate to the girl's parents that they consent to their daughter's marriage with him.

Usually, there is no question that the parents will agree, because once the girl has spent more than a couple of hours with the man, the physical and sexual integrity of her virginity will be questioned. She will then have difficulties finding another man. Her social status, her reputation – her behavioural virginity – is damaged regardless of whether she actually lost her physical virginity or not. Her reputation reflects on the whole family's reputation. The kidnapped girl will then be pressured both by her parents and by the kidnapper's family: 'What will the neighbours say? Who else will marry you now? If you leave this man, we will lose our honour, our reputation.' Under these conditions, the girl will have little choice but to consent to marrying her kidnapper.

Bride kidnapping is forbidden by law. Today it is a crime, just as it was under Soviet rule. In the Criminal Code of the Soviet Republic of Georgia (1960), a specific article was dedicated to it: 'Kidnapping for the Purpose of Marriage' (article 134), and was punishable with a prison sentence of at least three years. Since 2004, when Saakashvili was elected, bride kidnapping, as an 'illegal deprivation of liberty', is punishable with prison sentences of from two to ten years (Criminal Code of Georgia, article 143). Non-government organisations such as Amnesty International (AI) and the World Organisation against Torture (OMCT) have campaigned to have bride kidnapping recognised as a specific offence but the Georgian parliament has yet to pass such a law.

In Tetritskaro, the police registered eight kidnappings in 2009, but none ended in a court trial or a conviction. Charges in all eight reported incidents were withdrawn by the victim's family to avoid social stigmatisation and disgrace. In one of my interviews with a man, twenty-three year old Suliko mentioned that victims of involuntary kidnappings do not report the cases to the police not only because of social stigmatisation but also to avoid prison sentences for the kidnappers:

> Suliko: '[The kidnapper] begged the girl to stay, don't do this, stay, because they knew that Lika [the kidnapped girl] did not want to stay and all of them would be put in prison. Later, the housewife [where they hid the girl] came and persuaded her to stay: "Daughter, you have to stay now". And Lika went outside, looked at all the boys and said, "OK, I will stay because of you".'

Suliko said that Lika married her kidnapper to save him and his friends from prison. Although she liked her kidnapper, she was not in love with him. She agreed to the marriage to avoid damaging anyone's reputation.

Social degradation, loss of a good reputation and the fear of rumours concerning the girl's physical integrity are sources of social pressure. Virginity is seen as the basis for marriage and once a girl has been kidnapped there is little chance that she will be able to marry someone else.

Bride kidnapping is not simply an 'illegal deprivation of liberty'. It is a premeditated action by the kidnapper, who knows exactly what the consequences of his actions will be. He is safe in a society where bride kidnapping is still thought of as a peccadillo and seldom ever dealt with in court. Considering the norms of behaviour for women, men can be sure about the woman's decision.

Kalishvilobis Instituti – 'Institute of Virginity'

This practice of bride kidnapping might seem inconsistent in a country that has experienced a transformation such as has taken place since the so-called 'Rose Revolution' under President Mikheil Saakashvili (2004–2013. See Lilli Di Puppo in this volume). Modern attitudes towards virginity and women's rights and liberties have in fact emerged – and are held consistently by some people in the region that was studied. But there are also people in Georgia, who continue to legitimize bride kidnapping and virginity. They do so, on the basis of religion and tradition.

The issue of virginity is a lively point of discussion in Georgian talk shows and in internet chats.[6] An interesting phenomenon that has emerged in this context is the *kalishvilobis instituti*. This can be translated as an'institute of virginity'. But this not so much a physical institute as an emerging social institution – it is a sign of women's behaviour in modern Georgia.

A Georgian woman is considered pure and even adored as sacred as long as she remains a virgin until marriage in all three of the aspects outlined above. The value of virginity is culturally constructed and its value is stimulated artificially. This has a financial aspect as well. Interviews with hospital staff in Tbilisi revealed that an increasing number of men had begun to demand medical certifications of their bride's virginity. Just as in countries where virginity is of cultural and social value (such as in Turkey, Armenia, Iran or Iraq) virginity has become a business. It is also possible to perform hymen reconstruction surgery at a cost of between two hundred and five hundred dollars.[7] In October 2010, it was argued in a talk show on Rustavi 2, a major Georgian TV channel, that this operation is performed much more frequently than, for example, cosmetic nose surgery, which is also done very often in Georgia (on plastic surgery in Georgia see Bolotnikova, 2010).

The performance of this operation ensures that a woman bleeds upon intercourse on the first night of marriage. A women and her family is willing to spend a lot of money to ensure that this social norm is fulfilled.

Conclusion

I have deconstructed virginity as it is perceived in Georgia and shown that the appearance of virginity is much more important than physical virginity. It is a constructed norm of behaviour, of morality that is confirmed in society as a whole. Honour is in this respect not a static term – it is interpreted by society to demonstrate honourable behaviour, to the neighbours and to society as a whole. Everything that does not agree with these norms is hidden or regulated within the family.

There is no sure physical way to prove one's virginity and most women are well aware of this but the fear of social consequences leads them vehemently to guard their (appearance) of virginity, going so far as to endure hymen reconstruction surgeries. Other, older, simpler strategies to fulfil the expectations of society exist in Georgia as well:

— 'What will happen if the bride does not bleed on the wedding night?'

6 See for example the chat on <http://vseobemlyushiy.ru/c-page-bfdchgg.php> or on <http://www.kinto.nl/forum/viewtopic.php?id=77> [Both accessed on 2 February 2011].

7 By comparison, a university professor at the University of Georgia earns about $500 a month.

> Tamuna (68 years old): 'That does not happen.'
>
> Maia (76 years old): 'Of course it happens. My sister did not bleed on the wedding night and she cried and cried. But her husband cut his toe and put the blood on the sheet for his parents, so that they could see the blood. She [Maia's sister] swore to him [husband] that she had never slept with another man.'

Another option to ensure an intact hymen is anal sex. Virginity, thus, has nothing to do with sexual abstinence. It is much more an issue of social relevance: 'The hymen (and its cultural analogues) functions as both metaphor and metonym for an array of ideas and beliefs about women, women's relations with and to men, and relations between men in cultural systems in which women figure as objectives of exchange' (Kelly, 2000, p.28).

Virginity is a sociocultural construct and is maintained in patriarchal societies. Surgeries to reconstruct the hymen keep up this construct: 'There are a thousand ways of losing the marks of virginity, without having to do with a man; there are, in like manner, a thousand ways of recovering them again, when it has been really lost by having to do with a man' (Bernau 2007, p.9). The possibilities have been discussed in medical literature since the eleventh century at least, when an Italian doctor, Trotula, suggested women place leeches on their labia (Green, 2002, p.42). While their effectiveness might be questioned, the mere fact that these suggestions were made, plays a role in the continuing social importance of virginity. And it is still vibrant today – a construct of gendered behaviour in the perception of honour and shame.

Some interviewees mentioned that many young women avoid discussions about sex before marriage and remaining a virgin until marriage, by getting married at a very young age. This has the consequence that the numbers of divorces has increased in the recent years (Dourglishvili, 1997). The couples soon find out that marrying at the age of fourteen or sixteen does not solve the problems of sexual behaviour – it creates new ones instead. Other young women are strong enough to ignore the social norms of traditional Georgian society. They use the opportunities provided by independent Georgia to emancipate themselves: through education and by working outside the country. They ignore the *kalishvilobis instituti* and enjoy a self-determined lifestyle: also in relation to their sexuality. Yet, it remains difficult for many women to escape traditional morality about proper behaviour for a woman, especially with regard to virginity:

> Natia (45 years old): 'There is a canon that says that you have to marry a virgin.'
>
> — 'Did this canon change with the generations?'
>
> Natia: 'No, it is still like this. Everybody that lives according to tradition and has an ordinary family conforms to the canon.'

— 'Why is it so important to be a virgin?'

Lamara (A fifty or so year old doctor at a hospital in Tbilisi): 'It makes no sense, it is tradition. The woman is sacred. The Georgian woman always differed from other women. The woman is a sacred figure in the family, a mother ... The woman is a woman and the man is the leader of the family. Times are changing now and there is gender equality among youth. Women move forward and earn money as well as men.'

References

Apridonidze, S., et al, 2006. *Georgian English Dictionary*. London: Garnett Press.

Bernau, A., 2007. *Virgins: A Cultural History*. London: Granta.

Bolotnikova, S., 2010. Georgians Rush to Plastic Surgeons for Western Noses. *Pravda.Ru*, 11 November 2010. Available at <http://english.pravda.ru/health/10-11-2010/115714-plastic_surgeons–0/> [Accessed 22 March 2012].

Dourglishvili, N., 1997. *Social Change and the Georgian Family*. Tbilisi: United Nations Development Programme.

Giordano, C., 1994. Der Ehrkomplex im Mittelmeerraum: sozialanthropologische Konstruktion oder Grundstruktur mediterraner Lebensformen? In: L. Vogt and A. Zingerle, eds, *Ehre: archaische Momente in der Moderne*. Frankfurt am Main: Suhrkamp, pp.172–92.

Green, M., 2002. *The Trotula: An English Translation of the Medieval Compendium of Women's Medicine*. Philadelphia: University of Pennsylvania Press.

Hilgers, M., 2006. *Scham: Gesichter eines Affekts*. Göttingen: Vandenhoeck und Ruprecht.

Kelly, K. C., 2000. *Performing Virginity and Testing Chastity in the Middle Ages*. London: Routledge.

Mars, G. and Altman, Y., 1983. The Cultural Bases of Soviet Georgia's Second Economy. *Soviet Studies* 35(4), pp.546–60.

Soyağacı, S., 2010. Çağdaş Türkçenin Etimolojik Sözlüğü [Family Tree of Words: Etymological Dictionary of Contemporary Turkish]. Istanbul: Adam Yayınları.

Schiffauer, W., 2008. *Parallelgesellschaften: Wie viel Wertekonsens braucht unsere Gesellschaft? Für eine kluge Politik der Differenz*. Bielefeld: transcript.

Trier, T. and Turashvili, M., 2007. *Resettlement of Ecologically Displaced Persons Solution of a Problem or Creation of a New? Eco-Migration in Georgia 1981–2006*. Flensburg: European Centre for Minority Issues.

Peristiany, J. G. ed., 1974 [1966]. *Honour and Shame: The Values of Mediterranean Society*. Chicago: University of Chicago Press.

Pitt-Rivers, J., 1966. Honour and Social Status. In: J. G. Peristiany, ed., 1974, *Honour and Shame: The Values of Mediterranean Society*. Chicago: The University of Chicago Press, 19–77.

Wheatley, J., 2009. *The Integration of National Minorities in the Samtskhe-Javakheti and Kvemo Kartli Provinces of Georgia*. Flensburg: European Centre for Minority Issues.
Wild, V., Poulin, H. and Biller-Andorno, N., 2009. *Deutsches Ärzteblatt* 2009. 106, 8: A 340–41.

Chapter 9
Moral Breakdown among the Georgian Svans: A Car Accident Mediated between Traditional and State Law

Stéphane Voell

At first glance it was not a special case. The accident happened in July 2009 in the municipality of Tetritskaro in Kvemo Kartli, southern Georgia. Svans live in many of the villages in this region. They came to Kvemo Kartli at the end of the 1980s, for various reasons. The majority were resettled here as a result of natural disasters in the highlands of Svaneti. Others arrived because of difficult economic conditions in their home region. Many have lived in the municipality of Tetritskaro for more than twenty years, together with other Georgians, Azerbaijanis,[1] Armenians, Greeks or Ossetians. The non-Svans look to the Svans with a certain degree of reservation. Svans have their 'own tradition', I was told. They have their law and treat all problems within the village with their elders (*makvshi*) or mediators (*morval*). It is said that sometimes they have recourse to blood feud (see Lavrenti Janiashvili and Natia Jalabadze in this volume). I had the impression that the Svans tolled a fearful respect and that one should avoid problems with them. Yet, the car accident in which the young Svan (David M.) killed another Svan (Irakli K.) did not at first look like a special case.[2] The tragic incident lead to a court trial in the course of which, David M. was sentenced to five years in prison. There was no blood feud and everything appeared normal.

In 2009, I was involved in a study of Svan traditional law in Kvemo Kartli.[3] Svan legal practice has been described repeatedly since the nineteenth century, but only in the context of Svaneti itself (for example Gabliani, 1925; Koehler, 1999; Davitashvili, 2002). Today, at a time when probably more Svans live outside of Svaneti than in their home region, I was interested in the degree to which

1 The terms 'Azerbaijanis' and 'Azeris' are used synonymously in the literature.

2 All names in this chapter have been anonymised.

3 The fieldwork took place within the framework of the research project 'The Revitalisation of Traditional Law in the Republic of Georgia' (2009–2011, project leaders: Stéphane Voell and Mark Münzel, financed by the Volkswagen Foundation) at the Institute for Comparative Cultural Research, Department of Cultural and Social Anthropology of the Philipps-University Marburg (Germany) and the Ivane Javakhishvili Institute for History and Ethnology, Tbilisi.

traditional law was present in Svan villages in Kvemo Kartli. This is a region, which in Georgia generally is perceived as a lowland region, even if, objectively speaking, the altitude of the Svan settlements around Tetritskaro is not much lower than in Svaneti itself. In the municipality of Tetritskaro, the state administration and the police are in control of the situation and the local population appears to be quite pleased with this state of affairs. But, when speaking with the Svans in their villages, stories about their traditional law come easily. Even young people can recall prominent cases in Svaneti and explain in detail what traditional law would foresee if, for example, a theft would take place.

In the anthropology of law, one generally works with case studies. I tried to collect case studies of specific incidents in which traditional law was referred to in order to overcome the conflict in question. I was told many stories about traditional law but I could not record many such cases. Other Georgians were not surprised. They predicted that the Svans would never get concrete about any case that they had resolved according to their traditional law; the Svans would not let an outsider look into their cards, as it were. And, in fact, after ten months of research in a four-person Georgian–German research team, it did seem that narratives about traditional law where much more prominent than conflicts in which these Svan legal conceptions played a significant role (Voell, 2012b).

But, I did hear about a few concrete cases, and the car accident described in this chapter is one of them. As the matter rolled on, I was able to collect a significant number of details about this incident, which was dealt with both by official legislation and informal legal practice. At the beginning it was only a car accident: one respondent said something about the case, which lead to my asking questions of another person based on this first bit of information. It slowly became clear that apart from the official criminal procedures other proceedings were taking place – in the shadow of the formal criminal trial. I observed that there appeared to be fears among both Svans and non-Svans, as well as the police in the region, that the case might lead to a blood feud, and some actions in response to these worries had already been undertaken. I spoke to Svans from various villages around Tetritskaro, to lawyers, members of the state administration, a former state attorney, and even asked the court for a copy of the official trial transcript. The case, so I thought, was a chance to describe, also on a general level, how references to traditional law might 'come out' in special situations and how to explain them. A death in a car accident is a special situation. The car accident was a point at which 'local notions of morality' (Zigon, 2008, p.72) were manifested.

Italo Pardo, in regard to law and morality, writes that 'what is legal is not always broadly regarded in society as moral and legitimate and what is illegal as immoral and illegitimate' (2004, p.5). Georgian state law may be respected in Svan villages in Kvemo Kartli, but this state law may not be fully accepted as 'moral and legitimate' there (which, of course, can be said of other villages as well, as I will discuss below). I think that the connection of morality to law can be a useful point of departure: using the concept of morality is for me one more attempt to find an adequate description of the practice of traditional law in Svan villages in Kvemo

Kartli (Voell, 2013; Voell, et al., 2014). Traditional law is present, it is practised: but it is only a very loose and often inconsistently used legal frame of reference. I think 'morality' can describe this practice in which, for example, a conflict treated in court according to state law is not accepted by the Svan population as meeting the moral dimensions of their traditional law. Therefore, I want to describe the car accident as a 'moral breakdown' in the sense Jarett Zigon (2008) used the term and in relation to the definition of morality proposed by Catherine Wanner (2011). People are not always conscious of their moral principles, but in intense situations in which a deep feeling of injustice towards specific issues emerges, a moral breakdown may occur. This leads to an alternative process taking place beside the official court trial that mediates the conflict on a moral level.

Utilising approaches to morality by Zigon and Wanner, I will introduce the conceptual framework. As my central approach, I will then introduce Zigon's concept of 'moral breakdown'. This is followed by a brief description of the setting and the resettlement of the Svans to Kvemo Kartli. Then, I will describe the case as presented in the official transcript of the trial. The 'facts' presented in court are of course only one reality, though I will nevertheless take the official one, as a point of departure. Furthermore, I will give an account of the different narratives attached to the case and how references to traditional law were made alongside the official trial. In the conclusion, I will argue that in the Svan case in Kvemo Kartli, traditional law should not be understood as a 'functioning' legal framework but as the expression of a Svan notion of morality. Narratives and occasional references to traditional law in social practice reflect a profound feeling of injustice embedded in a Svan legal imaginary.

Morality and Moral Breakdown

Jarret Zigon was among the first to attempt to develop an anthropology of moralities. He explored the dimensions of morality in religion, law, gender, and in narratives, yet nevertheless remains surprisingly vague in regard to what morality actually is. He describes morality 'as the acquired attitudes, emotions, and bodily dispositions of a person throughout their life' (2008, p.17). These are principles and rules that take effect in a 'bodily way of being in the world' and are constantly reshaped through social experience. Morality entails a 'kind of habitus', that is, 'unreflective and unreflexive disposition of everyday social life'. In day to day life, one does not think constantly about whether one is acting morally, one simply does it.

If I understand Zigon correctly, and understand his description of morality as a 'kind of habitus' it supports my impression that morality as embodied dispositions is an 'internalisation' of something. Through socialisation, the individual internalises socio-economic structures as dispositions of action, that is, something like the 'habitus' of Pierre Bourdieu (1972). Morality is, then, one's framework for social practice, which stands in a constant dialectical relationship to the social field.

Catherine Wanner is more concrete. She describes morality as a 'shared understanding of commitment to certain core values or practices' (2011, p.215). If morality is not observed, a feeling of injustice arises. This commitment consists in some form of loyalty towards the group with its own traditions, canons, histories, values and practices, and provides a framework for self-motivation and self-policing. She refers here to Zygmunt Baumann and his conception of morality as *für sein*, a concept he borrowed from Martin Heidegger, that is 'to be there for somebody' (2011, p.216; after Baumann 1993, p.13). Morality means to feel some responsibility for others. It contains an 'emotional' moment, that is morality means to cultivate a moral component that leads individuals to react in – and here appear to be coming to the core of 'morality' – a consistent and foreseeable way towards injustices.

In accord with Wanner, I conceive of morality as this shared understanding of core values or practices, a set of beliefs on how things should take place among people. Elsewhere, I used the term 'ideology', that is a connected set of moral concepts that are bound to a specific group, to describe a similar phenomenon. I wanted to describe the traditional law, *kanun*, of Northern Albania (Voell, 2004), and presented its 'ideology' as objectively detached, as uninfluenced by everyday life and as a source of robust but not fixed values (Fine and Sandstrom, 1993). Here, ideology was also part of the 'habitus' of traditional law (Voell, 2003). But, morality is probably a better notion to grasp the value systems underlying traditional legal frameworks such as in Georgia and Albania. In the latter, there appears to be a special word for morality, the concept of *besa*. In its most complex form it incorporates the concepts of honour, loyalty, faith, assurance for safe conduct, and truce, and is something like the cultural conscience of northern Albanians. Important acts and pledges of *kanun* are sealed with *besa* (Schwandner, 1993, pp.8–13). Something like *besa* is also inherent in Svan traditional law.

From an ideal type point of view, one can delimit four dimensions of Svan traditional law (*limorav*), even if some of them are no longer in use today (Voell, 2012a). Traditional law has, first, a social dimension: village life was framed by a segmented clan structure with elders (*makhvshi*) at each level of the organisation. The people met in village or regional assemblies to decide on important issues affecting the community. The second dimension is the processual and performance component of traditional law. Based on precedents and some explicit rules, mediators (*morval*) discussed conflicts and negotiated each problem one by one. In general, at the end of a reconciliation process, there followed public acknowledgement of the achieved agreement, which had to be sealed by an oath on an icon (see below). The third dimension of traditional law is religion. Svans, like most Georgians, are Orthodox Christians, but they apply many folk religious elements in their religious practices outside the official church liturgy. Chosen elders are also religious leaders during celebrations at shrines. Oaths on icons are taken at these shrines or in churches when the priest is absent. The final dimension of Svan traditional law is, I would suggest, this local sense of morality. Conceptions of honour and the necessity to maintain one's integrity in the village are important for Svans. Morality is based on mutual respect in the village (at least it has to appear to be so) and the belief in the importance of, and solidarity within, the lineage (*gvari*). Conflicts inside the village have to be treated at this level, that is, after a conflict a form of equilibrium has to be returned to the village by Svan mediators.

It gets interesting when this moral worldview is challenged, because generally, people are not constantly thinking of their moral standards. These are manifested only after a 'moral breakdown' or an 'ethical dilemma' (Zigon, 2008, p.18). This means that if someone's morality is challenged, or – in Wanner's terms – if someone is confronted by some form of injustice, one's conceptions of morality suddenly come into the foreground. In these moments 'that shake one out of the unreflective everydayness of being moral' (Zigon, 2011, p.11), morality starts to be what Zigon understands as 'ethics'. The latter is the acknowledgement of a moral breakdown, if subconsciously practised, morality is challenged and one is forced to think about it (Zigon, 2008, p.18). Ethics are in a sense the tangible manifestation of morality, a 'kind of stepping away to question and work' on morality. Once morality is palpable, once the individual becomes conscious that something is happening that he feels to be treated unjust, once morality becomes ethics, a special situation is framed. The moral breakdown frames, according to Zigon, a 'creative moment', because 'by performing ethics people create … new personhoods and enact new moral worlds' (2011, p.11).

Wanner notes that in post-Soviet space one could have the impression that people fell into a moral vacuum after the end of the Soviet Union. The, at first glance, strong socialist ideological frame of reference fell apart and left the local population in a moral void. But reality was different: the weakening of the dominant ideology only made it possible to see more clearly that other conceptions of morality were present. Neither socialism nor postsocialism managed to control fully all conceptions of morality that were already in existence. There were always a multitude of moralities. The moral breakdown in the years of transition simply made it more visible. The plurality of 'core set[s] of values and practice' to which individuals and groups are attached (2011, p.214) was always present in different configurations.

But the interrelation of these various conceptions of morality remains unclear. Does a person follow their own morality as internalised bodily disposition? Does one choose in specific situations, consciously or subconsciously based on specific needs, a specific morality or are there in these arenas of moralities some which are stronger? And how does this work? The suggested parallels to some ideas inherent to legal pluralism are intended (see Introduction to this volume). Zigon does so himself when he writes that in times of radical change it can happen that there are situations where there is no state law, or some distance to state law emerges. This happened in the first years of postsocialism: 'often … local notions of morality fill in where the state's law is impotent' (2008, p.68). In situations where the state is 'weak', in situations of 'multifarious social, political, and economic contingents' (2008, p.69) morality is often the only 'compass' (Wanner, 2011).

In Georgia, one cannot say that the state is weak (see Barbara Christophe, Elizabeth Cullen Dunn and Austin Cowley in this volume). On the contrary, since 2004 the government of President Mikheil Saakashvili made important changes, especially in law enforcement and the juridical systems (see Lilli Di Puppo in this volume). The police are in control in Kvemo Kartli and infractions of the law are generally pursued according to official rules. At this local level, corruption is not possible and the local population accepts the police and its work. The Svans in the municipality of Tetritskaro also consider the police to be important. The latter, patrol regularly in their villages and many Svans are themselves police officers. But still, if a conflict arises in a village, from a small fist fight, to discussions about irrigation, family issues, or petty thefts, local elders continue to have words to say. But, in other more significant cases, the police are present and control the situation. This does not mean, however, that any formal trial in court results in the full 'resolution' of a problem. The morality of formal state law apparently does not conform completely to Svan morality.

Zigon delimits three 'aspects' (2011, pp.8–9) that help to describe situations of multiple moralities. First, he names the institutional aspect, the claim of an institution to the truth or the rightness of a particular morality. Institutions like the state have a certain power to influence views on morality, but they are not in a position to control it completely. Second, there is the public dimension of morality, those conceptions of morality not influenced directly by an institution but are conveyed in the media, in protests, or everyday articulated beliefs. Finally, there is personal, embodied morality, that is, the dimension of morality at the core of his definition of morality, that is, morality as a kind of 'habitus'.

With the car accident among Svans in Tetritskaro, multiple realities suddenly became palpable. The institutional aspect is provided here by the state, which includes the local court and the police. But then, there is another aspect of morality, between the institutional and personal, but not quite in agreement with Zigon's much too broadly defined 'public' morality. In Georgia, one can find moralities related to ethnic belonging. But to speak of a Svan morality is just as misleading as Zigon's public morality. As will be revealed in the following, Svans are far from being a homogenous group. But for the sake of simplicity I will speak of a Svan morality. The mutual existence of these moralities, that is of state and Svan dimensions of morality, is revealed only in the case of a moral breakdown.

Svans and Their Resettlement to Kvemo Kartli

Svaneti is situated in the north-western part of Georgia and is the highest inhabited region of the country. The Svans have their own language (Svan), which is in the same linguistic family as Georgian, but the latter cannot understand it. The Svans are considered Georgians, a definition that the Svans share.

Svaneti basically consists of two steep gorges and the surrounding mountains. The Enguri gorge, with the little town of Mestia, is called Upper Svaneti. This is the most prominent area of Svaneti, known for its numerous fortified towers (*koshki*). The upper part of this gorge is also known as 'Free Svaneti', a former autonomous region, ruled by clans with their own legislation. Czarist Russia made an end of Free Svaneti in 1876.

The lower part of the Svaneti, along the river Tskhenistskali with the municipality of Lentekhi is, consequently, called Lower Svaneti. The Svans of Upper and Lower Svaneti have very different histories. The Lower Svans were always integrated into the prevailing governments. Communication between the people in the two gorges was generally difficult because of the high mountain range separating them.

Svans settled in various other parts of Georgia, too, and in the nineteenth century a larger population settled in the valley of the river Kodori. This region is located in the breakaway region, Abkhazia. The Svans lived there until 2008, which means that it was the last piece of land in Abkhazia still controlled by Georgia. During the events of the 2008 war between Georgia and Russia, which was mainly focused on South Ossetia, Russian and Abkhazian forces managed to gain the control of the region. The Svans living there had to flee. Many of them resettled in the municipality of Tetritskaro.

Kvemo Kartli is in southern Georgia. It is one of Georgia's multi-ethnic regions in which Georgians are not in the majority (Wheatley, 2005). Today, around 44 per cent of the population are Georgians and 45 per cent are Azerbaijani. The latter have been living in this region for a long time. There are also other ethnic groups present, such as Armenians, Greeks, Russians and Ossetians. Apart from larger settlements, the villages in Kvemo Kartli are generally 'ethnically' homogenous villages. The percentage of Georgians living in Kvemo Kartli grew rapidly in the late 1980s.

At that time, in the winter of 1987, there were massive and enduring snowfalls in the mountainous parts of Georgia. In Svaneti, around 2,000 houses were destroyed, 85 Svans died in avalanches and under collapsed roofs, and around 16,000 families had to be relocated (Nizharadze, 1999; Trier and Turashvili, 2007). The government quickly organised the relocation of large parts of the population to various regions of Georgia, and especially to Kvemo Kartli, planning to resettle them there permanently in numerous new villages. Svan representatives were also involved in the planning process. The houses were easily constructed ready-made concrete buildings, all resembling one another. But the resettlement was greatly affected by political events in the Soviet Union and the Georgian declaration of independence in 1991. Financial resources and the building materials no longer reached the construction sites in the new Svan villages. Many Svans had to finish building their houses and to organise their relocation on their own. In some of the Svan villages in Kvemo Kartli, one can still see half-finished houses, empty plots and some foundations of what was supposed to be a public building.

The victim of the car accident I will describe was living in Chivchavi, one of the villages built after the heavy snowfall at the end of the 1980s. The population of Chivchavi originates from several neighbouring villages from Lower Svaneti.

Many villagers knew each other well before arriving in Kvemo Kartli and have now lived together in Chivchavi for more than twenty years.

Abeliani, the village in which the driver of the car involved in the accident lives, is also populated by Svans. But this village has a different history. Abeliani was once a Greek village, but its population fled Kvemo Kartli as a result of the nationalist rhetoric that emerged especially in the first years of Georgian independence. They fled because of difficult economic conditions and emigrated to the North Caucasus and to Greece. Svans settled in abandoned villages like Abeliani in the early 2000s. This time the resettlement was economic in nature, the people fleeing the poor economic situation in the highlands of Svaneti. Svan families arrived in Abeliani one by one and bought the houses from the Greeks leaving the village. By 2008, many Svans from the Kodori valley had found new homes in Abeliani and other similar villages.

The 'first generation' of migrants, who arrived in Kvemo Kartli because of the catastrophe caused by snow are called 'eco-migrants'. Ecological reasons forced them to leave Svaneti. The second group were Svans who left their homeland for economic reasons. A third group of Svans had to leave the Kodori valley because of the Georgian–Russian war.

The Case

The accident happened on 13 July 2009 at around 10 pm in the centre of Tetritskaro, a small town of around 4,000 inhabitants (2002 census), around sixty kilometres from the Georgian capital Tbilisi. It is the main town of the rural district ('municipality') with the same name. The town is described by many Georgians from Tbilisi as a healthy and 'ecologically clean' place. Numerous city inhabitants have their dachas in the area and spend their summer weekends in Tetritskaro or in one of the surrounding villages. David M. from the village of Abeliani crashed his Opel Vectra into Irakli K. from Chivchavi, who was walking on the footpath. Irakli K. died shortly after the accident.

David M. had gone to Tetritskaro with his friends that afternoon. Tetriskaro is around six kilometres away from his home village of Abeliani. David M. emphasises that he was sober when he left his house. The four of them had decided to spend the afternoon at a lake near Tetritskaro. The young men left Abeliani and on the way to the lake stopped in Tetritskaro, where they bought three or four two-litre bottles of beer. They drove past Chivchavi which is four kilometres away from Tetritskaro and arrived at their destination at the lake some three kilometres further on. At the lake they drank the beer. After some time at the lake they were driving back to Abeliani but stopped in the village of Chivchavi. Near the churchyard at the edge of the village they met two other young men, Otar K. and Zurab K., who invited them to a *supra* in their house. This is a Georgian banquet with a number of formal drinking rules and many toasts (see Mühlfried, 2006). It can be a large, festive and very formal event, but also a rather small and casual affair. It was probably the latter kind of *supra* here.

In other testimonies during the court trial it was said that the men from Abeliani met Otar K. and Zurab K. already at the lake. Be that as it may, they accepted the invitation. They went to the house of Otar K. and Zurab K. and began drinking wine. They drank around two litres. The driver, David M., assured the court that he only drank two glasses of wine.

Earlier that evening, Irakli K. who was from Chivchavi went to the city of Tetritskaro to take a walk in the city centre. Irakli K. is from the same lineage (*gvari*) as Otar K. and Zurab K., David M. and his friends' hosts. Around 5 pm or 6 pm Irakli K. met some friends in Tetritskaro near the courthouse. He would die in Tetritskaro a few hours later. They went to the schoolyard to play volleyball.

After the *supra*, David M. and his friends went back to their car and drove in the direction of Abeliani. It was already dark and David M., who was driving, was, so one of his passengers to the court said, giddy, but far from drunk. Tetritskaro is between the two villages, that is to get back home, David M. and his friends had to drive through Tetritskaro. The main street, which is still called Stalin Street, is a wide and straight boulevard, inviting drivers to not to look too closely at their speedometers. David M. was driving very fast on Stalin Street within the city precinct. The court report mentions a speed of 140 km/h. David M. finally slowed down, but suddenly his windshield turned white. He must have hit something.

It was almost dark and Irakli K. and his friends were walking on the footpath of Stalin Street. Irakli K. was on his way back to Chivchavi and was trying to get a lift. The young men were playing with their mobile phones and listening to music but not really paying attention. This may be why they did not hear David M.'s car approaching. Irakli K. was walking on one side of the street with one friend while a third young man was walking on the other side of the street. The latter suddenly heard the noise of a collision, looking around he saw that Irakli K. had been hit.

David M. told the court that he had hit something but could not see what had happened. He did not realise what he had crashed into. He had hit a pedestrian on the footpath. It was Irakli K. At that point, David M. wanted to stop the car but he could not do so because the brakes were not working anymore. The car continued along Stalin Street until it hit a curb and jumped onto the footpath. Then it stopped.

Irakli K.'s friends ran to his aid, stopped a passing car and began bringing the injured friend to the hospital in Tetritskaro. Irakli K. was barely breathing. It was too late. He had sustained a serious head injury; his left arm and his right leg were broken. He also had a serious haematoma and numerous other injuries, all of them listed in the transcript of the trial. Irakli K. died before arriving at the hospital.

After the Opel Vectra finally came to a stop, a number of people gathered at the accident site. The car stopped near the central square in Tetritskaro, that is, close to the museum, the courthouse, the regional administration, and around three hundred meters away from the police station. David M. was frightened. Irakli K. and his friends were unconscious and seemed to be seriously injured. In court he admitted that he did not have his driver's license with him and because of this he fled the scene of the accident.

Around 10 pm in Chivchavi, the home village of Irakli K., Akaki K.'s wife told him that there was some commotion in the village. Somebody was running around from house to house, but what was it for? Akaki K. was Irakli K.'s father. He went outside to see what was going on. His cousin stopped his minibus and told him that an accident had happened in Tetritskaro. On the way to town the cousin told Akaki K. that his son was involved and had broken his foot. But when they arrived in the hospital emergency room in Tetritskaro, Akaki K. discovered that his son was dead. His friends told him that Irakli K. had been hit by a car in the centre of Tetritskaro. Because of the accident his son's neck had been broken. Every part of his body showed some form of injury. When he asked who had caused the accident, they told him that David M. was the culprit. He was told that David M. was drunk and had been driving his Opel Vectra at high speed down Stalin Street.

David M. was arrested three days later by Lasha B. Latter. was employed by the Ministry of the Interior and Irakli K. was his mother's cousin's son. When he heard about the case, via internal ministry communication channels, he decided that the car accident was the fault of David M. He consulted the ministry databank, found David M.'s picture, and printed it out to take with him. It was the picture from David M.'s driver's license. On 15 July, while driving through a village on the way to Tsintskaro, he passed a young man on the side of the road. This village is around twelve kilometres from Tetritskaro. He thought he recognised David M., made a U-turn and drove back. He asked him who he was and the young man provided a name. But when Lasha B. showed him the picture he admitted that he was the man in the picture. Lasha B. called the police and invited David M. to sit in his car to wait. There was no resistance from David M.

The trial took place in late November 2009. The judge sentenced David M. to five years' jail and revoked his driver's licence for two years.

Narratives of the Car Accident

One day, walking around the village of Chivchavi, I stopped at the cemetery.[4] Some of the graves are marked by small models of Svan towers. This is noteworthy because the Svans from Chivchavi are from Lower Svaneti and in this region these towers are rare. They are a symbol of Free Svaneti, a once quasi-autonomous region of Upper Svaneti with a clan-based traditional system of law. Svan towers on graves of Svans from Lower Svaneti thus look somewhat contrived. But most of the graves are the usual Georgian graves with dark, almost black gravestones, surrounded by a low fence. Some include a small table for offerings. At Easter,

4 My research in the municipality of Tetritskaro would not have been possible without my Georgian field assistants Nika Loladze (2010) and Sandro Shanidze (2009).

many people will come to commemorate the deceased members of their family. The graveyard is relatively empty because the village of Chivchavi is rather new. Because of this emptiness, one grave catches my eye. This grave appeared to be new. Many fresh flowers were placed around the black gravestone. As usual, there is a picture on the gravestone. It is the picture of a young man. It is the grave of Irakli K., who died in the car accident.

I was merely curious and so, during my first conversations in Chivchavi, I asked about the young man in the graveyard. Initially, nobody would tell me much about the incident. I learned that Irakli K. was not married. He was the only son in the family and had one sister. His parents are old and their only son was their pride and joy. He had graduated from university with a law degree only weeks before he died. He wanted to join the army but on the day of the accident he had heard that the government would not allow him to enlist.

In the following conversations in Chivchavi and in Abeliani the accident became a standard issue that I would address. First, I was told that the accident was nothing special. It was only an accident and David M. from Abeliani had simply not been paying attention. Because of this, Irakli K. had been killed. Then people said that, yes, the driver had probably drunk too much. In addition, he had been racing through Tetritskaro. He could not steer the car anymore and he ran the other Svan over. It was a tragic accident, but it happened because he was drunk and driving too fast.

Then, slowly, other elements in the case that were not reflected in the court transcript entered into conversations with local Svans. Someone from Chivchavi suggested that another person was actually driving the car and not the person who had been convicted. Does this mean that David M. was falsely convicted and that he was covering up for someone else? An official from the municipal administration negated this immediately. The police did everything correctly, I was assured. I did not hear any further suggestions that it was not David M. who had been driving. But I had another element to include in my conversations about the case.

The local representative (*gamgebeli*) for Abeliani had his own questions. 'Yes', he said, it had been an accident, but for him it remained incomprehensible that the driver, David M., was in such a state. The *gamgebeli* was surprised that David M. had been drinking since he had never drunk before in his whole life. David M. had just recently settled in the village of Abeliani with his family. The *gamgebeli* did not know him well, but he had seen David M. several times and had judged the boy as intelligent and reserved. A relative of David M. explained to me that he had admitted to even more misbehaviour before the court, much more than he had actually done. David M. appeared to be saying 'I did it!' more often than he had to because he felt guilty and he wanted more punishment for himself. He regretted the accident. I could not find any point in the court transcript that would support this statement, but I think that the people of Abeliani wanted to tell me that David M. was in fact a good person and that the incident was completely incomprehensible.

A Svan from another village near Chivchavi claimed that David M.'s friends from Abeliani had forced him to take drugs. He said that David M. was a very good boy and never drank. On that day he had smoked marihuana and consumed other drugs. I was told that he was not drunk but high. That was why David M. could not see the other boy and ran into him. No drugs were mentioned in the court transcript. Some stories like these might also be rumours. I will never find out what really happened on 13 July 2009 in Tetritskaro, but the narratives about the event remain of interest because they provide insights into the moral dimensions of Svan traditional law.

The main street in Tetritskaro is wide and straight and seduces a driver to open the throttle. But there is something else. Irakli K.'s friends said during the trial that they did not hear the car approaching, which is quite surprising considering the car was apparently going so fast. Another thing might have taken place. Many drivers in the region, after having arrived at a certain speed, turn off their engines in order to save gas. David M., driving at a speed of 120 km/h in the city centre, may have turned the engine off. Thus the car made little noise.

The first person to tell me that traditional law and blood was an issue in this case was a local policeman. In the court transcript it is mentioned that the driver, David M., had been arrested three days later. But the policeman told me that this was not true. The culprit knew exactly what would follow after such an accident. He was afraid of blood feud, said the policeman. That is why David M. fled the scene of the accident. Someone apparently told David M. that he knew that 'they' would kill him. The policeman said that because he was afraid of blood feud, David M. surrendered to the police, but not to the police in Tetritskaro. He fled to Tbilisi and turned himself in there, the policeman claimed. He is sure that somebody helped him to hide after the accident. Since the accident happened almost in front of the police station, one might wonder why the police let him go. But the policeman said that there were many people on the scene and they could not keep an overview of everything. At that time it was more important to look after the injured people.

With this information I could question the Svans in Abeliani and Chivchavi directly. I asked more openly about what had happened and why the driver had fled the scene of the accident. The answers were more or less the same among all the Svans: If David M. would have turned himself in to the police in Tetritskaro they – the family of the victim – would have killed him. The Svans from Chivchavi wanted to have a blood feud, I was told. That is why David M. fled to Tbilisi, far away from the influence of the family of Irakli K. Another Svan from Chivchavi told me that the police had arrested the culprit immediately, but that he was taken away from Tetritskaro and imprisoned in Tbilisi. The police did not want to tempt the villagers to avenge the dead boy. My respondent concluded with a sigh that the family of the victim had wanted to go the 'traditional way' in this conflict but that the police had been faster.

A villager from Chivchavi also suggested that the family of Irakli K. wanted to have recourse to traditional law, even if David M. had been tried and found guilty and had been sent to jail. He did not know what might happen after David M. is released from prison. The conflict might break out again.

But it was not only David M. who was afraid that the incident might have escalated in some way. The car accident also had consequences for his family. David M. and his family had just recently come to Abeliani having resettled there from Svaneti. One of their relatives told me that someone from the lineage of the victim, Irakli K. came from Chivchavi to their house shortly after the accident. This person asked the family of David M. to leave the village of Abeliani as soon as possible. 'In the days after the accident', he continued, 'the head of the family of the victim was angry and was "really crazy". He went mad because of it. He might have set fire to the house of David M.'s family. Nobody knows.' The family wanted to avoid any escalation and decided to follow the advice of the messenger from Chivchavi leaving the house they had just bought in Abeliani. A neighbour from David M.'s family said that members of the family came by from time to time to visit Abeliani, but that they no longer live in Abeliani.

A former state attorney at the regional court in Tetritskaro explained that the Svans have 'this kind of tradition'. One could say that they have 'a dual system of law'. The Svans respect state law, but that is often not sufficient for them. The Svans usually employ mediators in such cases to avoid an escalation. This was also the case for the car accident in Tetritskaro.

A relative of David M.'s reported that: 'we sent mediators to Chivchavi to meet the family of the victim.' Unfortunately, I was not informed who these people had been. Thus I was unable to talk to them directly. The mediators went to Chivchavi and were received by the family of Irakli K. But apparently the mediators returned to Abeliani without any concrete results. At least one relative of David M.'s, however, is not angry about this and even sympathises with the other family. 'They only had one boy and this boy died. After some time will have passed', he continues, 'maybe in one or two years, we will send the mediators to them again. Then, the family of the victim will hopefully accept the mediation and everything would be normal.' Both families would then reconcile.

'Without reconciliation', so another villager from Abeliani reported, 'the problem would continue. The families and maybe even the villages would continue to live under a black cloud. Should David M. get out of jail before they reconcile they should avoid one another.' If so, 'this Svan tradition and this is a very terrible tradition', would become manifest. He concluded: 'They should not meet each other again in this life.'

I was interested in knowing how such mediation might work. An elder from David M.'s family said that in such cases, several elders from both sides would discuss the case. The elders would sit together, but the negotiations would not be about compensation, like in old Svaneti. In the past it was usual to pay some form of compensation (*tsori*), which had to be understood as a kind of counterbalance for a loss of manpower in the highland subsistence economy. Nowadays, nobody would pay or even accept *tsori* anymore. The family member of David M. said that one need only imagine how it would be, if someone would say something like:

'Sorry, I killed your son, but here is some money.' There will be no compensation but surely a gift during the ceremony of reconciliation. The reconciliation might also include that a member of one of the families involved become godfather for the child of another. Godparenthood is a strong link for Svans. It even precludes intermarriage between the families. 'But one thing that will definitely take place', as the elder from David M.'s family explained, 'is that in the end there will be an oath on the icon'.

The oath at the end of a reconciliation process is the formal public performance of the agreement made. Oaths have to take place inside a church or churchyard, or at a shrine. There are different forms of oaths, but they all have in common that the parties involved make a vow on an icon, which is an important act for Orthodox Christian Svans. If, for example, someone is accused of having committed a theft, the elders of the village can ask the suspect to swear on an icon that he did not did steal the object in question. The oath has to be accompanied by the oaths of guarantors who support the oath of the suspected person. In this case, the oath absolves the suspect of any suspicion. In the case of reconciliation, the elders invite the parties in conflict to step before the icon. If the mediation process is successful and the families of David M. and Irakli K. agree to meet and reconcile, both sides will swear on an icon that the case is closed. The oath is then solemnly performed in front of God and the community. The elders pronounce that both parties accept the agreement made, and the people present repeat these words. The oath on an icon is generally followed by a *supra*.

Conclusion

In the beginning it was a normal accident. And in the end it was also a normal accident. It was normal because the Georgian legal regime works properly and the perpetrator was convicted to five years in prison. In the end it was also a normal accident for the Svans: the case was not only treated in court but was debated by the Svans in a process parallel to state procedures, in order to achieve reconciliation.

The driver of the car, David M., fled from the scene of the accident because he was apparently afraid of a blood feud. The formal court transcript says something different but a member of the police pointed out that David M. ran away to Tbilisi in order to hide from potential avengers. I do not know if revenge was really an option, but the police did not it rule out.

After the trial ended, the family of David M. sent mediators to the victim's house, in vain. They were not received. The victim's family in turn sent a representative, who asked them to leave the region. Was the risk that the situation would escalate really that high? David M.'s family, at least, did as asked and left the village.

In the end, some form of reconciliation will have to take place. The parties have to be brought together again and maybe they will even seal their reconciliation with godparenthood. An oath on the icon and a large banquet (*supra*) will probably take place to conclude it. It is not clear when this will happen. The time David M. will spend in jail is something like time-out, but before his sentence ends the reconciliation has to be concluded. If not, I was told, the culprit would not be able to walk the streets of Tetritskaro in peace, whatever that means specifically.

The car accident is, then, a real 'moral breakdown' as Jarett Zigon defined it. Svans and non-Svans generally say, when asked about the situation in Kvemo Kartli, that there is no risk of blood feud among Svans anymore. But in out of the ordinary events, incidents that challenge the 'unreflective everydayness of being moral' (Zigon), morality becomes observable. The commitment of the group to its traditions and values is revealed and provides a framework for self-motivation and self-policing (Wanner). The Georgian state and the formal legal framework are respected by the Svans, but this is not considered sufficient from a moral point of view.

But is the discontent with the moral dimension of state legal practice, especially when it comes to homicide, where the state judges rationally in a situation of grief and anger about the experienced loss, not an absolutely normal phenomenon? Is the Svan reaction towards this accident somehow special? A lawyer in Tetritskaro told me: 'You know, in cases of car accidents, such extra-court arrangements like for the accident in July 2009 are quite common. The parties involved always try to deal with the problem on their own.' The family of the culprit generally tries to speak with the other side in order 'to improve the situation'. Often in rural areas, the parties involved had good relations before and if such an accident happens, so the lawyer said, they speak to one another outside court in order to find an arrangement. Then, in court, they tell the judge that they have a good relationship and ask the court not to punish the accused person too harshly because it would strain that relationship.

One could cite Paula Garb, who did research on local legal conceptions among Abkhazians in the 1980s. She writes: 'A villager had killed a fellow villager in an automobile accident. The Soviet court convicted the driver of involuntary manslaughter and sentenced him to a prison term. Relatives of the deceased, believing that they needed to take their own action in accordance with the traditions of blood revenge, appeared to be preparing some retaliatory action against a member of the convicted man's family. The elders who told me this story said they did not really think a retaliatory murder was imminent, but that talk about taking action was the family's way of showing its high value of Abkhazian traditions, a mark of honour in any Abkhazian community, then and now' (Garb, 1995, p.3).

The Svans do not have a monopoly on extra-legal procedures accompanying formal court trials. They can be found in many places in Georgia and beyond. But the actions the Svans take are embedded in a specific Svan legal imaginary. This is the formal procedure of sending elders to the other party and taking the oath on an icon. But this imaginary has spilled over to non-Svans as well, who think they know how Svan traditions work and contribute in their way to this specific Svan form of extra-court procedures. The police or even ordinary people outside the Svan community also refer to the Svan legal imaginary when speaking about such cases among Svans. The police were very cautious in the described case because they feared a possible act of revenge. The Svan legal imaginary appears to be nourished by both the Svans and people on the outside.

I have deliberately shifted to using the idea of a Svan legal imaginary. This is because, first, there is no functioning traditional law in the Svan villages of Kvemo Kartli. The segmented clan structure is falling apart. The younger generation has liberated itself from their elders, who in turn do not have many other possibilities to enforce their point of view. But, maybe these very same young Svans will rediscover their traditional law in the future. Secondly, Svans from very different regions, that is, from Upper and Lower Svaneti, and from the Kodori Gorge live together in Kvemo Kartli. While from the outside they may appear as one group, they live side by side, but they are suspicious of each other. Conflicts between Svans from different regional origins or with different resettlement biographies, like in this example of a moral breakdown involving Svans from Upper Svaneti (Abeliani) and Svans from Lower Svaneti (Chivchavi) can be treated on the basis of traditional law only with difficulty, because it is generally bound to a specific group. The Svan groups are condemned to draw on the lowest common denominator, and that is not a common legal frame of reference but merely a Svan legal imaginary.

References

Bauman, Z., 1993. *Postmodern Ethics*. Malden: Blackwell.

Bourdieu, P., 1972. *Esquisse d'une théorie de la pratique*. Paris: Seuil.

Davitashvili, G., 2002. *Samediatoro sasamartlo svanetshi* [Courts of Mediation in Svaneti]. Tbilisi: Tbilisis Universitetis Gamomtsemloba.

Fine, G. A. and Sandstrom, K., 1993. Ideologie en Action: A Pragmatic Approach to a Contested Concept. *Sociological Theory* 11(1), pp.21–38.

Gabliani, E., 1925. *Dzveli da akhali svaneti* [Old and New Svaneti]. Tbilisi: SSSR Sakhelmtsipo Gamomtsemloba.

Garb, P., 1995. The Return of Refugees Viewed through the Prism of Blood Revenge. *Anthropology of East Europe Review* 13(2), pp.41–4.

Koehler, J., 1999. Parallele und integrierte Rechtssysteme in einer postsowjetischen Peripherie: Swanetien im Hohen Kaukasus. In: E. Alber and J. M. Eckert, eds, *Settling of Land Conflicts by Mediation*. Berlin and Frankfurt: GTZ, pp.246–66.

Mühlfried, F., 2006. *Postsowjetische Feiern: Das Georgische Bankett im Wandel*. Stuttgart: Ibidem.

Nizharadze, L., 1999. *Svanebis migratsia da misi gansakhlebis arealebi* [Svan Migration and their Areas of Resettlement]. Tbilisi: Tbilisis Universitetis Gamomtsemloba.

Pardo, I., 2004. Introduction: Between Morality and the Law. In: I. Pardo, ed., *Between Morality and the Law: Corruption, Anthropology, and Comparative Society*. Aldershot and Burlington: Ashgate, pp.1–18.

Schwandner, S., 1993. *Funktion und Bedeutung der 'Besa' in Vergangenheit und Gegenwart.* Institute for East-European Studies, Berlin.

Trier, T. and Turashvili, M., 2007. *Resettlement of Ecologically Displaced Persons Solution of a Problem or Creation of a New? Eco-Migration in Georgia 1981–2006*. Flensburg: ECMI.

Voell, S., 2003. The Kanun in the City: Albanian Customary Law as a Habitus and its Persistence in the Suburb of Tirana, Bathore. *Anthropos* 98(1), pp.85–101.

Voell, S., 2004. *Das nordalbanische Gewohnheitsrecht und seine mündliche Dimension.* Marburg: Curupira.

Voell, S., 2012a. Local Legal Conceptions in Svan Villages in the Lowlands. *Caucasus Analytical Digest* 42, pp.2–4.

Voell, S., ed., 2012b. Traditional Law in Georgia. *Caucasus Analytical Digest*, 42.

Voell, S., 2013. Oath of Memory: The Taking of Oaths on Icons in Svan Villages of Southern Georgia. *Iran and the Caucasus* 17(2), pp.153–69.

Voell, S., Jalabadze, N., Janiashvili, L. and Kamm, E., 2014. Identity and Traditional Law: Local Legal Conceptions in Svan Villages (Georgia). *Anthropological Journal of European Cultures*: 23(2), pp. 98–118..

Wanner, C., 2011. Multiple Moralities, Multiple Secularisms. In: J. Zigon, ed., *Multiple Moralities and Religions in Post-Soviet Russia.* New York and Oxford: Berghahn, pp.214–25.

Wheatley, J., 2005. Obstacles Impeding the Regional Integration of the Kvemo Kartli Region of Georgia. In: *ECMI Working Paper 23*, pp.1–49.

Zigon, J., 2008. *Morality: An Anthropological Perspective.* Oxford and New York: Berghahn.

Zigon, J., 2011. Multiple Moralities: Discourses, Practices, and Breakdowns in Post-Soviet Russia. In: J. Zigon, ed., *Multiple Moralities and Religions in Post-Soviet Russia.* New York and Oxford: Berghahn, pp.3–15.

Chapter 10
Dagestani Experiences of the State[1]

Iwona Kaliszewska

The North Caucasus is the most unstable region in the Russian Federation. It is ridden by numerous interior political and social conflicts. The Republic of Dagestan, the most multi-ethnic and most southern republic, is at the moment on the verge of a domestic war. The social and political crisis, which is ongoing, clashes between power structures (local police; FSB: Federal Security Bureau/ Federal Security Service, Федеральная служба безопасности; federal army) and Islamic militants, clan and ethnic divisions, corruption and high unemployment, has resulted in a search for new authorities and alternative ways of life. Some have turned to Sufi brotherhoods, some to mafia-like organisations, some join the Islamic militants, others – perhaps the majority – withdraw from public life and live according to *sharia* law in their local communities (*djamaat*)[2] both in the cities and in the villages. The *djamaat* have introduced penalties for selling and drinking alcohol, smoking, gambling or even playing music, and not wearing a veil. State officials, administration, and police are either ignored or not let into these communities. They lost their authority over the local imams long ago. Local laws based on *sharia* are being introduced and legitimised as being intrinsic to local morality and tradition (on local law and morality see Stéphane Voell in this volume). The inhabitants of the communities hardly resort to the state institutions. Some even reject state-paid jobs, claiming that they do not want to participate in a 'corrupt system'. Others, however, profit from it and get paid for the job not done or fake certificates indicating some kind of handicap to receive extra money. They live in a self-created, insular safe community turning their backs on the world outside. What they are trying to escape is the 'state of emergency', the violent world of constant detentions and arrests of those accused of being terrorists, who are sometimes chosen at random from those who pray piously.

One could describe places like Dagestan as 'failed states' (see also Barbara Christophe in this volume), 'local forms of sovereignties' (Humphrey, 2004), or

---

1 In 2012, I worked on my contribution to this volume at the Institute for European, Russian and Eurasian Studies at George Washington University thanks to a grant from The Kościuszko Foundation.

2 *Djamaat* are communities based on kinship and territorial ties; they consist of *tukhum* (from Persian: families), which derive their origins from an actual or fictitious ancestor. In Dagestan, the *djamaat* are rarely bigger than one village. See also Kapustina in this volume.

local 'chieftaincies' (Derluguian and Earle, 2009). But though Dagestan appears to be 'stateless', the state is omnipresent with police blocks, borders, arrests, and tortures. The state is simultaneously absent and strongly present in people's everyday lives. Local narrations about the state are full of references both to unjust violence and to the 'good old times' of the 'orderly state' and of powerful leaders. Interiors of homes are often decorated with both posters from Mecca and posters of Putin, and of proud sons serving in the federal army.

'The state is like a sideshow and has two faces: one legitimate, the other criminal, corrupt and murderous; one rational, the other irrational and magical', writes Diane Nelson (2004, p.135). 'In the one the state means the people, our representatives; in the other the state is against the people constantly assessing the risk of our rebellion it is always ready to repress. With one face the state is a regulator, creating and maintaining standards by normalising; with the other it is a freak show functioning precisely through its abnormality, its awesomeness, its massive differentiation from the everyday' (2004, p.135). I aimed to look at the state in Dagestan through this framework. Yet, when I turned my focus from the state to people's experiences of state practices, a slightly different kind of framework emerged from my field material, namely that of the simultaneous shortcomings and the excesses on the part of the state. This outlook can increase our understanding of the play between people's experiences and imaginings – grounded in the cultural and political context.

In my chapter, I want to look more closely at the way people experience state practices in Dagestan which is on the peripheries of the Russian Federation. How do local people experience the practices of state representatives in times of the so-called 'fight against terrorism'? What triggered my interest in people's experiences of state practices was an initial puzzlement? Why do people who seem to perceive the state as a source of violence, and support the introduction of *sharia*, put Vladimir Putin's posters on the wall and praise the old days of the USSR? Is there any kind of legitimacy invested in the state even if it is regarded as violent or absent?

My first experience of Dagestan was of a place distant from 'the centre', not fully controlled, where people silently resisted the state (Scott, 1985). When I started my research in 2004, there was hardly any reliable information about the contemporary situation in the region. There was a feeling of both structural and geographical isolation (Kaliszewska and Falkowski, 2010). I was expecting a strong local identity tied to local languages and villages of origin. Over thirty languages spoken in the region made the republic even more 'distant' and 'exotic'. There was a feeling that there was no functioning state or barely any. Even in the Dagestani capital of Makhachkala everyday life seemed to unfold on its own, alongside explosions and shootings. There was a feeling of being duped by a state which tries to hide from the observer what is really happening (Nelson, 2004, p.129). I was looking for signs of resistance, yet why should resistance be the only mode through which the agency of people in the margins is seen (Das and Poole, 2004, p.20)? I found signs of resistance, but it was intermingled with loyalty to the state and a belief in Putin. This puzzled me even more and I was encouraged to take a closer look at the ways the state is experienced and perceived in Dagestan: which is on the margins of the Russian Federation.

In the following, I will show that in peripheral and conflict-prone places like Dagestan, peoples' experiences of the state can be conceptualised in terms of the simultaneous shortcomings and excesses of the state. I believe that this framing, applied to the post-Soviet setting, can inform anthropological conceptualisations of state margins and so-called 'failed states'. I will show that on the one hand, the state is experienced as a source of violence and local state practices are very often silently or openly resisted, or made up for with the help of *sharia*. On the other hand, regulatory state practices are longed for and the state is still invested with some hope. I will also show that local practices of introducing *sharia* are locally interpreted in terms of building order, and motivated by care for the society and the state. In other words, the shortcomings of the state are made up for, and excesses disdained and sometimes resisted.

I did not want to base my chapter on one specific event. In order to grasp the multitude of experiences of the state in everyday life, I refer to selected narrations or examples which one could encounter in the everyday lives of the people. Firstly, I show how people experience the state's excesses: how the practices of state officials are being experienced as a source of violence, chaos and disorder. Then, I have a closer look at what is perceived as a shortcoming and how it is interconnected with the processes of peripheralisation. The interplay between the shortcomings and the excesses of the state is the main focus throughout this chapter.

The Excesses of the State

In Dagestan and in general in the North Caucasus, the practice of 'fighting against terrorism' conceals many practices connected with local historical and social contexts rooted in the Russian political system. State practices within the so-called 'fight against terrorism' are being experienced and those experiences shape the image of the state. Living in a place where violence touches upon many aspects of everyday life; where contact with state officials is avoided – the state (seen through the prism of practices/dealings of the state officials) is seen as a source of unjustified violence. On a rhetorical level, the 'fight against terrorism' is being rationalised by the politicians as a necessity, but in everyday life where those dealings and rules are put into practice, the state loses its legitimisation, and state officials are seen as a source of violence and chaos, not order.

Violence had been present in my interlocutors' lives long before I chose to look more closely at that aspect of their reality. Via the online news agency 'Caucasian Knot', I had read about extrajudicial killings, kidnappings and tortures. I listened to the narrations of my interlocutors, yet I could not grasp it all, without touching upon at least a small piece of their experiences. Without personal experience of 'meeting the state' it would have been difficult for me to understand their hatred, frustration and disdain for state representatives. (Involuntary) visits to the FSB and the police stations became an intrinsic part of my fieldwork. I did not experience the hell of detention centres, but the mere fact that I walked down corridors where every door potentially could have been a place of torture made all accounts very tangible for me. In numerous interrogations I needed to prove that I was not a spy or 'Wahhabi ally' and I was forced to show all the photos I had taken. I was annoyed and felt disdain for the people interrogating me in the name of the state, during times of the so-called 'fight against terrorism'. After some time, I understood why among my interlocutors the mere mention of *mentovka* (from *ment*, a colloquial word for a policeman) or of the ROVD recalled memories of violence, and invoked fear. As my knowledge grew, and while I heard more narratives of violence and persecutions, my own feelings of fear became stronger – I was afraid of being stopped at the checkpoint or in the street. I changed my phone number from time to time; I tried to improve my local dress so as not to stand out. I believe such experiences helped me to grasp a piece of my interlocutors' experiences; to grasp a piece of their fears.

From 'Not Our War' to Direct Experiences of State Violence

During the eight years when I carried out my fieldwork in Dagestan (2004–2012, around two months per year), narratives of state practices changed. In 2004–2007 the 'far away war' was recalled from time to time when one heard an explosion or shooting. But it was 'somebody else's war': 'Oh no – not again, probably some special operation. They are outdoing the *boioviks*' [local denomination for Islamic militant] hunting', said Gasan, a little irritated by the July 2006 traffic jam. 'There was once a special operation', he recalled. 'A BTR [armoured transporter frequently used in special operations] arrived and started shooting at the building; other artillery arrived too. They surrounded the building. A crowd gathered around: "Go and shoot there! More to the right! Look he is at the window!", commented the people pointing at the windows of the building under attack. And, as always turns out in such cases: two *siloviks*[3] were killed and all the *boioviks* escaped. This is crazy' [*drudom*, literally: 'It's like being in a funny farm']. – State violence seemed to be annoying; it was laughed at, yet the necessity of 'fighting the terrorists' was not contested. The state monopoly on violence was not challenged.

However, over time, narratives have changed. In 2009–2010 violence in state practices became more evident. The link between violence, torture and the corrupt practices of state officials became more obvious. Disdain and condemnation of state practices were the common element of the narratives: 'They bomb a flat for three days – are there any *boioviks* there at all? They are paid per hour in a KTO

3 A *silovik* is a representative of the power structures (*sila*, power).

(zone of a counter-terrorist operation),[4] so it is profitable to keep on shooting. *Boioviks* will be found afterwards and the commanders will get their stars.' The intentions of state officials became a contested point: 'They called them *boioviks* again', a woman commented sadly while sitting in a *marshrutka* (minibus) when the driver said that four *boioviks* had been killed in the shooting they had heard ten minutes earlier when the *marshrutka* got stuck in a traffic jam in Makhachkala.

Death and violence became more tangible. The link between the shootings I heard and the people kidnapped and tortured became more direct. More and more often, sometimes in a low voice, I was told about 'our boys', being tortured while being forced to admit that they were *boioviks*. I was also told about the bodies of young men, all with traces of torture. They had fallen into the hands of special operations troops trying to prove that the young men belonged to the Islamic underground. Instead of distant, abstract narrations of somebody's cousin being kidnapped by unidentified people in *lazik* (local denomination for cars of the Ulyanovsky Avtomobilny Zavod/UAZ make), which are frequently used by the police or FSB in the region, I heard sad, tangible narratives of people known, loved and missed. Violence was occurring in unexpected locations, unpredictably and in the midst of 'normal' daily life. It had become tangible, close, felt and feared.

State Practices, State Violence in Spaces

Police blocks on streets, borders and places where special operations had been held not only embodied violence but were also the places where violence was expected and anticipated (Jeganathan, 2004). Those were not only places like detention centres and police stations but also checkpoints and zones destroyed during KTOs. Such spaces became part of the urban space in Makhachkala. Many of them were not visible at first sight: hard to distinguish from buildings being renovated or torn down for some other reason. Yet, they were present in the lives of city inhabitants, experienced through their bodies and senses. In October 2010, a Dagestani friend wanted me to join her for the wedding of her colleague. I called her to learn about the meeting place.

> – 'Let's meet at the junction of Engel Street and … this street, near the bazaar', suggested Lena.
>
> – 'Where is this', I asked?

4 A KTO is the zone of a counter-terrorist operation: a temporary state of exception (to use Agamben's term), with all places and things belonging to it. A KTO is introduced in different places, at different times. It delineates the state of exception (for more, see Raubisko, 2011).

> – 'It is where the special operation took place. The one I told you about. You go up at the bazaar and then on the right you will see the bombed house: the whole floor burnt out. I will wait for you nearby'. (field material)

Places like the above-mentioned invoked memories of violence, sometimes very subtly and unconsciously. Only after some time was I able to tell the difference between renovation and the aftermath of a KTO. It took me a while to begin to spot bullet holes in the walls near the newly installed plastic windows. Very often there were no longer any visible traces of the special operations, yet the memory of violence was there. 'Turn near the shop which has been burnt and then go on for a while and you will get there', a friend of mine explained, pointing the way to a place where a Muslim shop had been set fire to two years before. At the time of my visit, however, a new building had been built, leaving no traces of what had been before for those passing by.

The most frequently 'visited' places and the most difficult to avoid were the checkpoints. Built during Soviet times in order to control people and migration flows, they are still in service today, especially in the south of the Russian Federation. Nowadays, they aim at securing the inhabitants of the Russian Federation (from other inhabitants of the Russian Federation, as one of my informants joked). They are built on roads at the borders of the city, on the borders of the regions, near tunnels, reservoirs and many different objects regarded (now or in the times of the USSR) as strategic. Typically, they include a little building or a small tower. There is always a barrier/gate and speed bumps. On the bigger, or for some reason more strategic police blocks, there are sandbags. Behind the sandbag walls there are soldiers in bulletproof vests with cocked rifles. Some checkpoints look like the borders between two hostile states.

The mere existence of checkpoints is justified by the necessity of reducing violence. The 'fight against terrorism' is implemented through numerous arrests and searches at the checkpoints. Yet, almost every checkpoint can be avoided by travelling around it, and car searches can be avoided through bribery. Checkpoints up until recently were simply seen as 'places for the collection of bribes'; now they are also 'places where violence is anticipated. To drive through the checkpoint is to remind oneself why it exits' (Jeganathan, 2004, p.69), reminding oneself of the possibility of attack, of shooting. Violence is also anticipated by the soldiers standing on the police blocks, or police controlling people and cars: 'The checkpoint lies at the boundaries of a target. As such, it delineates and focuses attention on the target. If the logic of the anticipation of violence creates a plethora of shifting targets that flicker and move like shadows across the landscape with each explosion or threat then the checkpoint is an attempt by an agency of the state to control that flickering movement and announce in no uncertain terms: "this is a target". The irony of this situation must be more than apparent' (Jeganathan, 2004, p.69). The checkpoints on all roads entering the city delineate the city as a goal. A masked policeman standing in front of the ordinary building delineates it as a goal, suggesting that 'an important' figure is living there – such places then become places where one expects violence. 'The very embedding of a checkpoint in different ways indexes and suggests the terrain of anticipated violence. Each is a nodal point in the map of anticipation each reconfigured by it, I can think of no better places where the state performs the magic of its illegibility with such breath-taking precision' (Jenganathan, 2004, p.72).

In May 2009, I was travelling by *marshrutka* (minibus) from Grozny to Makhachkala. Trying to start a conversation with a woman next to me I asked: 'Where are we now?', expecting to hear the name of the village. 'We are approaching the Severnyj checkpoint', said the woman pointing in the direction the bus was driving. Then I asked again. 'We passed an entry post to Khasavyurt', she answered. A year later, approaching Makhachkala, I was making a phone call to my friend to explain where I was and was told: 'Tell her we are passing the entry checkpoint to Makhachkala', this despite the fact that the checkpoint was no longer there (which puzzled me and made it harder for me to identify the place).

Spaces and roads were experienced as being divided by checkpoints. Checkpoints, armed men, and burnt parts of buildings became an intrinsic part of everyday life: an intrinsic part of the relationship between the state and the individual. Armed state officials appeared and disappeared, marking spaces which should be avoided. 'My neighbour says that when she sees a *lazik*, she crosses the street so as not to pass by it. She is afraid that the car will explode', said Gula, when we met for tea in October 2010 after a summer full of explosions. 'Even the *marshrutka* try to keep a distance from them' (field material, 2010).

State Violence and Bureaucratic Practices

A day before my departure in May 2010, my old fieldwork friend asked me about the progress of my research. I answered jokingly that it would not be bad if I had talked to some more women who wear the hijab.

> – 'I don't have any friends who turned to religion' (*udarilis v religiyu*), answered Mariam. 'What do you need that Islam for?' She emphasised over and over again that I had chosen a strange topic to explore.
>
> – 'Mariam, what about your cousin Zumrut? She wears a hijab. Maybe Iwona will meet her today?', said Mariam's mother joining our conversation.
>
> – 'I don't know any Zumurt.'
>
> – 'The one whose husband was killed a month ago.'
>
> – 'Aaa, right …', answered Mariam a bit annoyed by the long farewell (field material, 2010, names have been changed).

We met Zumrut not far from her place of work where she spends most of her day to sustain herself and her five year old. She was around twenty-five. Her husband, Murat, had renovated houses and flats. He had had his own small business. One day he did not come back home in the evening. The next day, Zumrut was interrogated in the ROVD (Regional Section of the Ministry of Internal Affairs, Районное Оттеление Внтуренных Дел), her house was searched, and things were stolen. She was forced to sign a paper saying that her husband had belonged to an Islamic underground organisation. Then, they gave her his corpse, full of scars from torture, and told her that he had wanted to detonate a bomb. Zumrut knew that the charges were false but she would not go to court. 'I don't want to see all those ugly muzzles again', she said with disdain. 'Allah will punish them all!'[5]

Zumrut was not informed about the investigation. Maybe the 'credible testimony' – a paper signed by Zumrut – was sufficient to bring the investigation to an end: 'The terrorist has been caught.' Many young people, who like Murat ended up in detention centres, were tortured and testimonies were forced out of them in the face of unbearable pain. In the North Caucasus torture has become the most popular means of extracting testimonies. It has become like a bureaucratic practice. The use of electric shocks and the pulling out of fingernails are just some of the methods used after which a 'typical suspect' pleads guilty; pleading guilty becomes the main evidence which makes it possible to close the case: 'Torture, one might argue, has become a routine and repetitive bureaucratic practice, authorless and seemingly independent of its practitioners, in that the latter are drawn and subscribe to it as a widely accepted way. In this respect, torture is no different from other bureaucratic procedures performed from day to day … , despite the horror it provokes. It is only in the bodies of the tortured and in the suffering of their loved ones that torture reaches its limit, in their eyes bearing testimonies from the other side, from beyond death … , in their words: "I will not survive another time"'(Raubisko, 2011, based on Sharma and Gupta, 2006, pp.11–13, and Kvedaravicius, n.d.).

During the so-called 'fight against terrorism', quick results are needed by politicians and high ranking officers. Results are produced by ordinary employees of the ROVD. They are ready to extract testimonies in the most efficient way; they do not want to lose their jobs. Very often they lack the skills to operate within the law. Therefore, lawless activities are being used to comply with the regulations required by law (see Raubisko, 2011, writing about Chechnya). During a couple of years, the perceptions of state dealings have considerably changed; representatives of the power structure started to be perceived as propagators of senseless violence. They were no longer trusted (unless they were members of kin). They became potential persecutors who ought to be avoided and for whom human life seemed to have no value.

5 Condemnation of violent practices and disdain for state agents and their violent practices can be seen as a certain kind of resistance (for more, see Raubisko, 2011).

In March 2011, one evening a year later, I was watching TV with Mariam's family and admiring the big TV set, which had been bought recently by Mariam's father. In the news, Vladimir Putin was speaking about an explosion in a metro station in Moscow the year before. He used words like 'liquidate', and 'neutralise', which had become an indispensable part of the 'fight against terrorism' rhetoric. His speech was about the necessity of the fight against terrorism and the mobilisation of all means to 'wipe out' the terrorism. 'Yes, he is totally right, terrorists should be liquidated', commented Mariam's mother! Yet, during the previous meeting, she had spoken with compassion about Zumrut and her husband and had pitied her and condemned the practices of the power structures. Is the state Vladimir Putin or Dmitry Medvedev speaking about in their public speeches invested with some kind of trust, while the practices of local state officials somehow detached from it? Is it the regulatory face of the state that becomes visible (and presumably longed for) on the TV screen: the very face which is perceived as lacking in everyday life, where the excesses of state practices are more visible and tangible? Or is it the 'magic' of the state project, to use Veena Das's expression (2007)?

I came across a very similar perception of state practices when visiting a flat rented by two young Salafi female students. They told me with disdain about corrupt practices at the university, about their friends being kidnapped by unidentified state officials. A strong condemnation was heard from their narrations. It was expressed with emotion, openly, leaving no space for excuses. I thought of it in terms of a hidden form of resistance. The excesses of the state's murderous practices was something they all had experienced (even if indirectly) and feared. Yet, not long after hearing their stories about local state practices and their encounters with the state, one of the women came up to the window where I was staying, pointed to the park, and said: 'Mukhu [Aliyev, President of Dagestan from 2006 to 2010] is living not far from here. Sometimes we see him strolling around the park here with his wife', she said, as if boasting a bit that such an important person was living in the neighbourhood.

It seems that although the state, through the practices of its representatives, was experienced as a source of unjust violence, it was supported by the whole system of bureaucratic practices. Its 'magical mode' (Das, 2007) did not cease to operate in everyday life. The excesses of state practices were condemned, or, as in the case of Zumrut, silently resisted, yet the shortcomings of the state's regulatory face made people long for an order which could be achieved by any means, even violent ones.[6] It is the 'distant abstract state' that is invested with desire for justice, not 'the state' represented in local state practices, perceived locally not as the 'state' but as an 'aberration' of what the state should be. It seems that two different kinds of imaginaries are at play here.

---

6 Similarly, for people on the margins in Guatemala, Nelson shows that the state is identified as the perpetrator of a terror which comes to be invested with a desire for justice (2004, p.119).

I could not help thinking about Zumrut. I asked about her after supper. Mariam's mother told me that Zumrut's brother had been killed recently; that he had been in hiding after Zumurt's husband was killed. She said that the body had not been released. 'Maybe he was a *boiovik* after all. I heard on TV that the bodies of *boioviks* are not given back to the families', she added to my surprise.

Longing for Order, Experiencing the Shortcomings of the State

The collapse of the Soviet Union was a great shock for most Dagestani and other Soviet citizens. As elsewhere in the former USSR, some ethno-national revival movements emerged. Yet, in Dagestan, unlike many other republics, neither did they last for too long nor did they have considerable social support; their character was not really separatist. Leaders of the revival movements were soon co-opted into the government. Representatives of both old nomenclature, and new, young and charismatic leaders created a system based on ethno-parties, ensuring proportional participation of all 14 titular ethnic groups in the republic. The system was a very unique example of culturally sensitive political participation (Ware and Kirsiev, 2009) and it might have helped to resolve conflicts over territories (between groups resettled in Soviet times like Chechen-Akkins, whose territories had been given to Laks and Avars). Yet, it was prone to corruption and loyalties linked to *djamaat*. The ongoing war in Chechnya, and drug and human trafficking only caused the situation to deteriorate. The majority of the population started to expect a solution from the federal centre. Putin's rule was connected with big expectations. For a short time, after his first election in 2000, the situation was slowly becoming somewhat better; the state provided citizens with basic security, and salaries and pensions were eventually paid on time. The centralization politics of Putin brought some order in the beginning. The side-effect, however, was the pathological system of loyalties/dependencies between Kremlin and Dagestani elites. Local politics ceased to exist; elections became a total fiction. 'Elections? Today? Oh, he will get 101 per cent anyway. I have no idea why they bother to organise it anymore. Waste of money' (Kaliszewska, 2011) – commented one of my informants (for village elections in Dagestan see Ekatarina Kapustina in this volume). Soon after, citizens, engaged in politics in the 1990s (both at the local and at the republican level) were kept away from the elites and their decisions. From the local elites the Kremlin expected loyalty to the ruling party (expressed for example in huge election rates). The Kremlin also did not want the Dagestani problems to spread to the other republics. Elites profiting from the money from the central budget were not interested in providing society with basic needs. Neither were they interested in any changes, especially changes of regime, ruling party, and so on. They had (and have) enough means also to suppress any alternative political activity.[7] Pathological systems of dependency had been growing, leading to the situation where hardly any work for common good was done, yet the additional 'tax' was sent up to the bosses, who sent it further up the line. Public money was stolen not only among the elites but even at the level of kindergartens.

Georgi Derluguian (2005) characterises peripheral places. The processes he identifies – taking as a case study the republic of Kabardino-Balkaria – are similar in Dagestan and other North Caucasian republics. The places he considers as peripheral are the zones with too many 'corrupt' officials bound by various forms of patronage (Derluguian, 2005, p.226). Contemporary peripheral state officials can afford to be irresponsible towards their citizens. They offer very little in the way of public services. 'The problem is the detached autonomy of peripheral states from their own citizens, who do not matter much either as military recruits (because these states do not fight big wars), or as taxpayers (because these states derive their resources externally from aid, debt, and monopolies on export trade' (Derluguian, 2005, p.227).

'These states are, nonetheless, quite effective mechanisms for producing wealthy rulers in poor countries' (Derluguian, 2005, p.224). In peripheral states, national economies are polarised between sectors controlled by the local oligarchs and the majority of the populace. Its members are involved in irregular employment, petty trade (Derluguian, 2005, p.225) or, in case of the North Caucasus live on small bribes or half of their salaries (the other half is sent up to the bosses). They are paid from public money for the work, whether it is done or not done. Most Dagestani resources are divided between different clans. Lezgians are said to have control over the tax collection system; the Laks over the airports and rail transport, and so on. Yet, so called 'national elites' are not representing their nations anymore as was the case in the 1990s when the local system was introduced. Peripheries are – as Derluguian argues – no longer 'zones of imperialist domination'. Those are areas of structural weaknesses, vulnerable both to foreign economic exploitation but more commonly to the predatory behaviour by native elites (2005, p.226), which is especially true for Dagestan. The lack of trust in the state's institutions can be seen therefore as the product of processes of peripheralisation of the republic, an effect of both the collapse of the Soviet Union and of the neoliberal politics of its successor.

In peripheral places there is in general a very low degree of state penetration into society. Such states often resort to crude violence against their citizens precisely because they have few better means available to them (Derluguian, 2005, p.224) – which in part explains why the 'fight against terrorism' turns out to be so cruel and pointless and why any real perpetrators of violence are rarely caught. Kin,

7 The movements strongly criticising the *status quo* are the Islamic reformists called Wahhabi. Cast underground by their Sufi opponents and the government in the 1990s, they become both the illegal opposition and the scapegoat for the government: who attributes all failures to them. Yet, two decades after the collapse of the Soviet Union they regain certain power, especially in the cities, in a sense due to their uncompromising position.

clan, and neighbourhood loyalties are prevailing over trust and loyalty towards state officials.

The above processes help us to understand the reason and background to the inefficiencies of state dealings. But how are they experienced?

'Do you feel that the police provide security?' was a question in the sociological poll A friend of mine conducted in 2009. As my friend from the Academy recalls: 'Secure? How can I feel secure if they are unable to provide security for themselves?' wrote one of the interviewed.

The state is failing to provide its citizens with basic needs, was my first impression of the way the state operated on the peripheries of the Russian Federation. State representatives and members of local parliament were not even spoken about with disdain – they were hardly spoken about at all. Some of my interlocutors could not provide any names except for that of the president of the republic (or head of the national assembly). There was a strong emphasis on 'coping on our own'. 'The main thing is that the state doesn't disturb us when it doesn't help us.' Most state institutions, especially all kinds of 'inspections' were primarily seen as a nuisance, merely institutions for the collection of bribes, which have long since lost sight of their primary goal. Positions in those institutions were sold off for huge amounts of money, a payment later compensated in bribe collection. Driving licenses, sanitary certificates and even children for adoption were bought. In the case of a car accident both parties tried to resolve the problem themselves before the police arrived, so that 'the state is not paid extra money'.

In the following paragraphs I will describe the way people experience and make up for a lack of the state in everyday life both in Makhachkala and in the small village community in the Tsumada district. I show how seemingly anti-state practices like the introduction of *sharia* may be motivated by care for the community or even the state. I suggest that the way state is perceived and experienced bears much resemblance to the way the Soviet system colonised the systems of knowledge about state and society, through defining its role and its goal. In other words, I show that it is the Soviet imaginary that informs the experience and perception of the state in many ways.

Lack of State: Concern for Society

In Makhachkala the interplay between the shortcomings and the excesses of the state was very tangible. From narrations about the excesses of state practices my interlocutors smoothly switched to the shortcomings. They spoke with care about society and the state as a whole and tried to find ways out of the crisis. Below, I quote a lengthy narration by Rustam, aged 58, where he expresses his concern for society through the prism of Islam and modernist projects from Soviet times.

'In communist times', he recalls, 'communists, well, actually they killed my grandpa, but anyway those were the times when people were receiving their pensions, they could help their kids. And now? Now, can I help? The worst thing is the social injustice. It wasn't like that in Soviet times. If somebody earns little money, they tell you, "How can you go on living righteously; you cannot go on without bribing, can you?" If one is a moral man one should know that those circumstances, that mess, is just a trial, a kind of temptation. A man should in all circumstances look for a way out, a way God would like him to find. ... Our society doesn't create conditions for one's development. Young people wouldn't understand – why am I worse than a rich person? It is easy to push them [the young people] off the right track. They are like a wardrobe, half-filled with books and half-empty. Society should be responsible for young people. Now, the effort of bringing up young people has been abandoned. A young man gets a stream of information, but there's no filter, he doesn't know how to choose right knowledge. Censorship is needed. You can't show on TV that you can get away with murder.

If society doesn't take responsibility young men would rather accept negative information. They need an inside filter. Society should work hard on the soul of a young man. We human beings are made to live in society but if the society doesn't create laws which are compatible with the needs of our souls, then there is conflict between an individual and society. People need enlightenment. A man who is afraid of God and who has strong moral principles is better for all authorities and all systems, because he is afraid of the Creator. If a criminal breaks the law he thinks that he will get away with the crime and avoid responsibility. There is nowhere to hide from God. If there were more pious people, it would be easier to follow the law and life would be better in every state. A true believer is responsible; he knows he will be punished and he takes responsibility for every word he says. If we choose the path of justice and what is right we will be responsible in front of Allah, family and society ... There is a fight over minds and souls. True believers, who are God's slaves can't be the slaves of circumstances. Society forgets about it. The weaker the ruler, the weaker, more amoral and stupid the slaves he wants to have. Such people cannot tell him that the state doesn't fulfil peoples' basic needs. Society should educate and demand. If it educates but doesn't demand there's a mess (*bardak*). ...In Dagestan, a man's life is like the life of a fly – it doesn't have any value. The most important thing is to sell, to buy everything. Society should start believing in God. Man is not a machine; you can't turn his heart left and right. Man should have morality. If we want the world to be better, our laws should be surrendered to God's laws, and not the other way around.'

Narratives about the development or moral progress of society and calls for moral life and control over the morality of young people were a common element of the narrations of Dagestani Muslims. Some of my interlocutors thought that violence is necessary to change the situation; others like Rustam disapproved of it. When they criticised the current situation, they compared it not, as I had expected with an Islamic state, but very often with the idiom of a 'just state', for which the model of the Soviet state was set as an example. Experiences of Soviet modernisation or rather social memory of it must have had a great impact on contemporary narratives of the inhabitants of the former USSR – especially in regard to such topics as state, society, the future of society, and the goal society strives for.

The critique of the socialism project did not touch upon socialists' ideas but the incompleteness of some projects (Pine, 1996, p.134). Even if basic assumptions of the modernist project were not fulfilled, there was a great belief that the dreams could be fulfilled – maybe in a better, different system. Modernist practices and the way the Soviet state has functioned made many people perceive themselves as 'modern' – citizens of a modern, powerful state. (McBrien, 2009). It was especially vivid on the peripheries of the Soviet state such as in Central Asia or in the Caucasus. A very important idiom was the idea of the personified society which had some goal to achieve, which strives for something, which is constantly improving itself. Another important idiom was that of a new Soviet citizen – a better, modern man, relieved from all the cultural burdens of older times. Values such as gender equality, the fight with illiteracy and work for the good of society were strongly present in party officials' narratives that were future-based. In other words, it was the Soviet imaginary that informed the experience and perception of the state of my interlocutors. Important features of twentieth century modernist projects were the total, holistic solutions which were about to bring better lives to the masses. The rhetoric of progress, modernisation, the interplay of times of order and times of chaos and eventual collective morality, were strongly present in the narratives. 'Socialism was just a first step towards the development; it helped to merge the nations. Islamisation is the second step', said Rizvan, a man in his thirties. Islamisation was regarded as yet another step after socialism, in building a better, moral society – it was not regarded as resistance to the state, but rather as opposition to the status quo, regarded as 'no state' (again a look towards the Soviet imaginary of what the state is or should be).

Making up for the Shortcomings. Introducing *sharia*: Care for the Community

Practices of making up for the shortcomings of the state were even more vivid in small communities in the mountains. The interplay between the shortcomings and the excesses of the state looked slightly differently there. The shortcomings of the state were strongly felt and substituted for locally introduced and interpreted *sharia*, while the excesses were experienced from time to time when a bigger special operation had taken place in the region.

Small *djamaat* in the mountains have experienced the processes of peripherialisation considerably. 'We were left on our own, if it wasn't for Islam, we would have ended up split apart.' Although migration processes have considerably shaken the structures of *djamaat* with younger people leaving the village and marrying outside *tukhum*,[8] belonging to a 'noble' *tukhum* still bears

8 Kin, lineage. *Djamaats* usually consist of a couple or several *tukhums*.

some validity today. In Soviet times, *djamaat* structure was preserved under the structure of kolkhozes (for example the head of kolkhoz could have been the spiritual leader in the community). *Djamaat* not only adapted to the new structure of kolkhozes but also adapted the system to their traditions (Bobrovnikov, 1997). After the collapse of the Soviet Union, migration started to threaten the existence of *djamaat*. It became an important topic of public debate both in the cities and villages. Successful emigrants from the auls and villages sponsored the roads to the villages and invested their money in the organisation of village festivals. Mosques and local schools were being renovated with the help of prominent emigrants. It was them not the state who were relied on in cases of natural disaster, misfortune or the death of close kin. In the second decade of the 2000s, *sharia* became a new integrating factor for the communities. It was portrayed not so much as a comeback to ancestors' traditions but more as a way to discipline, and to order the life of the villagers, especially the younger ones.
Jamilat, a shopkeeper in Tindi (a village in Tsumada district) is quite a successful tradeswoman in her fifties. In her view:

> 'Nowadays, there is a mess/disorder everywhere. Here some war, there another. It is not that bad here yet, it is worse in the city: shootings, explosions, assassinations. Mafia, bandits, political affairs – it all comes from above. Why do they not stop it? Back in time they could do it. All the technology (army) is available at hand. They say the Wahhabi – nobody knows what is going on in reality, it is just a scapegoat. Even if there are really some *boioviks* in the forest, why don't they catch them? Stalin resettled the whole of Chechnya in two days and sent them to Kazakhstan, or elsewhere. And they cannot catch a couple of bandits? If there is an explosion they investigate, catch the innocent. Before, there were less police and fewer problems. Russia is the biggest country in the world – isn't there enough space for everybody? We work hard and they [the officials] get their money for free. But it is probably like that everywhere now.'.

Jamilat is a very religious person. She tries to pray five times a day and she believes that strong faith can make a person do good deeds. She would like all the inhabitants of Tindi and all the people in Dagestan to follow the faith, to act according to *sharia*. Then, she believes, things would change. She misses her merry life in the Soviet Union; the visits to the city and ostentatious weddings, yet she admits that it is only faith and *sharia* which can help order things in the end: 'The most important thing in life is to believe in Allah. He gives me strength, a will to live. If all people had more faith and believed in Allah, our republic, our country and the whole world, would look different.'

The imam in Tindi is a man in his fifties. He lives in a humble house in the centre of the village. The imam recalls how big a problem alcohol abuse had been in recent years. It became the reason for domestic violence, suicide, fights. 'Islam helped to unite the community', he recalls. 'There are still some who abuse alcohol and smoke, but they are old, you will not change them.' The imam consults the *djamaat* – a council consisting of the representatives of the main *tukhum*, a chief of administration and local police officer – on most of his decisions regarding village life. It is he whom people address in cases of conflicts. He tries to solve them according to *sharia*. First of all, he wants peace and order in the village. He enjoys authority though he is regarded as strict. What he forbids is the organisation of ostentatious weddings with loud music and the invitation of pop stars or bands. The imam, introduced penalties, both for drinking and the organisation of noisy events. 'These are the local rules, the *djamaat* agreed to them. We don't want to go against the law; we live in a secular state and want to obey the constitution.' The imam spoke about the USSR with respect: 'What was bad were the persecutions but it was bad to dismiss the whole thing – how do we go on living now?' He spoke with pride about World War II and emphasised the role of the Tsumadinians in it.

The head of the administration of Tindi admits that the imam has more say in the village. 'He is a clever man, he knows a lot' – he said with respect for the imam. 'But he consults the representatives of all the *tuhkum* on his decisions. Without them nothing happens in the village. This is how things are here.'

The imam of Tindi, Jamilat, and her family and many others of their age shared many ideas about the Russian state and its history with other inhabitants of the Russian Federation. An appeal for USSR modernisation projects was heard in their narrations. Its material artefacts like industry, factories, and airports in the mountains were recalled most often. The feeling of being closer to 'the centre' was of big importance too 'at that time we felt we participated in something but now?' 'There were tours (*putiovka*) to Zakarpatia, Moscow, Leningrad. And not there's nothing left of it [of life in the times of the Soviet Union].'

It seems therefore that the project of introducing *sharia* was less of an attempt to resist the state and build an 'Islamic state' (as is sometimes portrayed in the media), than an attempt to break the processes of peripheralisation, experienced as a demodernisation.

There are Islamic revival movements all over the world and similarities with the practices of Dagestani Muslims can be traced. Yet, the experience of living in the USSR and twenty years of post-Soviet reality gives the practices of introducing *sharia* another dimension that can inform our understanding of the state and its peripheries in the post-Soviet context. For my interlocutors, living according to *sharia* meant both: living in a state without corruption and living in an ordered space, with clear rules and regulations. Living according to *sharia* was presented by Dagestani Muslims as being good for the society and the state (both essentialised locally). Those practices were informed by care for the community or even the state. They were presented as intrinsic to local tradition, and to morality, yet not standing in opposition to the constitution (required idiom for state law and various state regulations). *Sharia* was perceived as good for moral well-being, superior to state law, then only because of its divine element.

Conclusions

It took me a couple of years to understand how and where to 'look for a state' in Dagestan. I 'decided' that there is no state and people are 'on their own' and suddenly I was being stopped at checkpoints, where the violent face of the state emerged. When I kept on listening to the stories like Zumrut's, or spoke to human rights defenders, I lost sight of the other side of everyday life. Tortures, persecutions and violence were the only idioms through which I saw the life of my interlocutors. Everything else seemed flat, uninteresting and first of all unimportant. Switching between the two zones – zones of shortcomings and zones of excesses of the state – was a schizophrenic exercise, yet it was the only way. And it was a local way, too. Dialectics of shortcomings and excesses were present both in narrations and everyday practices. Through that framework, Mariam's mother's emphatic solidarity with Zumrut and simultaneous praise of Putin's rhetoric on the fight against terror were easier to grasp. It was the Soviet imaginary which seemed to inform the perception of the shortcomings of the state and a longing for a strong emperor who would bring back order, like Stalin did in Jamila's eyes or Putin in Marima's mother's eyes. Likewise, the Soviet idiom of the state seemed valid for thinking about order and *sharia* – an alternative to no order, or chaos (an idiom for post-Soviet reality).

A closer look at the experiences of the state in everyday life can therefore inform us about the way the Soviet system has colonised some forms of knowledge – especially the very thinking about the state – as an abstract entity which acts upon society – which can and should discipline the individuals to be moral citizens. The growing importance of Islamisation processes contributed to the fact that Soviet notions were slowly being substituted for Islamic ones – presumably equally effective and powerful ones.

On the one hand, I tried to show that the practices and narrations of the Dagestani Muslims were not motivated by separatist ideas, or resistance. Those were rather, as Veena Das and Deborah Poole have suggested (arguing against Scott's focus on acts of resistance as the main expression of agency) the state's conceptual boundaries which were extended and remade (here with help of Islamic ideas) in order to secure survival or seek justice in the everyday (2004, p.20).

Ideas about common history and common past with former Soviet states and Russia prevailed; the necessity of the state's existence was not questioned. On the other hand, many everyday practices of the Dagestani Muslims reinterpreted declarations of loyalty and care. Many Dagestani Muslims truly believed in a state 'magic'; they would not question the necessity to obey the law; they would even call for stricter regulations and obedience executed through violent means. Yet, their everyday practices contradicted this (see Yurchak, 2006 regarding the last Soviet generation). An emerging idea about the longed for state encompassed both: social memory of social order in the USSR and new ordering practices inspired by *sharia*.

Many Dagestani Muslims considered living according to *sharia* as a condition for building a disciplined moral society. In times where a state 'regulatory face' (Nelson, 2004) was perceived as non-existent Islamic order and Islamic modernity was presented as an alternative – yet an alternative to the shortcomings of the state, to the status quo. The shortcomings of the state were slowly made up for with *sharia*.

In my chapter, I have tried to show that while Nelson's metaphor of a state like a sideshow, a state with two faces (2004, p.135) informs our understanding of the state on the peripheries, it can be equally informative to see people's experiences of state practices in everyday life through the framework of shortcomings and excesses.

Experiences of the state, of the violent status quo perceived through body and space brought in a 'murderous face' (Nelson, 2004) of state practices. They were perceived as unjust, unnecessary, and motivated by promotion and money. They were an excess – produced through bureaucracy and corruption, felt in space and body. The murderous face of the state appeared in unexpected moments, it was experienced as an excess. The regulatory face was pale and wrinkled. The older generation was waiting for a plastic surgeon to bring back its old looks with old tools; the younger was covering it up with green cloth.

The framework of shortcomings and excesses can, I believe, inform our understanding of the experiences of the state not only in Dagestan but also in different peripheral settings both in the former Soviet Union and elsewhere.

References

Bobrovnikov, V., 1997. Islam i sovietskoe nasledie w kolhozakh severo-zapadnogo Dagestana [The Islamic and the Soviet Past in the Collective Farms of Northwest Dagestan]. *Etnograficheskoe obozrenie*, 5.

Das, V. and Poole, D., eds, 2004. *Anthropology in the Margins of the State: Comparative Ethnographies.* Santa Fe and Oxford: James Currey.

Das, V., 2007. *Life and Words: Violence and the Descent into the Ordinary.* Berkeley: University of California Press.

Derluguian, G. and Earle T., 2010. Strong Chieftaincies Out of Weak States, or Elemental Power Unbound. In: K. B. Harpviken, ed., 2010. *Troubled Regions and Failing States: The Clustering and Contagion of Armed Conflicts*. Emerald Group Publishing.

Derluguian, G., 2005. *Bourdieu's Secret Admirer in the Caucasus: A World-System Biography.* Chicago: University of Chicago Press.

Derluguian, G., 2007. The Forgotten Complexities of the North Caucasus Jihad. In: B. Grant and L. Yalcin-Heckmann, eds., 2007. *Caucasus Paradigms: Anthropologies, Histories and the Making of the World Area.* Berlin: LIT.

Falkowski, M. and Marszewski, M., 2010. The 'Tribal Areas' of the Caucasus: The North Caucasus – An Enclave of 'Alien Civilisation' within the Russian

Federation. *Prace OSW.* Available at <http://www.osw.waw.pl/sites/default/files/PRACE_34.pdf> [Accessed 20 July 2011].

Humphrey, Caroline, 2004. 'Sovereignty': A Companion to the Anthropology of Politics, ed. by David Nugent and Joan Vincent. Malden, MA: Blackwell, pp. 418–36.

Jeganathan, P., 2004. Checkpoint: Anthropology, Identity and the State. In: V. Das and D. Poole, eds, 2004. *Anthropology in the Margins of the State: Comparative Ethnographies.* Santa Fe and Oxford: James Currey.

Kaliszewska, I., 2011. Wybory w Dagestanie: Demonstracja lojalności i pogardy [Elections in Dagestan: A Demonstration of Loyalty and Contempt]. *Nowa Europa Wschodnia*, 1(15).

Kaliszewska, I. and Falkowski, M., 2010. *Matrioszka w hidżabie: Reportaże z Dagestanu i Czeczenii [Matrioshka in Hijab: Essays from Dagestan and Chechnya].* Warsaw: Sic!

Kvedaravicius, M., 2008. *Dreaming Conspiracies: Experiencing Law in Post-Soviet Chechnya.* EASA Conference: Experiencing Diversity and Mutuality, Ljubljana, Slovenia, 2008.

McBrien, J., 2009. Mukadas's Struggle: Veils and Modernity in Kyrgyzstan. *Journal of the Royal Anthropological Institute*, p. 127–44.

Nelson, D., 2004. Anthropologist Discovers Legendary Two-Faced Indian! Margins, the State, and Duplicity in Postwar Guatemala. In: V. Das and D. Poole, eds, 2004. *Anthropology in the Margins of the State: Comparative Ethnographies.* Santa Fe and Oxford: James Currey.

Pine, F., 1996. Redefining Women's Work in Rural Poland. In: R. Abrahams, ed. *After Socialism: Land Reform and Social Change in Eastern Europe*, pp. 133–56. Providence, RI: Berghahn.

Raubisko, I., 2011. Life in a Negative – Positive Space: Moral Transformations in Post-War Chechnya. PhD. University of Oxford.

Raubisko, I., 2009. Proper 'Traditional' Versus Dangerous 'New': Religious Ideology and Idiosyncratic Islamic Practices in Post-Soviet Chechnya. Journal of the Anthropological Society of Oxford, [online] Available at <www.isca.ox.ac.uk/fileadmin/ISCA/JASO/raubisko.pdf> [Accessed 23 May 2010].

Scott, J. C., 1998. *Seeing Like a State: How Certain Schemes to Improve the Human Condition Have Failed.* Yale University Press.

Scott, J. C., 1990. *Domination and the Arts of Resistance: Hidden Transcripts.* Yale: Yale University Press.

Scott, J. C., 1985. *Weapons of the Weak: Everyday Forms of Peasant Resistance.* Yale: Yale University Press.

Ware R. B., Kisriev, E., 2009. *Dagestan: Russian Hegemony and Islamic Resistance in the North Caucasus.* New York: Sharpe.

Ware R. B., Kisriev, E., 2000. Ethnic Parity and Democratic Pluralism in Dagestan: A Consociational Approach. *Europe-Asia Studies*, 53(1), pp. 105–31.

Verdery, C., 1996. *What Was Socialism, and What Comes Next?* Princeton: Princeton University Press.

Yurchak, A., 2006. *Everything Was Forever Until It Was No More: The Last Soviet Generation.* Princeton: Princeton University Press.

Chapter 11
Informality in a Neopatrimonial State: Azerbaijan

Rail Safiyev

The ambitious purpose of this chapter is to sketch the broad outline of politics in Azerbaijan.[1] For this, I draw on ideas of informality and neopatrimonialism, which have to date been employed separately in such analyses. They appear here in combination with the argument that neopatrimonialism constitutes a superstructure of authoritarian domination whereas informality ties citizens into this superstructure. Neopatrimonialism is a form of political domination that shifts between public and private spheres, in other words, between formality and informality.

I will look at informal political manipulation in order to show how informality is conducive to tacit compliance with political rule. Another goal is to show how informality permeates everyday social practices of social interaction with the state. My conclusions are based on a general overview of the state institutions as represented in the media, combined with information gathered in interviews during fieldwork in Azerbaijan in 2008–2009. The images of the state that emerged may seem unconnected and only show different types of bureaucratic mismanagement, but they convey *pars pro toto* a comprehensive account of the state. The story of Agil Khalil, to which I will refer extensively, was reported by most newspapers of the country and my analysis of his case draws on these articles and an interview with Khalil himself.

A Quarrel over National Park Property and the Fate of a Journalist

In February 2008, a young reporter, Agil Khalil, had the misfortune to be in the wrong place at the wrong time. He could not have imagined that several days later he would be in the middle of a political scandal. At the time, the political climate in Azerbaijan was critical for oppositional parties. Their electorates were being intimidated and brutally repressed after protest rallies against the fraudulent election of 2005. Only the most fearless of journalists dared to dispute the unconditional exercising of power by the government. Many significant journalists were sentenced on charges of fabricated hooliganism or delinquency. That

1 I am deeply indebted to Andrea Weiss for her valuable comments on this chapter.

February, I was in the editorial office of the newspaper 'Musavat'. It was crowded with journalists, some of whom were on a hunger strike for the release of their colleagues. It was here, by sheer coincidence, that I gained my first impressions of Khalil's case while listening to the conversations of his colleagues. Some months later I interviewed him – after he had left Azerbaijan for exile to France.

The story began on 22 February 2008, Khalil went to observe illegal construction work in the city park, the 'Zeytunluq bağları' (Olive Garden).[2] After he could not find a responsible authority on site, he made inquiries among the workers to learn why healthy trees were being felled. Usually, the felling of trees was a sign that someone wanted to build a high-rise building or a villa. In order to justify their actions they simply burn the trees, as if by accident.

Suddenly, a car approached and two large men came got out. As soon as they learned that Khalil was working for an oppositional newspaper they began to beat him and attempted to suffocate him. Luckily, Khalil freed himself and fled. Arriving at the nearest police station he brought a charge against his offenders. It seemed at first glance that the police would investigate the issue and arrest his assaulters. Kids on the street had videotaped the event and this tape became valuable evidence, though as it turned out it was no help to the police but more of an obstacle. The videotape was posted repeatedly on the internet.

Journalists found out that the two thugs were in fact 'colonels' in the intelligence service. The newspaper, 'Azadlıq', reported that one of the colonels had personal contact with the Ministry of National Security (MTN) and that the MTN had organised his flight to Georgia.

The police detained a man who had allegedly faked ownership papers for the park. This was the director of 'Olive Garden Sovkhoz' and one of the colonel's brothers. He was released afterwards 'for lack of evidence' and disappeared as well.

Gradually, the police adapted its stance to the crime, a usual procedure in Azerbaijan. As soon as a crime becomes political, lower level decision-making makes way for the verdict of the minister.[3] In this case the police department waited for a personal decision by the minister and then distanced itself from the whole matter. But there were rumours that more influential clandestine powers were involved in the matter. Some sources said that the Ministry of the Interior had leaked information about the two colonels, supposedly to vilify the MTN as entangled in illegal business or – which would have been more risky for the MTN – to show that it was involved in business that was not 'sanctioned' by the authorities.

2 The 'Zeytunluq bağları' is a very popular park in Baku. It is located on Zarifa Aliyeva Street. Zarifa Aliyeva (1923–1985) was President Ilham Aliyev's mother.

3 The same thing happened at the Ministry of Transportation on 4 August 2009. Officials of the transport service beat a truck driver who refused to pay the 'usual fees'. The Information Office of the Transport Ministry announced that they were waiting for the minister's personal statement before commenting on the issue.

An important detail that can shed light on the particular severity of the MTN men's attacks against Khalil was the rivalry between these two security institutions, that is, the MTN and its intelligence service and the Ministry of the Interior and the police.

In 2005, three years before the incident involving Khalil, the MTN unmasked illegal activities in a department of the Ministry of the Interior. The department was involved in the murder of influential public persons, businessmen and celebrities. Arrests were made by the MTN, and high-ranking police officials up to the deputy minister were put on trial. The operation became a political campaign against an interior ministry that even before these events had little public prestige. Both the police and the Ministry of the Interior pretend to show their extraordinary loyalty to the president as the guardians of state order and guarantors of law, often profiling themselves in the media as the only executors of the president's decrees.

It also made headlines that Interior Ministry staff had been coercing and intimidating political opponents and had been involved in racketeering. The officials involved were dubbed 'werewolves with epaulets' by the public, implying their dual role on both sides of the law. Testimonies in the trial revealed that 'very important political forces in the country' (Agaev, 2006, p.198) had been informed about what was going on, all along. However, the case reached its climax when the criminals kidnapped the wife of the president of the International Bank of Azerbaijan demanding from her husband two million dollars. The bank director was said to have been a close friends of the 'family'.[4] The event signalled a shift; the activities affected the interests of the high elite directly. That said, most of the details of the case remained unclear.

In fact, all law enforcement agencies in Azerbaijan, that is, the MTN, the State Attorney and the Ministry of the Interior knew about these activities. The media skirmish when everything was over, was just about finding a scapegoat. The minister appeared to be the candidate when all of a sudden he revealed that in 1997 he had been instructed by the then president, Heydar Aliyev, to release a very dangerous criminal, Abuzarov, from prison. As he recalled, the mayor of Derbent (Republic of Dagestan, Russian Federation) had asked Heydar Aliyev for this favour. Abuzarov had kidnapped and killed two people. The minister argued that this had been done for the sake of the Azerbaijanis living in Derbent. Mistakenly or not, the minister tried to draw a parallel between the existence of the criminal organisation within the ministry and the illegal release of a very dangerous criminal, practically suggesting that such an organisation may have been a political necessity. Pro-government representatives in the parliament saw this as 'treason to the spirit of Heydar Aliyev' and demanded his immediate resignation. It was expected that President Ilham Aliyev (and son of Heydar Aliyev) would fire the police chief of the country at the next opportunity, which he did not.

4 In political language in Azerbaijan, *aılə* (family) is used as a reference for the Aliyev family and their friends.

In general, the investigation within the Ministry of the Interior brought disgrace upon the Minister of the Interior. The continuing rivalry between the MTN and the Ministry of the Interior was widely discussed in newspapers, allegedly revealing the secret plans of the Ministry of the Interior. In one of these articles, Agil Khalil's dizzy misfortune was turned upside down, so that now the Minister of the Interior was accused of organising a coup and embarrassing the country in the eyes of the world. The article also expressed the suspicion that Khalil had been instructed to investigate this issue (Yeni Çağ, 2008).

After the incident in February 2008, Khalil received anonymous calls that he assumed were from the MTN, with threats on his life unless he withdrew the charges against the colonels. He was pursued at every turn. He was offered a bribe by the State Attorney himself. But Khalil remained obstinate and did not accept the money. He was eager to proceed until all legal remedies had been exhausted.

Soon after, the police discontinued their investigation and kept a low profile. Investigations on the beating in February had been annulled earlier, because allegedly they were not based on facts. The police report states that 'the two men were only passers-by and had not been found to be linked to the property issue. They were disturbed by the extensive photograph taking and as they approached Khalil, he fell down on his back and began to cry. The medical examination did not show any grievous physical harm' (APA, 2008). The particulars of the crime were thus distorted many times until a desirable version had been arrived at.

On 13 March 2008, Khalil was attacked a second time. He was stabbed near the Court of Appeal in the middle of the day. The knife just missed his heart. Another investigation began. In their first statement, the police suggested a link between the first and the second case, which seemed obvious. However, after the State Attorney took over, such suspicions were put aside. A few days later, Khalil was interrogated for six hours. The interrogation was carried out by officials from the State Attorney's offices. In these interrogations they showed a faked video reporting Khalil's homosexual partnership with with a masseur, Sergey Strekalin, and tried to blackmail him. The intelligence services also faked telephone conversations to show that they had been in such a relationship for a long time. They threatened to show this video on TV and Khalil's alleged homosexuality public. These fabricated facts were to explain why Khalil had been attacked: Khalil had been unfaithful and Strekalin became jealous. Two days later, four state channels, including the official state channel, broadcasted the video.

The court trial was held behind closed doors, which was quite abstruse, since everything was disclosed to the public anyway. 'It is a very absurd situation. I claimed that this person had not stabbed me, and instead of rejoicing, he wanted to plead guilty for some unclear reasons', said Khalil later.

The Organisation for Security and Cooperation of Europe (OSCE) media observer, Miklos Harazsti, brought Khalil's issue to the attention of officials. Harazsti quoted the head of the State Attorney's office saying that he had personally ordered this slanderous video campaign (OSCE, 2008). Since Khalil life was perceived as being in danger – despite international interest and the provision of Ministry of Interior bodyguards – several embassies petitioned presidential officials to allow Khalil to leave Azerbaijan. Even after he was officially permitted to leave the border, police at the airport gave him a hard time while trying to examine his luggage. The two bodyguards from the Ministry of the Interior stopped them, seeing in it a contrived act of criminal orchestration. The situation turned violent culminating in one police officer drawing his gun and threatening to shoot. All this happened in the presence of diplomats and other passengers. After telephone calls between the American and the French embassy officials and the Office of the President, the border officer finally allowed Khalil to pass. Khalil lives in Paris today.

Informality, the State and Neopatrimonialism

Informality is defined by Levitsky and Helmke (2004, p.727) as 'socially shared rules, usually unwritten … created, communicated, and enforced outside of officially sanctioned channels'. Radnitz (2011, p.354) argues that this perspective reduces informality to the strategic choices or constraints of actors. He maintains that informality 'may emanate from occurrences that are informal but … not repeated in predictable, patterned ways'. To act informally is for Ledeneva (2006, p.20) a 'player's creative handling of formal and informal norms which breed into informal practices'. The concept of 'subversive institutions' also points to the fact that formal institutions can be the basis for informal action, which makes any rigid differentiation between informality and formality difficult (Gelman, 2010, p.7).

Misztal (2000, p.38) stresses the practicality and convenience of informality, making it possible for actors to determine and control interactive situations. She relies on a general sociological definition: informality is identified with co-presence, which 'utilises the duality of perception and communication' and is a feature of interpersonal, less routine, less rigid and less formal relationships that rely more on tacit knowledge than on prescribed norms (Misztal, 2000, pp.18–19). This definition fits well, as it points to the expedient use of formality and informality throughout human relations and includes a situational aspect. Because in Soviet times the official sphere did not provide political support and recognition, it produced a rather 'calculative and instrumental' attitude towards formal processes (Misztal, 2000, p.217). Consequently, in the post-Soviet context, informality continued to offer a myriad of options for the arbitrary instrumental use of power.

The question of the social basis of informality leads to the question of the role of a state that underpins such relations. Between the ideal of the state as formalised relations between citizens and knowledge, and that the state itself is immersed in informality, the imagination of the state reverberates for citizens every day. This is framed by Giordano (2007, p.43) as a public awareness about the abuse of people's interests by the state. As he notes, the immediate reaction is a rebellious infiltration of the state by practices such as clientelism, corruption, personal networks and criminality: in short, the increased informality of state rule.

By rethinking the state as 'not given and fixed, but producing a structural effect of appearance as if it were a discrete and relatively autonomous social institution', Gupta and Sharma (2006, pp.8–11) argue that the constitutive element of the state is the imprint of 'routine and repetitive procedures of bureaucracy'. In Migdal's (2001) state-in-society model, the state is woven into an image of a unified organisation that is at the same time being dismantled. As Darden (2008, p.54) notes, material incentives comprise the main catalyst for the organisation and integrity of the state. For Christophe (2005, p.36), such a state stimulates the infringement of (formal) state rules.

One approach to explaining this phenomenon has been offered by theories that suggest neopatrimonial rule as a factor for the inefficiency of the state, especially with regard to post-colonial Africa and Asia. These reflections on neopatromonialism are based in the Weberian sociology of domination, operationalised in regime analysis (Bratton and Van de Walle, 1994). Recently, the concept came to the attention of post-Soviet transitionalists who applied it to the resilience and adaptability of post-Soviet authoritarian regimes (Hale, 2005; Fisun, 2004).[5] But doubts remained if neopatrimonialism was not being too broadly applied, as a 'catch all' concept (Erdman and Engel, 2006, p.5) or if its analytical relevancy had been hollowed out (Therkirdsen, 2005).

Attempts have been made to render more precisely a definition of neopatrimonialism, and in the main there is broad acceptance to avoid an application that is too widespread. Erdman and Engel (2007, p.105) for instance, concretised neopatrimonialism as a form of domination that entails a legal bureaucratic apparatus but rests upon the distinctive application of public and private contexts. According to Theobald (1982, p.550), neopatrimonialism is 'a bureaucracy permeated by patron–client relationships, while the bureaucratic apparatus is constantly undermined and distorted'. Guliyev (2011, p.578) distinguishes neopatrimonialism from Rosberg's definition of personal rule and sees it as 'a set of informal institutions which are regularised, accepted and practised'. Hensell (2009, p.63) transposes neopatrimonialism onto the individual perspective of state actors, arguing that in a neopatrimonial state, the obstruction of formal rules became the sole accepted rule of the game; state practices are transformed into habitual 'patrimonial practices'.

Other students of this concept noted the broader effect of neopatrimonialism as routinised in behavioural norms and procedures beyond bureaucracy. Clapham (1985, p.63) claims that neopatrimonialism is the most salient type of domination in Third World countries because it corresponds to the normal forms of social organisation on the ground.

5 For Azerbaijan, see Babajew (2009) and Guliyev (2011).

Overall, the impression prevails that there are a variety of applications of neopatrimonial theory. For politics in Azerbaijan, it is necessary to focus on two of them. First, there is the peculiarity of the post-Soviet states focus on ideology. Gelman (2004, p.1027) identifies the ideological impact on the creation of 'formal and informal institutions' prior to the post-Soviet transformation, noting that liberal approaches to privatisation were early ideological inspirations. This ideology influenced actors in the transition period in Azerbaijan. For Ilkhamov (2007, p.67), formal institutions were constituent elements of Kerimov's regime ideology in Uzbekistan and neopatrimonialism was, so to speak, how the regime selectively employed formal and informal institutions, the strategy for creating ambiguities. Similarly, the ideology of recent governments in Azerbaijan encompasses abstruse and plastic forms of popularisation in the name of national unity, among them the cult of Heydar Aliyev and the so-called 'Azerbaijaniness', the etatistic notion of the state (see Babajew, 2009).

Second, neopatrimonialism is marked by patron–client relationships, which imply rewards for loyalty and regulate access to resources. However, it makes clients dependent on the goodwill of patrons and prompts them to reciprocal duties (Roniger, 2004, p.354). In such a framework, state actors are particularly vulnerable. Because of the unaccountability that is inherent to clientelistic frameworks, insecurity is a constitutive element. For that reason, ensuring increased security is a permeating strategy for everyone acting within a neopatrimonial environment (Erdmann, 2002, p.331). State actors and citizens must necessarily resort to patron–client relations, that is, to informality, 'in order to make their risks calculable' (Erdmann, 2002, pp.333–34).

The Meaning of Informality in Azerbaijan

The demise of the Soviet Union did not lessen but, on contrary, increased informality to the degree that it has gained a foothold in the state apparatus for capturing every interaction in Azerbaijan. As part of the Soviet Union, Azerbaijan was reputed to have been a hotbed of corruption, a fact that slowly came to light in the course of perestroika. Azerbaijani elites enjoyed autonomy and disposed of exclusive power to convert their administrative networks into secondary economic gains. Since the Soviet system constrained the opportunities for personal career advancement in the peripheries, informal politics emerged in the form of patronage networks as a form of power consolidation for the local leadership (Willerton, 1992, p.228). Double accounting (*dvoynaya bukhgalteriya*) was common in the economy of Soviet Azerbaijan; trust in formal institutions was broken and never returned. In the 1990s, democratisation processes weighed in against the quest for individual profit, which got the upper hand (Derluguian, 2005, p.222). Informal network groups occupying higher offices recreated the authoritarian institutional structures of the past (Koehler and Zürcher, 2003, p.167).

Today, informality is a much-used trope in correlating meanings in Azerbaijan, but as a social fact it unfolds from a long tradition reaching back into the Soviet past. One term for informality in Azerbaijan is *yazılmamış qanunlar*[6] (unwritten law), but this vernacular notion should not be confused with Ledeneva's (2001, p.7) 'unwritten rules', by which she means the knowledge needed to 'navigate' between formal and informal and between the rules and their enforcement.

Critically minded public activists, when they speak out against the deplorable situation in the official agencies of the state, resort to the Azerbaijan legal code or international law in their arguments. Due to the regular work of these social activists, knowledge of the discrepancies is widespread. But Soviet tradition has endured nevertheless, reaching the point of becoming an 'official' attitude toward the state marked by a 'formal' adherence to the letter of the law, which operates simultaneously with the open existence of informal structures. In this dichotomy, informality in the application of the law has been amplified to total ignorance of that same law. In an everyday encounter with legal stipulations, the spirit of the law has lost all practical implications beyond being a barely formalistic and technical apparatus that needs to be paid homage to, resembling ever more Russian *formalnosty*.

That said, informality is a market phenomenon and has taken on very structured forms. As Lomnitz concludes, 'the informal exchange ... take[s] the form of reciprocity, patron–client, or market exchange according to the motives, goals, degree of repression of the exchange, or culturally defined rules of obligation between partners' (1988, p.54) Just as in Russia, where blat has come to conform to market pressure, diminishing after commodity shortages were increasingly resolved (Ledeneva 1998, p.176), in Azerbaijan, informality has shifted from graft to a more pecuniary business. The informality reciprocity frameworks are the subject of the flexible attitudes. The informal exchange of favours, *tanışlıq, tapşırıq* (acquaintance, instruction) likened to blat in Soviet times has given way to an informal market. Under these conditions, according to one informant, personal 'sympathy for each other and personal acknowledgements no longer play a role'.

Political Dimensions of Informality in Azerbaijan

In Agil Khalil's case, the idealised version of formality is the basis of the stance of the media and local NGO's, those marginalised civil society activists. They struggle with such cases every day and their close relationship to international institutions enabled them a relative autonomy from the authoritarian state to do so. The relevance of outside powers should be not underestimated in maintaining this normative pressure on the Azerbaijani government.

---

6 Another form of informality in public consciousness is *qanunsuz* (unlawfulness), but it does not constitute an equivalency to the discrepancy between formality and informality.

With the collapse of the Soviet Union, enthusiasm for nation-state building and for climbing up the ladder of capitalist prestige, took hold. It was thought that the independent nation-state would quickly bear fruit, and the early 1990s were a period of predominantly Western-oriented constitutional reforms. Ideals of constitutionality were at the core of the model of the state, which was marked by human and civil rights and enshrined in a constitution.[7] A fairly free media was established and the foundation for a multi-party system was laid. The scales shifted in 2005, when new power holders with extreme financial resources emerged to shatter constitutional politics and dictate their rules.

There remains today a very minor group of oppositional and marginal independent media. The rule of law and the constitution have lost much of their charm. The state elite is only concerned with the preservation of its symbolic value, demonstrating pro forma their eagerness to be part of the 'democratic world'.[8] A quasi-democratic ideology is performed in the paradigmatic confrontation between the West and post-Soviet dictatorships. In the case study, it was presented in the phoney and ambiguous position of the presidential officials presenting the president ostensibly as a champion of the rule of law in the Azerbaijani state,[9] feigning cooperativeness in efforts to establish the truth behind Agil Khalil's case.

Politically sensitive cases like Khalil's are seen as hazardous and anticipate one reaction – direct intervention by the political establishment. In the reality of this state, political decision-making is at the ultimate discretion of the president. Any 'outside disturbers' like Khalil and his supporters are opposed by one orchestrated front on the part of the state apparatus, the latter consolidated to act as a unified political machine. In one of his speeches, President Ilham Aliyev made it very clear that ministers should not be political, that politics was the sole domain of the absolute ruler (EurasiaNet, 2005). The presidential administration's concern is uniquely the prevention of possible damage to the president's image, as he is in the predicament of having to maintain a rickety facade in representing a country looking toward Europe.

Why the situation involving Agil Khalil escalated to such an extent remains open. It might be that just in this case typical informal practices were externalised with the help of outsiders. Similar incidents before have not received as much attention. Behind the scene there exists the conviction that any turmoil within the state must be concealed from foreign observers and the presidential administration is successful in ensuring that the media tow the official line.

7 Thirty-seven articles in the constitution of Azerbaijan are dedicated to basic human and civil rights.

8 Identification with Europe and modernisation has strong roots in Azerbaijani political identity (Ismayilov, 2008), which is officially provided in a facade of democracy and rule of law.

9 The head of presidential administration, Ramiz Mehdiyev, is reputed to be an 'ideologue' of the regime. In oppositional media he is seen a dean of regime politics.

Paradoxically, informality becomes dysfunctional when it becomes the party line. The authorities have not relinquished their claim to formal power or their formalist ideology. The trial was pushed through, performed as accurately as possible. It was only in the last act – at the passport control at the border – that the state institutions inadvertently revealed the charade, the pure arbitrariness of the law and its enforcement.

Here, we may argue with O'Donnell (1999) that this is a case of *un*rule of law, revealing the informal patterns of the exercise of power. Likewise, Gelman (2004, pp.1021–1022) differentiates between the rule of law as 'dominance of formal institutions in the political arena' and the dominance of informal institutions as the *un*rule of law. The case of Agil Khalil points to the absence of judicial power and its substitution by informal practices – black PR and *kompromat*, as Ledeneva words it (2006). The political crisis could have been avoided if the police and secret services had completed their investigation on the basis of the law, but the law is seen here more as bureaucracy. In an environment of overwhelming informality, the law loses its validity and trustworthiness. The MTN, enmeshed in clientelism doubted the reliability of the police's performance. The police officials protecting Khalil, in turn, suspected the intentions of the border police when they demanded they search Khalil's luggage. Credibility is measured by other merits than in a functioning bureaucracy. Justice had no relevancy for the state officials, so they resorted to blackmail.

Economic Informality in Azerbaijan

When Agil Khalil went to report on the state of the 'Olive Garden', his goal was to examine the control of the private sector by state officials. The 'Olive Garden' property had been expropriated by illicit 'owners' – high ranking officers. Despite daily reports on the misappropriation of state or private property, the government turns a blind eye, either because of incompetence or unwillingness.

The Azerbaijan economy was formally liberalised in the 1990s, which does not essentially change anything since the factual state control of the economy was preserved by means of a regulated informal sector. Hart (2006, p.23) sees this informal sector as an antithesis to the 'bureaucratic form', which he describes as 'an attempt to manage markets and money through central bureaucracy and as an institutional effort to organise society along formal lines'. With some exceptions, I suggest that the state in Azerbaijan does not even enforce the 'bureaucratic form'. On the contrary, what we witness today is, to put it mildly, the informal taxation of the private sector by means of graft and embezzlement. Current challenges to the informal economy are responded to by the government with rhetoric. The government strives to make the impression that it is doing something to maintain its relationships with international donor organisations, but nothing more.

For instance, in 2008, the president abruptly confirmed the existence of informal payments in Azerbaijan in the presence of his ministers, making some critical remarks (Aliyev, 2008). In Azerbaijan, it is an open secret that there are some state institutions which include informal payments in their structures, for instance the State Committee on Property Issues, the Ministry for Taxation, and the Customs Service. Some departments of these ministries were entrusted with extortion activities, and institutionalised the allocation of informal payments to their staff in the form of what are known as cover salaries (*zərflə maaş*). After the president's remarks, the head of the State Social Protection Fund added 'we are not faced with such payments in the state sector. These are deeds of private companies' (Azadlıq Radiosu, 2010a). Some months later, one of the members of the ruling party confessed candidly that the head of state 'has to and actually keeps a tight grip on non-official economic activities and maintains surveillance on all economic transactions, even illegal ones' (Azadlıq Radiosu, 2010b), confirming the suspicion that the political elite had full knowledge of the transactions in the informal economy.

Informal agreements on salaries have a pragmatic aspect as well, since they consider market prices. I was told by one ministerial employee about the effects of an interruption in the transfer of informal salaries during an anti-corruption campaign in 2011. They were frustrated because official monthly wages do not suffice to cover the basic costs of living. The efficiency of informality lies in its comprehensive character, which is another reason why informality is met with consensus, providing for the economic survival of much of the disadvantaged population.

Here, Hart's separation of an informal economy from the bureaucratic form may not apply because interdependencies exist between these two sectors, the state itself being an integrated part of the informal economy. The power of the ministers rests on clientelist relations, graft, and economic profiteering – and these co-exist side by side with the bureaucratic apparatus. For actors, it either necessitates compliance with the informal rules for accessing such rewards or forces them out.

Informality shapes the economic power of the state. The emic notion of 'bureaucratic oligarchy' (*məmur oliqarxiyası*), is an example. Infrastructure projects, construction of government buildings, Party infrastructure, parks and entertainment centres, museums named after the 'national leader' Heydar Aliyev, and Olympic centres are a common distribution mechanism in a patrimonial state and a significant economic factor. The failure of bureaucracy is replaced by economic incentives that result from oil revenues.

Clientelist structures based on informal networks offer alternative mechanisms within the administration that transcend formal bureaucratic efficiency. Clientelism maintains the clandestine, less rigid channels of asset allocation, keeping the knowledge about them in obscurity and controlling all material incentives.

That those bureaucrats in Azerbaijan have the monopoly over hotels, construction companies and even the informal administration of the local political executive is a well-known fact. *De jure*, private companies are registered in the name of relatives, friends, colleagues or employees who hold lower posts and depend very much on their higher ranking managers. This is not questioned nor is it investigated. Drawing on Clapham (1985, p.48), who describes this oligarchic understanding of public office as neopatrimonial, it can be said that in Azerbaijan public office is understood as the private property of an office holder. If one takes a look at the on-going discourse in society, one can easily discern the types of relations based on the symbolic and personalised characteristics of its officials. In the media or in public, entire ministry apparatuses are reduced to the names of the respective ministers, who personify their ministries as if they were their owners.

In Azerbaijan, lucrative economic spheres remain outside the control of the security services. Meanwhile, the latter have their internal economy. Similar to what Hensell (2009, p.177–96) argued for Georgia's police of the Shevardnadze era, the police in Azerbaijan has its own economic system based on recruitment, extortion, and daily police controls. In the eyes of the public, police controls are associated with nothing more than collecting money from the residents of houses, vendors and firms. The purpose of the police is not to control but to extract wealth and thus they are interested in a certain degree of informality on the market. The results can be seen in the public presentation of the police, their latest model BMWs underline the 'prestige and power' of an entire ministry.[10]

The same can be said for the MTN, which is the local successor of the KGB. Little has changed in the new ministry and they continue to gather compromising materials on Azerbaijani citizens.[11] Access to such information is another key tool for controlling the population (Di Puppo, 2004, p.50).

Conclusion

The conflict that emerged with Agil Khalil at the centre was an example of bureaucratic oligarchy dividing the spoils of office. The struggle was about the respective significance in the hierarchical order and about who was more loyal to the president. The main pillar of bureaucratic oligarchy is the trust that results after years of working together and loyalties based on beneficial patron–client relations. The most successful oligarch is the one who places his own people in controlling positions in the administration or in auxiliary companies. Like a spider, he sits in his web of trust relations spanned cautiously across the enormous expense of his network.

But such neopatrimonial relations do not equate with state officials having inviolable property rights, even though they have, to all intents and purposes, privatised the economy for themselves. Just as in Georgia, the political elite in Azerbaijan ensures that there is just enough disorder to create insecurity among lower ranks, thereby ensuring their instrumental power over public servants and

10 Many of my informants were employees of the Ministry of Energy and the Ministry for Labour and Social Services

11 Interview with a state employee.

making them compliant to the rules of the inherent hierarchy. An anti-corruption campaign is an example of such a control instrument of the state, which is utilised for the purposes of disciplining officials (Christophe, 2005). The insecurity of state actors is part of the particular effectiveness of informality, which constitutes a non-fixed set of rules and creates insecurity for state agencies. It positions the ruling elites over those who are lower in the hierarchy.

The case of Agil Khalil is a lesson about the informal and formal in the state, in which Khalil and all the officials he encountered are trapped. Formal structures are the opportunities for sanctions that are imposed by officials. At the same time, informality is constantly reproduced by formal laws and sanctions.

Neopatrimonialism for its part provides a frame for informality and defines who profits how much and where. In this power game, insecurity plays a vital role, the patron ensuring the insecurity of his client and thus cementing the system.

References

Agaev, R., 2006. Azerbaydzhan: Perekhodnyy period shtrikhi k portretu nezavisimoy respubliki [Azerbejdzan: Transition Period, Towards an Image of an Independent Republic]. *Vestnik Analitiki* 26(4), pp.187–200.

Aliyev, I., 2008. Nazirlər Kabinetinin 2008-ci ilin 9 aylıq sosial-iqtisadi inkişafının yekunlarına həsr olunmuş geniş iclasında Prezident İlham Əliyevin yekun nitqi [Closing Remarks by Ilham Aliyev at the Meeting of the Cabinet of Ministers on 9 Months' Social Economic Development in 2008]. Available at <www.president.az> [Accessed on 13 October 2008].

APA, 2008. 'Azadlıq' qəzetinin müxbiri Aqil Xəlilin 'Zeytun bağı' adlanan ərazidə döyülməsi ilə bağlı cinayət təqibinə xitam verilib [The Criminal Prosecution for Assault on Reporter of 'Azadliq' in the Place of the so Called Olive Garden Has Been Stopped] 21 March 2008. Available at <http://az.apa.az/news.php?id=97275> [Accessed on 14 April 2012].

Azadlıq Radiosu, 2010a. Dövlət idarələrində 'zərf maaşlar' yox imiş! [There Were No 'Cover Salaries' in State Offices!], 29 April 2010. Available at <www.azadliq.org/content/article/2027480.html> [Accessed on 09.03.2014].

Azadlıq Radiosu, 2010b. Nizami Dzhafarov vo vsem mire yest' vzyatki [Nizami Jafarov: Bribes Exist All Around the World] 9 August 2010. Available at <http://www.azadliq.org/content/article/2120719.html> [Accessed on 14 April 2012].

Babajew, A., 2009. Politische Transformation im postsowjetischen Aserbaidschan: eine historisch-institutionalistische Analyse. PhD thesis. Mannheim. Available at <https://ub-madoc.bib.uni-mannheim.de/2925/1/Dissertation_Babajew.pdf [Accessed on 12 April 2012].

Bratton, M. and Van de Walle, N., 1994. Neopatrimonial Regimes and Political Transitions in Africa. *World Politics* 46 (4), pp.453–89.

Christophe, B., 2005. *Metamorphosen des Leviathan in einer post-sozialistischen Gesellschaft: Georgiens Provinz zwischen Fassaden der Anarchie und regulativer Allmacht*. Bielefeld: transcript.

Clapham, C. S., 1985. Third World Politics. Madison: University of Wisconsin Press.

Darden, K., 2008. The Integrity of Corrupt States: Graft as an Informal State Institution. *Politics and Society* 36, pp.35–60.

Derluguian, G. M., 2005. *Bourdieu's Secret Admirer in the Caucasus: A World-System Biography*. Chicago: University of Chicago Press.

Di Puppo, L., 2004. Corruption as an Instrument of State Control in Georgia. *Osteuropa Forum* 21. Available at <http://www.oei.fu-berlin.de/publikationen_old/boi/21_boi/03_forum/08_di_puppo/index.html> [Accessed on 9 March 2014].

Erdmann, G., 2002. Neopatrimoniale Herrschaft – oder: Warum es in Afrika so viele Hybridregime gibt. In: P. Bendel, A. Croissant, and W. Rüb, eds, *Zwischen Demokratie und Diktatur: Zur Konzeption und Empirie demokratischer Grauzonen*. Opladen: Leske and Budrich, pp.323–42.

Erdmann, G. and Engel, U., 2006. Neopatrimonialism Revisited: Beyond a Catch-All Concept. *GIGA Working Papers* 16. Available at <http://www.giga-hamburg.de/de/system/files/publications/wp16_erdmann-engel.pdf> [Accessed on 9 March 2014].

Erdmann, G. and Engel, U., 2007. Neopatrimonialism Reconsidered: Critical Review and Elaboration of an Elusive Concept. *Commonwealth and Comparative Politics* 45(1), pp.95–119.

EurasiaNet, 2005. Rovshan Ismayilov: Azerbaijan: Two More Officials Sacked, 19 October 2005. Available at <http://www.eurasianet.org/departments/civilsociety/articles/eav102005.shtml> [Accessed on 14 April 2012].

Fisun, A., 2004. *Postsovetskie politicheskie rezhimy: neopatrimonial'naya interpretatsiya* [Post-Soviet Political Regimes: Neopatrimonial Interpretation]. Kharkov: Konstanta.

Gelman, V., 2004. The Unrule of Law in the Making: The Politics of Informal Institution Building in Russia. *Europe-Asia Studies* 56(7), pp.1021–1040.

Gelman,V., 2010. Podryvnye instituty i neformal'noe upravlenie v sovremennoy Rossii [Subversive Institutions and Informal Governance in Contemporary Russia]. *Politeia* 2(57). Available at <http://www.politeia.ru/content/pdf/Politeia_Gelman-2010-2.pdf> [Accessed on 14 April 2012].

Giordano, C., 2007. Privates Vertrauen und informelle Netzwerke: Zur Organisationskultur in Gesellschaften des öffentlichen Misstrauens. Südosteuropa im Blickpunkt. In: K. Roth, ed., *Soziale Netzwerke und soziales Vertrauen in den Transformationsländern*. Zürich: Lit, pp.21–51.

Guliyev, F., 2011. Personal Rule, Neopatrimonialism, and Regime Typologies: Integrating Dahlian and Weberian Approaches to Regime Studies. *Democratization* 18(3), pp.575–601.

Gupta, A. and Sharma, A., 2006. Introduction: Rethinking Theories of the State in an Age of Globalization. In: A. Sharma and A. Gupta, eds, *The Anthropology of the State: A Reader*. Oxford and Malden: Blackwell, pp.1–41.

Hale, H. E., 2005. Regime Cycles: Democracy, Autocracy, and Revolution in Post-Soviet Eurasia. *World Politics* 58, pp.133–65.

Hart, K., 2006. Bureaucratic Form and the Informal Economy. In: B. Guha-Khasnobis, R. Kanbur and E. Ostrom, eds, *Linking the Formal and Informal Economy: Concepts and Policies*. Oxford: Oxford University Press, pp.21–36.

Helmke, G. and Levitsky, S., 2004. Informal Institutions and Comparative Politics: A Research Agenda. *Perspectives on Politics* 2(4), pp.725–40.

Hensell, S., 2009. *Die Willkür des Staates: Herrschaft und Verwaltung in Osteuropa*. Wiesbaden: VS Verlag für Sozialwissenschaften.

Ilkhamov, A., 2007. Neopatrimonialism, Interest Groups and Patronage Networks: The Impasses of the Governance System in Uzbekistan. In: *Central Asian Survey* 26(1), pp.65–84.

Ismayilov, M., 2008. Azerbaijani National Identity and Baku's Foreign Policy. *Azerbaijan in the World ADA Biweekly Newsletter* 1(1)

Koehler, J. and Zürcher, C., 2003. The Art of Losing the State: Weak Empire to Weak Nation-state around Nagorno-Karabakh. In: J. Koehler and C. Zürcher, , eds, *Potentials of Disorder*. Manchester and New York: Manchester University Press, pp.145–73.

Ledeneva, A., 2001. Unwritten Rules: How Russia Really Works. Centre for European Reform. Available at <http://www.cer.org.uk/sites/default/files/ publications/attachments/pdf/2011/e246_unwritten_rules-2203.pdf > [Accessed on 11 March 2014].

Ledeneva, A., 2006. *How Russia Really Works*. London: Cornell University Press.

Lomnitz, L. A., 1988. Informal Exchange Networks in Formal Systems: A Theoretical Model. *American Anthropologist* 90(1), pp.42–55.

Migdal, J., 2001. *State in Society: Studying How States and Societies Transform and Constitute One Another*. Cambridge: Cambridge University Press.

Misztal, B., 2000. *Informality: Social Theory and Contemporary Practice*. London and New York: Routledge.

O'Donnell, G., 1999. Polyarchies and the (Un)Rule of Law in Latin America: A Partial Conclusion. In: J. E. Mendez, G. O'Donnell, and P. S. Pinheiro, eds, The (Un)Rule of Law and the Underprivileged in Latin America. Notre Dame: University of Notre Dame Press, pp.303–37.

OSCE, 2008. Press Release: OSCE Media Freedom Watchdog Calls Baku Trial 'Fake', Aimed to Discredit Opposition Journalist and Protect his Real Attackers. Available at <17 July 2008, http://www.osce.org/fom/49925> [Accessed on 25 September 2012].

Radnitz, S., 2011. Informal Politics and the State. Review Article. *Comparative Politics* 43(3), pp.351–71.

Roniger, L., 2004. Political Clientelism, Democracy, and Market Economy. *Comparative Politics* 36(3), pp.353–75.

Theobald, R., 1982. Patrimonialism. *World Politics* 34(4), pp.548–59.

Therkirdsen, O., 2005. Understanding Public Management through Neopatrimonialism: A Paradigm for All African Seasons? In: U. Engel and G. R. Olsen, eds, *African Exception*. Aldershot: Ashgate, pp.35–51.

Willerton, J., 1992. *Patronage and Politics in the USSR*. Cambridge: Cambridge University Press.

Yeni Çağ, 2008. Prezident seçkiləri üçün qanlı plan hazırlanır [Bloody Plotting for Presidential Elections]. *Yeni* Çağ, 24 March 2008. Available at <http://www.yenicag.az/article.php?storyid=736> [Accessed on 26 July 2009].

Chapter 12
Elections in Armenia: Western Models and Local Traditions

Levon Abrahamian and Gayane Shagoyan

The chapter presents the political history of elections in Armenia since 1988, that is, from the late-Soviet period to the first years of independence up until recent times, including the 2013 presidential and Yerevan municipal elections. The text is composed of four parts. In the first and second part, the introduction of the institution of elections and its uneven and sometimes paradoxical development is retraced. We will see how this institution, an acquisition of the mass rallies of the late 1980s, which resulted in the independence of Armenia, transformed soon into an instrument of acquiring and reproducing power. This is similar to what happened elsewhere in former Soviet space, where it was mainly introduced from the West. We will follow the development of this 'endemic' institution and discuss the encounter of Western and local models of elections. The third part analyses elections in the village and the political and social consequences of the introduction of this institution in rural regions. The fourth part deals with Western models related to the institution of elections, from mythological and imagined ones to pretexts for and sophisticated techniques of falsifications. Our analysis is close to a political anthropological study. It discusses political issues and events with an anthropological perspective, involving not only official figures and data, but also prejudices, rumours and gossip related to elections.

Political 'Festival' and the Institution of Elections

In a number of earlier publications one of the authors (L.A.) has discussed the stormy rallies of the late 1980s in Armenia that gained the general name of the Karabakh Movement[1] – as a kind of a festival that could have but did not terminate in possible social changes (Abrahamian, 1990a, 1990b, 2006, pp.217–43). Such

---

1 The movement is named after the Nagorno-Karabakh Autonomous Oblast in the Azerbaijanian SSR with the majority of the Armenian population claiming unification of the oblast with the Armenian SSR in 1988. This claim was supported in Armenia and rejected in Azerbaijan and Moscow. It developed from constitutional rallies to bloody war in Karabakh and the de-facto independence of the former oblast and currently unrecognized Nagorno-Karabakh Republic.

estimations or, rather, predictions were based on the analysis of the social structure before, during and after the 'political festival'. Here, we will not go into a discussion on whether the rallies of 1988 (and the Karabakh Movement in general, as well as future rallies of 2008 and 2013) could be considered as a revolution (from historical, economic, political perspectives),[2] or a protest or a national liberation movement, but will base our analysis on the 'festival' typology of the original rallies, referring interested readers to the already cited publications.

Actually, we need to refer to the study focused on the 'festival' mentioned, to state that however problematic the building of democracy and civil society could be considered in post-Soviet Armenia (Abrahamian and Shagoyan, 2011, 2012, pp.12–13, Ishkhanian 2008, p.20), during the rallies of 1988 a kind of a civil society was nevertheless built in Yerevan. But this was a carnivalesque civil society born in the square (Abrahamian, 2001) that many participants of the rallies mistook for the real one, with whatever meaning they invested into this concept. 'We were others at that time' – this is the standard nostalgic motto of the people recalling their experience of 25 years ago. A subsequent remark often would be that we have already had civil society, which we contrived to miss. Given the characterisation of the rallies as a 'festival', one could conclude that the end of the festival would also mean that civil society in the square had come to its end. This was actually just what happened. Real civil society, or rather its very draft and preliminary version became something to be formed step by step during a long process (see Ishkhanian, 2008), which is still continuing. However, in 2013, a new and supposedly 'already shaped' version of civil society could have been spotted in the same square during the presidential post-electoral rallies. This time this civil society was not a result of the political 'festival' in the square, but the product of the institution of elections, which in its turn was once a product of the 'festival' that happened here in 1988. We will briefly outline the emergence of this festival product and its fate throughout the last 25 years. In an earlier published article, we characterised this process as a 'history of unfairness' (Abrahamian and Shagoyan, 2011–2012, pp.13–31). Here we will follow the general line of this article, but with another perspective we will try to trace the 'Western' and the 'local' in this history of unfairness.

Although the institution of democratic elections in Armenia is usually considered to have begun after the presidential elections of 1991 (Ishkanian, 2008, p.36), that is, beginning from the period of independence, it actually should be dated to October 1988, when two deputies had to be elected to the Armenian Supreme Soviet to replace the ones who had passed away. The electioneering took place in the square, where people learned for the first time about their election rights. This

2 See Marutyan, 2009, pp.276–78, p.281, p.2013. The idea, or rather the term of 'revolution' became especially popular in 2013, being used not only by those politicians and theorists who tried to put this term into a modern political context, but also by 'leftist' oppositionists, their 'rightist' opponents, and journalists in general. We leave the discussion of this aspect of the rallies for another occasion.

knowledge became available from activists who formed so-called constitutional groups. They put out little tables here and there around Theatre Square, where the rallies were taking place, featuring information pamphlets containing excerpts from the Soviet Constitution and other documents concerning the elementary rights of Soviet citizens. Interestingly, these seeds of juridical society were sown in the same 'table' way as the first seeds of private commerce – numerous tables with various types of goods spread piecemeal all over Yerevan and Armenia, in general, in the early 1990s (Abrahamian, 2006, p.242).

The two candidates, Ashot Manucharyan and Khachik Stamboltsyan,[3] were the first deputy candidates proposed from below, and not appointed from above by the authorities according to unwritten law in the Soviet Union, which included Soviet Armenia. They won the electoral competition against communist and Soviet protégés, who lacked the experience of their competitors in gaining the audience's sympathy, according to the new square rhetoric. It should be stressed that the authorities were not yet ready for real electoral fighting and corresponding ballot manipulations, as became a rule during later elections. Speeches of the newly elected deputies were enough to change the general atmosphere in the Supreme Soviet, the Armenian parliament of those times. Interestingly, the Armenian parliament, formed according to Soviet – in theory, democratic – principles, represented all social strata. One could find there not only communist functionaries, but also prominent figures in culture and science, and ordinary labourers and employees as well.[4] The speaker of parliament, for example, was an industrial worker who, together with other deputies, finally adopted a set of revolutionary resolutions on 24 November 1988. Thus, as the people in the square started to learn about their electoral rights, deputies began to realise their rights and liabilities according to the constitution. Of course, not all deputies were ready for such revolutionary changes. During those first manifestations of civil rights, deputies did not necessarily feel their obligations as strongly as their rights. Thus, to summon the Supreme Soviet session, an action took place which actors themselves playfully labelled as *deputatavors* (literally 'hunt for deputies'): voters found out the names and addresses of their deputies, passed them their mandates, and forced them to go to the session, in some cases against their will. This occurred especially when summoning the session on 24 November, which

3 In November 1988, Rafael Kazarian joined this list, and in 1989 more activists of the movement, including the future first president of Armenia, Levon Ter-Petrosyan, were elected as deputies following the same model.

4 The parliament in question had the following composition (according to 1985 data; it was elected by 99.99 percent of voters, who formed 99.99 percent of registered voters): 42.6 percent were labourers, 8.6 percent collective farmers, together comprising 51.2 percent; 63.9 percent of deputies were Communist Party members and candidates; 36.1 percent – unaffiliated; women – 35.8 percent; people under age of thirty – 18.9 percent (Sovetakan Hayastan, 28 February 1985). Interestingly, this list does not mention the intelligentsia, who seemed to be hidden among the 48.8 percent of non-specified deputies.

was not approved by the communist authorities. In one case a deputy, a collective farmer by occupation – declared that she was appointed to the position of deputy and could not understand what the voters who were 'hunting' wanted from her. In another case, a deputy, a high-ranking Soviet authority, was said to be invited forcibly to enter into his state-provided car. Then, some activists moved it by pushing it to the square where the rallies were taking place, and one of the authors (L.A.) witnessed how they helped the deputy to move to the Opera House which was located at the same square where the parliamentary session had to take place, which he was reluctant to participate in. His actual or potential voters held him under the armpits and his feet hardly touched the ground. This carnivalesque 'hunt for deputies' was nevertheless followed by a parliamentary session which adopted a number of historical decisions.

The parliamentary debate method proved to be so effective that an activist of the Karabakh Movement assured Levon Abrahamian that this first Armenian experience inspired the Polish trade union 'Solidarność' leaders to turn from the strategy of struggle using strikes, to the parliamentary approach (Abrahamian, 2001, p.128, Marutyan, 2013, p.14). As for Armenia, this first parliamentary 'revolution' was so out of the ordinary and dangerous (for Soviet rules in general), that by the end of its work a state of emergency was declared in Yerevan.[5] All the adopted decisions were annulled by communist authorities, to be readopted at one of the first sessions of the newly elected parliament (Abrahamian, 2001, p.131). Although these first elections and subsequent parliamentary sessions could hardly be labelled as democratic in the strict sense, they nevertheless extended the kind of carnival-like civil society that was built in the square.[6]

Relevant is the development of electoral education: during the 1988 electoral campaign, voters learned about their civil rights from the 'constitutional tables' in the square, while in preparation for the 1990 election, voters could get their political education from newspapers, which published considerable information on how to vote. Though the parliamentary elections of 1990 took place in Soviet Armenia, they already reflected the post-Soviet situation. Indeed, the elected parliament had to function during the first four years of independence. While the former two by-elections involved a few candidates for a number of parliament

5 The state of emergency was said to have been imposed because of turmoil in some regions, where violence against local Azerbaijanis occurred in late November as a reply to the anti-Armenian actions in Azerbaijan, specifically in Kirovabad (now Ganja). However, while it was natural that a state of emergency was imposed in turbulent areas, it was not clear why it was necessary to impose it in Yerevan, especially during the parliamentary session, which continued past midnight.

6 On another election, the May 1989 by-election of three additional deputies from Armenia into the Supreme Soviet of the USSR, which usually is not taken into account when evaluating the history of democracy in Armenia but which also can be considered a key point in developing the institution of elections see Abrahamian and Shagoyan (2011–2012, pp.15–16).

seats, the 1990 election involved over 1500 candidates for 260 parliamentary seats (newspaper, *Kommunist*, 1 May 1990). In this sense, it entailed quite a new phase in democracy in Armenia, demonstrating peoples' high politicisation and freedom of participation in electoral procedures.

Although the 1990 elections had a touch of revolutionary and populist anti-communist enthusiasm, members and candidate members of the Communist Party constituted 73.3 percent of the deputy candidates (*Kommunist*, 1 May 1990) and more than half of parliamentary seats. This might indicate that elections were in fact free and fair, especially as it was politically correct to vote for the All-Armenian Movement (AAM), the most popular and, for the next several years, the ruling political movement.[7] Though in Yerevan people, as a rule, were just voting against communists, in villages and smaller cities and towns, communist candidates turned out to be much more popular and some were able to win against the charismatic leaders of the AAM.[8] Nonetheless, the high figures of communist preferences are misleading, since some of these communists were also Movement activists. For example, the future second and third presidents of Armenia, Robert Kocharyan and Serzh Sargsyan, were party functionaries in Nagorno-Karabakh and others at least sympathised with the Karabakh Movement. Let us remember that Armenia was still a part of the communist system, and many participants of the rallies were far from being anti-communist dissidents.

Many communist deputies elected in the provinces were local authorities,[9] 'big men' of local Soviet structures, not ideological followers of communist ideas. Actually, they could not have become 'big men' without undergoing a communist 'initiation'.[10] In the same manner, many unaffiliated people such as schoolteachers and white collar office or cultural workers were potential communists.[11] The quota

7 For example, in *Kommunist* (18 May 1990). Beginning with the 2008 presidential election, an animated broadcast on television visually taught voting procedure. People watching this animation before the 2009 mayoral election joked that in the second part of this clip it would be good to show how the ballots would later be manipulated by falsifiers.

8 During the first congress of the AAM in 1989, its founders classified themselves as a movement, not a political party. Its program was adopted in August 1988, during the peak of the rallies, when most Armenians in Armenia considered that they belonged to or somehow represented this movement. Beginning in the mid-1990s, people differentiated between the nostalgic AAM of 1988 and the devalued AAM political party. In 2013, the latter's juridical successor claimed to be the 'Armenian National Congress' (ANC) party.

9 We use this word as it was understood in 1990, in the sense of a respectable and competent person. During the elections that occurred in the last few years, this word came to be understood as 'criminal authority' in regard to deputies or their supporters.

10 Communist Party membership in Soviet Armenia as a kind of a rite of passage, see Abrahamian, 1993–1994, pp.15–16.

11 In comparison, the 1985 parliament had considerable numbers of labourers, while during the 1990 election only 3.8 percent of the registered candidates were labourers, and 93.8 percent constituted office workers, who had not been taken into consideration in the 1985 parliament structure.

of new party members was not high in such professions, and they were awaiting their turn to undergo 'initiation' for a better life. At the end of the communist era, many formal communists readily entered other parties (Abrahamian, 1993–1994, p.27, FN 5). Some AAM candidates won the campaign through their constituencies being located in their place of residence or their natal village. These became not really a competition of political platforms but a matter of 'blood' affiliation. In rare cases in Yerevan, winners were not AAM protégés and were even opposed to AAM. However, their success was not principally due to their opposition to the AAM platform: they used the same Karabakh and other nationalist rhetoric but seemed to do this better than their opponents.

In sum, the definition 'democratic' could be ambiguous in these early elections. They nevertheless could be classified as 'free and fair' in a stricter sense than that used by foreign monitors regarding later elections. We have given more attention to these early elections because the situation at 'the beginning' can often explain a lot about future developments.[12] The 1990 election revealed an essential difference in democratic processes in cities and villages which is still a major problem in the development of the institution of elections, and hence democracy and civil society. In Armenia, in the provinces, people vote as their village mayor or respected elder or relative advises. (We will see this in more detail in a further section.) The 1990 election also presaged the 'protest vote', since these early elections became the general model for later elections – in 1996 (against Levon Ter-Petrosyan) and in 2008 and partly in 2013 (against Serzh Sargsyan).

Elections in Post-Soviet Armenia: 'Free but not Fair'

Although the 1991 presidential election was, and still is, rightly characterised as free and fair (Ishkanian, 2008, p.36), it nevertheless did not display the pronounced emulative spirit of the first elections. Levon Ter-Petrosyan, the future first president of Armenia, was too popular for protest at that time, so that the democratic nature of the elections had very little chance of being challenged.

Quoting Armine Ishkhanian (2008, p.36), 'in every election thereafter, beginning with the 1995 parliamentary elections up to the most recent May 2007 parliamentary vote [we update this to the February 2008 and 2013 presidential votes: L.A. and G.S.], elections have become, or are perceived as having become, steadily more corrupt and less "free and fair".' It is not our aim here to present an exhaustive analysis of the elections or discuss in detail each election, their correlation with observers' estimations, the authorities' or 'the opposition's arguments against or in support of them. What we try to present below is rather an anthropological perspective of the history of elections in Armenia. This history is, as a matter of fact, at the same time, the history of the unfairness of elections (see

12 Concerning the same principle regarding violence, see Abrahamian, 1999, pp.59–75.

Abrahamian and Shagoyan, 2011–2012, pp.13–31),[13] which, however, seemed not to be 'seen' by foreign observers.

The 1995 parliamentary election, we think, was a turning point in this history. It was declared free but not fair by the Organisation for Security and Cooperation of Europe (OSCE) monitors' newspaper (*Azg*, 7 July 1995), however, it could be classified as both not free and not fair. This election seemed to pave the way for the rich and sophisticated machinery of falsifications used during the next elections. By 'not free' we do not refer to voting in villages, which, as we will see in the next section, continues to be far from free. The 1995 election could be classified as not free because candidates were not registered as freely as during the 1990 election. At first glance, this could be considered as a step in harnessing the uncontrollable mass desire to run for deputy, but actually the 'strict checking' of the proposed candidates' documents by voting district commissions, which were responsible for the preliminary registration, gave an unsupervised and effective means of eliminating serious competitors of the 'true' candidates. According to Gurgen Boyajyan, a member of the Central Electoral Commission, who, together with five other members of the commission, did not sign the final resolution on the election results, about 1,000 candidates were not registered without serious grounds.[14] However, more than 1,900 candidates were nevertheless registered – for the 190 parliament seats, still a rather high figure, compared with 1,500 candidates registered for the 260 places during the 1990 election.

Beginning with the 1995 election, falsifications became institutionalised. This election seemed to be the first to use appreciable ballot stuffing. While in the 1990 election, isolated cases of stuffing were aimed not towards changing the results of voting but towards ensuring the voting itself (in a sense they were 'following' the future improved law of voting), the 1995 ballot stuffing was deliberately aimed at falsifying the results. The 1995 parliamentary election ran parallel to the referendum on the new constitution, but the electoral quorum for the referendum was higher than that for the parliamentary election. The initial participation requirement was of no less than one third of the number of registered voters,[15] while the second had no special numerical regulation. The new constitution was to become the first constitution of independent Armenia and was of particular importance for the president, while the opposition considered this draft ('Levon's Constitution') imperfect and authoritarian and was campaigning against it.

13 A further more detailed archival and/or investigatory report, is hoped, will become part of the history of democracy in Armenia, see a detailed analysis of the Russian experience in post-Soviet elections in Smirnov 2008. The only publication we know of that deals with similar problems in the Armenian electoral sphere is a booklet on the 2007 parliamentary election (Zhamakochyan and Gyulkhandanyan, 2009).

14 Personal communication. See also Petrosyan 1999, the author estimates over 700 candidates were not registered.

15 According to Article 113 of the 1995 constitution, this number was no less than one-third of registered voters; in the 2005 constitution it was reduced to one-fourth.

By that time, Levon Ter-Petrosyan had the opposition of recent comrades-in-arms. Electoral commissions of different levels were therefore eager to ensure a voters' quorum, at least. It could be obtained by additional ballots – following the experience of the 1990 election. We do not know whether these ballots were falsified in favour of the constitution or were stuffed unsigned, in 'naive' zeal to make the elections effective. In any case, even if the referendum was 'fair', it had an unexpected by-product: for the parliamentary election, the extra ballots representing voters who 'participated' in the referendum meant 'participating' also in the other election. These were the ballots, as some of our informants think, that were falsified in favour of the ruling AAM candidates. Some more sophisticated but less large-scale falsifications were said to be successfully tested during these elections, but we need not go into the details here.

From this moment on, those who were at the administrative helm at the time were 'doomed' to win the next elections. This became a general rule irrespective of their political orientation. Also from this point on, civil society in Armenia was tasked with a new aim – the institution of free and fair elections. For veterans of the AAM, this goal had already been attained by the 'revolution' of the late 1980s but had been lost after the 1995 parliamentary election and especially after the 1996 presidential election.

Armenians have a general opinion that the 1996 presidential election was falsified in a rather crude manner. Primarily, falsification was considered to have been achieved by stuffing ballots in favour of Levon Ter-Petrosyan. But other, no less crude methods, for example army detachments voting many times in different polling stations, were also thought to have been realised. Further, this election was a typical election 'against' – this time against the first president. His opponent Vazgen Manukyan, who claimed to be (and actually was) the winner, never again got such a high percentage of votes during future elections, whether parliamentary or presidential. When Levon Ter-Petrosyan again entered big politics in 2007, for many people, including our interlocutors, it was difficult to forget these falsifications and believe that he would really introduce the institution of free and fair elections, as he claimed during his electoral campaign. It is also significant that he never apologised for the 1996 falsifications during the campaign, although many people waited for an apology. He did publicly apologise for other misdeeds, especially for his personnel policy, that is, his introducing the future second and third presidents into the power-holding structures of Armenia.

During the presidential election of 1998, the main competition was between Robert Kocharyan, the former president of the unrecognised Nagorno-Karabakh Republic, the incumbent prime minister of the Republic of Armenia, and Karen Demirchyan, the former communist leader of Soviet Armenia. Results were contested and ambiguous. Those who voted for Demirchyan were positive that their candidate had lost the voting as a result of his opponent's falsifications, while those who voted for Kocharyan and were later disappointed in their choice usually blamed themselves and not the falsifiers. But even among the pro-Kocharyan voters one could easily spot those who were positive that falsifications had not taken place. Thus an opponent of Karen Demirchyan, who was anxious about the latter's obvious popularity during the election, tellingly paraphrased the well-known words of the poet Yeghishe Charents (1897–1937) on the salvation of Armenian people into the following phrase: 'Armenian people, how great it is that your choice is not in your hands'. Indirect evidence of Demirchyan's advantage over his opponent is that during the electoral campaign, especially in rural regions, royal features were routinely attributed to him, while Robert Kocharyan was perceived only as a high-ranking official (Abrahamian, 2006, p.212). Although the 'king' did not regain his 'throne' officially in the presidential election, he nevertheless returned to power the next year: Demirchyan was elected speaker of the new parliament in 1999.

The 1999 parliamentary election may have been unique, in contrast to the list of elections that were increasingly unfair. That election seemed to be free and fair, and in any case was not cloaked in rumours, 'evidence', and suppositions. We did not note any tales about the inclusion of names of the deceased in voter lists – a common violation attributed to the election organisers, that is, to the authorities, during other elections.[16] The only explanation we noted for this strange reappearance of a free and fair election was an assumption that the authorities decided to avoid falsifications to legitimise the power of Vazgen Sargsyan, the authoritative prime minister and former defence minister, who successfully formed an alliance with Karen Demirchyan. The point that Demirchyan's presence in this alliance (named 'Unity') was sufficient for victory was viewed by my interlocutors as more indirect evidence of his victory during the recent presidential election. However, this much-anticipated return of the 'king' lasted only a short time – Demirchyan was assassinated together with Sargsyan and six other deputies during the terrorist attack on the Armenian parliament on 27 November 1999.

The ghost of the assassinated king returned during the 2003 presidential electoral campaign. Karen Demirchyan returned in the form and image of his son Stepan Demirchyan. Like his father, the son became a presidential candidate opposing Robert Kocharyan, now the incumbent president. The tight election required a second round, and took on legendary significance. The son not only fitted the mythological archetype of a prince coming to avenge his father, but also resembled the adored king in his appearance, manner, and voice. Although he headed the opposition at that time, one suspects that his great popularity and alleged victory[17] was as much a result of this resemblance and mythological schema as derived from his political rhetoric. Though Western observers came to their usual

16 A popular joke on this theme noted that a person was very offended by his deceased father, who came to their own polling station to vote but did not visit his son's house.

17 Although he officially lost this second round, many people still think he won it; some informants even present numerical 'evidence': the number of ballots that brought this opponent to victory were thought to be correlated with the number of potential voters (300,000–500,000) that were absent at that moment. These figures correlate with the emigration situation in post-Soviet Armenia; see Kharatyan, 2003.

conclusion as to how the elections were conducted, which could be formulated as 'not very fair, but not unfair enough to influence the elections', there were also some foreign observers who noted violations during the election. Interestingly, the present day president Serzh Sargsyan, who was Defence Minister of Armenia at that time, answering to this Western criticism on TV, made a statement that 'we have different mentalities'. This statement was much discussed – for example, at the meeting of the opposition on 11 March. A Western observer made a remark in his interview on Radio Azatutyun (Liberty) on 14 March concerning this statement that one could hardly find a people with a mentality that would enjoin election falsifications. The future president referred, obviously, to unintentional ('rural') violations to be discussed in the next section, rather than to the intentional falsifications organised by the authorities. This seems to be the first articulation (even if implicit) of the contrast between Western election standards and 'local traditions'. In any case, one may think, the level of falsification was so obvious that the Constitutional Court, which rejected Stepan Demirchyan's claim of infringement, was 'forced' to recommend a referendum on President Kocharyan's confidence vote to be held the next year (Concort 2003). The demonstration of protesters demanding this recommended referendum was broken up severely on 12 April 2004.

The 2003 and 2007 parliamentary elections were marked by the process of the parliament's criminalisation. People gossiped about the nicknames of deputies, and opposition newspapers were eager to list them. Any person with a specific nickname was suspected of having a dark past. That was why Khachatur Sukyasyan, an oligarch and deputy, forestalled journalists by releasing a TV documentary where he discussed his nickname 'Grzo', tracing its previously unknown past to his peasant ancestors, thus moving it into a non-criminal context.

These elections were thought to be the start of mass bribery as the main machinery of elections. The 2007 election especially, was considered to be the champion on the scale of *entrakasharq*, a neologism designating 'voting bribe'. Each new electoral process made people state that precisely this recent experience should be classified as the most falsified election.

A referendum in November 2005 on constitutional reforms was remarkable for several reasons. President Robert Kocharyan was eager to pass these reforms, since they were demanded by the Council of Europe as important improvements to the 1995 Constitution, which the council considered as inadequately aligned with European standards. This referendum was the second attempt, after the first one failed on 25 May 2003. The council attributed the failure to the fact that the authorities, who were focused on the parliamentary election (on the same day as the referendum), did not pay enough attention to advocating the constitutional reforms (Council of Europe 2005). Let us recall the 1995 constitution ('Levon's Constitution') referendum, when the first president was so eager to have constitutional support for his authoritarianism (Abrahamian, 2001, p.119) that it triggered, we hope inadvertently, the first mass falsifications. This was particularly significant as it involved voting for the first post-Soviet parliament. In contrast,

Robert Kocharyan did not pay as much attention to passing 'his' constitution in 2003, being too busy to form 'his' parliament.

After some serious criticism from the 'European Commission for Democracy through Law' (The Venice Commission) that resulted in commensurate improvements, a draft of the reforms was finally approved by the Venice Commission. However, the parliamentary opposition (Ardarutyun (Justice) Alliance) was against the reforms, since it wanted to present its own amendments to the constitution, competing with the ones proposed by the parliamentary coalition which was holding power. The opposition project was not realised. Further, demonstrating once again a vote of no confidence in President Kocharyan[18] by denying 'his' constitution, the opposition called for a boycott of the referendum. The referendum, which needed more than fifty percent of votes for constitutional reforms from one third of the registered voters, was held on 27 November 2005. Contrasting figures were reported: the official number of participating voters comprised 1,503,568 (65.3 percent), 1,403,430 of whom (93.3 percent) supported the reforms, while opposition activists, who counted people as they entered polling stations, claimed that their number was much lower (Abrahamian and Shagoyan, 2011–2012, p.45, FN 47), which was not enough to provide the required one third. The official figures, which recalled Soviet era elections, were so improbably large that people were discussing not the possibility of falsification, but the meaning of the message the president intended to send by publishing such figures. Everyone that we have interviewed was sure that the results were falsified. A supporter of the opposition interpreted it this way: European experts would have been satisfied by more probable, lower figures, so this message was not addressed to them but to the opposition, with the meaning 'you may protest as much as you like; I can give any figures, even improbable ones'.[19] This supporter referred to the criminal world, where a similar language of subordination and domination is widespread. Actually, the criminal element plays a specific role in the modern worldview of Armenians. It also embraces the institution of elections; it could even be said that there are three distinctly co-existing layers in the functioning of this institution – democratic/civic ('Western'), 'traditional' (mainly rural – to be discussed in the next section) and 'prisonous' (based on criminal ethical order) (Poghpatyan 2013).

In the 2008 presidential election, the first president of Armenia, Levon Ter-Petrosyan, re-entered politics after ten years of silence. It seems that in Armenia, ten years is necessary before a political leader can return in another guise, and for people to forget undesirable events from the past and remember (or imagine) happier

18 As we have already noted, the peaceful demonstration, demanding fulfilment of the referendum envisaged by the Constitutional Court after the debated presidential elections of 2003, was violently broken up on 12 April 2004.

19 Following this 'numerical tradition', the present day president, Serzh Sargsyan, said during the 2013 presidential campaign that 'we will "strike" any figure we need' meaning the number of pro-voices. The word *khpel* (lit. 'to strike'), which he used, was immediately used as a deterrent in numerous oppositional sites and Facebook pages.

ones. Thus Karen Demirchyan recalled the 'happy' Soviet times and Levon Ter-Petrosyan remembered the unforgettable political 'festival' of 1988. Meanwhile, people had to forget the former's lack of popularity in 1988 and the latter's demise in 1996, as well as the 'dark and cold years' of 1992–1994. While Demirchyan did not need to manipulate people's memory – it happened by itself – Ter-Petrosyan had to manage this during his electoral campaign. He used his rhetorical skills and, more importantly within the context of this chapter, appealed to the need to uproot the existing unfair electoral machine in order to establish democratic elections. That was why those who voted for him included not only his fans from the rallies of the late 1980s and AAM veterans, but also people who were ready to forget 1996 in exchange for free and fair elections that would allow them to elect a better president, if needed. However, his supporters considered the election unfair, utilising the arsenal of previous electoral falsifications and introducing new ones.[20]

The evolution of the machinery of falsification is a sign that some opposing forces existed that needed to be overcome by such elaborate methods. Attempting to force Armenia to be a little more European, local civil society (different NGOs, opposition parties, journalists), and some foreign organisations tried to improve the institution of the elections and get rid of falsification. However, every achievement in providing free and fair elections is followed by a new and more sophisticated trick that tries to get around it. It is not only civil society that needs to be evaded, but also the voters who are eager to take 'electoral bribes' and then vote for someone else. That model of 'freedom from bribed voting' was endorsed by Robert Kocharyan during his 2003 presidential campaign. He said that if somebody offered you a bribe to vote for him, take it and vote for whomever you like. Thus, he admitted the reality of bribing and even suggested a tricky way of counteracting this negative phenomenon.

Despite the 'official' declaration of freedom to bribe and cheat (repeated by other candidates during other campaigns, including Serzh Sargsyan in 2008), it was not welcomed by deputies and their electoral teams. Thus the introduction of the so-called 'carousel' was aimed not only at falsifying elections, but also at controlling a bribed falsifier: a voter received a bribe only after bringing back a blank ballot instead of the signed one, which he/she had to drop into the box. But this method requires a manipulation with blank ballots and is risky. So they began to use cell phones with cameras: voters had to photograph the ballot with the 'right' mark; after the image was checked, they got the bribe – about 5,000 drams ($17–18). Thus cell phones superseded the 'carousel method' of cheating which had involved the more seemingly criminal stealing of blank ballots. However, here too some counter-cheating was said to have taken place: people used a short piece of black thread to imitate the tick marking the required candidate, took a photograph and then put a real ink tick beside the name of their own candidate. This means we must expect more sophisticated methods of overcoming this

20 For the new machinery of falsifications during this and 2009 Yerevan City Council elections see Abrahamian and Shagoyan, 2011–2012, pp.25–31.

counter-cheating (which actually took place) and expect new counter-counter-cheating. These interrelated processes seemed to be so troublesome that during the 2009 campaign, control over bribed voters seemed to be not as well organised as in previous years; bribes were said to be given out without a guarantee, hoping for a sense of 'fairness' from the bribed voters.

The 2008 presidential elections were also considered unfair by many in Armenia, this opinion being supported later by new evidence from the West (see newspaper, *Armenia Today*, 2 September 2011). The protest rallies that followed the election had a dramatic ending – ten people including two policemen were killed during the alleged clashes with police with this unsolved case continuing to be the focus of local and international attention. The latest presidential elections in 2013 were no exception to the 'rule' – we will return to this event in the last part of the chapter.

In 2009, and later in 2013, the institute of elections also embraced the Yerevan City Council *avagani* (elders' council); its elected members had to elect the mayor later. This was the first direct election at this level. It was considered a new step towards democratic society by the Council of Europe and included in the constitutional reforms of 2005; previously each city district had elected its local *avagani*. All Yerevan citizens were involved in this new event concerning the capital city. Slogans calling on residents 'to begin with the city', both during the 2009 and 2013 electoral campaigns had a special meaning that could be traced to the requisite opposition between city (city residents, citizen) and village (countrymen). During the 1988 rallies, this contradiction almost disappeared, as a result of the solidarity of the 'festival' and unity manifested by the 'carnival-like civil society' created in the square. But the gap returned when the 'political festival' was over (Abrahamian, 1990a, pp.82–3). In post-Soviet Armenia, this contradiction became especially evident because of the contrast in voting, and in the institution of elections in general, in the city (Yerevan) and provinces (especially in rural regions).

Elections in the Village and the Intensification of Kindred Relationships[21]

In general, elections in the village are clearly differentiated on the basis of opposition between the local and the national, all-republican ones. Local elections are aimed at forming local power-holding structures – election of the *gyughapet* (the village mayor), *avagani* (members of the elders' council), while the all-republican ones form the structure of the National Assembly (the parliament), elect the president

21 This section utilised the framework of the project 'Globalization Processes in the Contemporary Armenian Village' which was sponsored by the John D. and Katherine T. MacArthur Foundation (Grant no. 06 86346 000 GSS). See, for more details, Abrahamian 2008. Cases in this section are mainly from two villages Gosh and Tatev, though evidence from other villages is also used.

and also realise passages of important all-national authorisations (referendums, constitution). For villagers, it was the local elections that were the main ones, since the presidential elections, for example, as one informant noticed, 'have little meaning for us regardless of the result'. While elections of the *gyughapet* are such a topical problem that, as a rule, they run openly: the person to be elected should see with his[22] own eyes who voted for him, and how. We recorded a case, where a woman mechanically folded the ballot paper into halves before dropping it into the box and, by doing so, worsened forever her relationship with the newly elected *gyughapet* who could hardly believe that she had voted in his favour. It should be noted that all the people who told us about the open elections were aware of their illegality, but could not do anything about it, since the person to be elected and the voters, as a rule, were kindred, to one extent or another. The democratic institution of the *gyughapet* and *avagani* election, which came to replace the institution of assignment from above during Soviet times, brought a sudden intensification of the structure of blood relationships (see Sahakyan, 2002, pp.130–33): one had more chances to become a head of a village if one had a large number of blood relatives and relatives by marriage – in one case a candidate won due to numerous relatives on his wife's side. As one informant noted, if you have lots of kinsfolk, you are a *gyughapet*, if you have not, you have no chances of becoming a *gyughapet*. Another informant told of a case when both candidates happened to be relatives: 'This led to quarrels and misunderstandings within one group of kinsfolk, which divided into two camps. And the village too divided into two camps'. In some cases, the principle of voting for kindred carries over to the ideal of the institution of the election as being strictly independent and anonymous, to its logically anticipated antithesis – becoming totally dependent and non-secret. For example, we recorded a case during some elections where there were four persons in the list of candidates for the *avagani* who happened to be relatives of the informant, who had 'only two votes in her home'. In order not to offend the candidates, the extended family of the informant distributed the votes of the relatives (far and close ones, including the grandmother and a relative from another polling station) in such a way that each candidate was supported by one vote. 'You see, as all such people proposed themselves as candidates; we couldn't refuse anybody', the informant commented as she explained the motivation behind her actions. As for the parliamentary and presidential elections, this way 'elected' *gyughapet* can demand the villagers vote openly for the candidate who is imposed upon them from above, from the regional authorities; and who is imposed upon the region from the capital. However, elections at the village mayor's command are directly dependent on his authority. In one case with a rather weak *gyughapet*, the country-wide elections could be estimated as maximally democratic. In another case, where the mayor was not tough enough, the village which was known for its rebelliousness exhibited oppositional behaviour in the best of revolutionary

22 The *gyughapet* is predominantly a position for a man so we will abstain from gender neutral language in this case.

traditions. One more case showed that practically all the village, including the *gyughapet*, could stand against the dictatorial regional and central authorities, not because of its revolutionary opposition nature, however, but as a sign of support for their respectable co-villager who had fallen into disgrace with the Yerevan authorities. This was the case with the village of Dzorakap (Shirak Province), where the 700 voters, including the electoral commission members, boycotted the 2003 parliamentary election protesting the illegal imprisonment of their fellow villager, the former detention facilities chief (Dzorakape boycotum e, 2003). This episode could also be classified as village ('blood') solidarity with an oppositional-type touch.[23] Where they failed to conduct open elections (this usually happens in big villages and regional centres), various means of controlling the results of elections were used – from direct falsifications and psychological pressure (in one case this was realised by someone from a local authority who was gazing heavily at the voters entering the polling place) to sophisticated tricks, which the naïve foreign observers could hardly even imagine. However, artful falsification, as we already know, is used mainly in the city, where it came to replace the democratic experience of the first elections of the late 1980s and early 1990s.

It should be noted that the methods of falsifying the elections that had found acceptance in the village are an innovation: before the conventional theatricalised 'elections' assigned from above by deputies of Soviet time, the Armenian villages knew very democratic elections, which some of our informants of the older generation were aware of. Thus, an old woman compared present-day elections with the pre-Soviet ones: 'What takes place today has nothing to do with elections. Those are some games. How did they elect in olden times? Suppose that they had to elect one of the two candidates. They put on their tall *astrakhan* hats, and people approached with kidney beans. They couldn't write, so if they wanted to vote in your favour, they dropped their beans into your hat; if in the other person's favour they dropped beans into his hat. The winner was the person who had more beans in his hat. This was the way of electing, for example, the *kyokhva*, the village headman. While in present-day elections they come to an agreement beforehand and divide people into groups.'

It is interesting that during elections in the village people often do not even realise that they are committing an infringement. One informant expressed his indignation at our conceding that they might be manipulating elections, while it was he who had told us about some of these manipulations though he never admitted that they were actions of this kind. It is also characteristic that the villagers enter into 'fair' negotiations with the candidate to be elected into the parliament, these negotiations resembling haggling, on what concretely he/she should do for the village in exchange for the villagers' votes: build a road, repair a bridge, or set up

23 It is remarkable that in 2008 these village protesters were involved in already apparent civil society-related activities: they supported the independent 'GALA' TV channel in Gyumri, and during the 2013 presidential elections they gave their votes to an independent candidate.

a big parabolic dish antenna, and so on, as was the case with the village of Gosh. And the decision was accepted at a general meeting, observing all the rules of communal democracy.

All this demonstrates that elections in the village, which were actually an export from the city, where they were, as we have already mentioned, the main attainment of the democratic movement of the late 1980s, in the end became one of the effective instruments for manipulating the results of elections country-wide, when it was needed to influence the undesirable voting in those polling places (mainly in the centre of the city), where it was difficult to realise falsifications. On the other hand, this democratic institution imposed from above led to the intensification of blood relations and 'kindred inequality'. As an informant has noted regarding the institution of elections in the village, 'there is nothing positive in these elections, they are not for us'.

As noted, in the provinces, people vote the way their local authorities and/or respected relatives advise them to. Since these two categories usually coincide (a person with more relatives has more chance to become village mayor), it could be said that the institution of elections, an accomplishment of the 'Armenian revolution', strengthened blood relations in the village and the decline of democracy. In this context, the election of city mayor gained another significant aspect: it could be a unique chance to vote without the 'non-democratic' impact of the vote in the provinces. Authorities usually won the decisive 'casting vote' in favour of their candidates in the provinces. A hierarchy pyramid worked quite well here: from an authority in Yerevan – to the province governor (*marzpet*) – to the village mayor – to the voter. In this sense one can understand the authorities' 'democratic' decision to focus, for the Yerevan mayoral election (of 2009), on voters who had resided in Yerevan for at least one year. A 'non-democratic' discussion had questioned whether a villager who had lived in the city only for one year could know the needs of the city and, consequently, decide what kind of a mayor Yerevan would need. Another manifestation of the 'capital (city) – provinces (village)' opposition during the election was an interesting event reported by Radio Liberty correspondents on the morning of polling day. Suspicious looking cars and vans with festively attired people, allegedly on their way to a picnic or elsewhere, were spotted in Gyumri and Vanadzor, heading towards Yerevan. This added grounds to rumours that the current election was to be falsified with additional fake voters. There were a number of versions of how this fraud might be achieved. People from the provinces (or some of them), were thought to be those fake voters, although reporters did not trace their itineraries in Yerevan. Whatever the scenario and underlying cause,[24] it is significant that the provinces were to be used for falsifications in the capital. The same model was said to be used during the last 2013 Yerevan mayoral elections. In a sense, the failure of the opposition candidates both in 2009 and 2013 elections showed that Yerevan was still 'not

24 The most popular version was that this was a gesture of gratitude by provincial authorities for some previous comparable service from the capital authorities.

enough' of a real city to realise the closeness of the concepts *polis* and politics, city and citizens, in the way that these conceptual relations were articulated during the electoral campaign.

Waiting for Help from the West

There is an old Armenian idea of looking to the West for help in critical situations. Actually this is rather a strategy for survival. In the fifth century, during the anti-Persian rebellion, this was the expected help from Byzantium. Since the late eleventh century, the time of the Seljuk invasion and the Crusades, expectations of rescue from the West were based on a series of visions and prophesy which were traced back to the famous vision of Nerses the Great, the Catholicos of Armenia in the fourth century (see Hovhannisyan, 1957, pp.16–17). In the eighteenth century, Armenians of endangered Nagorno-Karabakh looked to Russia for help (the West being substituted for the North); in the beginning of the twentieth century, during World War I, Western Armenians were expecting rescue from European countries, and at the end of the century, during the Karabakh Movement, again from Russia. The diaspora, being located mainly in the West and embodying Western values, now becomes the most recent expression of this universal strategy of survival (Abrahamian, 2006, pp.338–39). And, although this strategy never seemed to help Armenians survive in the past, it continues to feed Armenian dreams of survival now, by inviting 'wise' ministers from the diaspora, observers from the West and, quite recently, a presidential candidate with a Western (American) background.

Interestingly, there seems to be an inner division into East and West within Armenian society, which is not connected with the geographical structure of Armenia, but may sometimes coincide with it. Following N. Adonts (1948), we can characterise this dichotomy according to two tendencies, which seem to have been distinguishable at least since the fifth century. These two opposed trends represent, respectively, the trend towards rebelliousness and towards prudence, the first trend more associated with the Mamikonian family, and the second more accentuated in Bagratuni generations. These two trends may correlate with the East–West differentiation of Armenia, although they may change places, as well as switch between these two high-ranking families. One may speculate on the necessity of such an intrinsic dichotomy for a nation; when conditions are continually changing, having the flexibility of both orientations simultaneously allows for the possibility to choose the best approach depending on the situation. Though such an ambivalent mechanism of national survival might sometimes be dramatic for the nation itself, as was the baneful animosity between the Mamikonian and Bagratuni lines, Adonts connects the prudent trend of the Bagratunis with the rise of the lower middle classes and the growth of towns, which need stability as a principal component for their survival, and the Mamikonian's rebellious spirit with the traditionalism of the feudal lords. In short, the prudent trend was opposed to the rebellious trend as the centralised power was opposed to the parcelled feudal structure (Adonts, 1948, pp.46–7).

Be that as it may, the two trends also continue to exist in modern times, when there is no opposition between feudal and centralised social structures, though there are some typologically correlating divisions, including the Armenian homeland and diaspora dichotomy (Abrahamian, 2006, pp.331–35), which continue to feed this model. In a rough approximation, this conventional inner division creates an impression of a more advanced 'civilised West' within Armenian society, which tries to follow the civilised West.

Concerning elections, the Western trend in Armenia actually represents 'prudent' Western style democratic traditions, though the institution of elections was, as a matter of fact, introduced as a result of the 'rebellious' movement of the late 1980s. The actual West, mainly various European state and non-governmental organisations, were naturally eager to support, sometimes with a mentoring touch, this 'Western' trend in Armenia. At present, the local 'non-Western' ('feudal') trend has to survive the 'Western' institution of elections, however reluctant it is to accept this situation. One may compare the already cited statement of the future president of Armenia about the specific national mentality of Armenians as an argument against the Western criticism of falsifications during the elections in 2003; while also in 2003, the Constitutional Court of the Republic of Armenia passed a decision stating that 'voter lists already signed and filled by voters are considered one of the elements of secrecy of the ballot and are not subject for publication' (Decision 2003, no. 412, 15). This prohibition was intended as a means to protect the rights of those citizens who do not participate in the elections and would like to keep this secret. In Western countries, one can find a wide spectrum of attitudes on this point, however the Constitutional Court followed the position approved in October 2002 by the Venice Commission claiming it the only Western thing Armenia should follow (To Understand the Mechanism 2013). The reason for this 'Western' orientation is that by defending the rights of the voters in such a way, the authorities can use the ballots of the migrants, officially represented in the lists of voters: the number of migrants estimated at being from 300,000 to 500,000 people. This estimated number increased naturally over the following years and migration rates continue to be the focus of discussions and criticism at both official and non-official levels – this theme is obviously one of the most popular in modern political and academic rhetoric. Requests for change in this area are the main demands in almost all the opposition electoral programs including the presidential elections of 2013, since the number of the missing voters, whose rights the authorities are eagerly defending, compose just the amount of falsified ballots necessary to reproduce existing power. The presidential elections of 2013 demonstrated that this mechanism of power reproduction can successfully work despite the obvious prevalence of opposition supporters – the map of pro-authority voters is much more dense in the regions famous for their high numbers of migrants (Suleymanyan, 2013; Lying Numbers, 2013). One could say that the

Western-oriented institution of democratic elections is being hindered by some tricky, but 'Western' ways.

The last Western manifestation related to elections was the 2013 presidential electoral campaign conducted by Raffi Hovhannisyan, the presidential candidate of American descent who used an unusual hand-shaking greeting policy during his campaign.[25] This totalitistic and slightly maniacal hand-shaking was widely discussed and ridiculed but strangely enough it provided an unexpected result: among other reasons (not to be discussed here), this close communication with potential voters gave the candidate an opportunity to become the second candidate with a high amount of ballots or even the most, as his supporters claimed and independent estimations calculated. However, it was considered to be the 'Western way' of campaigning by the Western candidate, giving hope to his electorate of help from the West, thus adding a new case to the long list of the expectations of help from the West. Even the degree of inconsistency in his speeches and deeds was interpreted sometimes as Western: behaviour unfamiliar to Armenians.

Thus, Western trends are being introduced into the 'endemic' institution of elections in Armenia, either together with Western, or Western-oriented leaders, or by manipulation with Western, or what are claimed to be Western, models.

Conclusion

The institution of elections in post-Soviet Armenia was one of the few acquisitions of the mass rallies of the late 1980s. The first democratic elections in the former USSR were actually realised during these rallies, which displayed many of the characteristics of a festival. Being a product of a 'carnival', civil society that was born in the square, it was soon transformed into an instrument of acquiring and reproducing power. We have outlined the history of this festival product throughout the last 25 years, which in a sense could be called a 'history of unfairness': beginning with the 1995 parliamentary elections, each new electoral process was considered by people as the most falsified election to date. As a matter of fact, those who were at the administrative helm at the time were 'doomed' to win the next elections. Thus, civil society in Armenia, which was born in the square together with the institution of elections, had a new and relevant task – that of acquiring the institution of free and fair elections. However, every achievement in providing free and fair elections was followed by a new and more sophisticated trick that tried to get around it. The most sophisticated trick was introduced by the Constitutional Court of Armenia in 2003 as a Western 'civilised instruction' (The Venice Commission's recommendation to keep in secrecy the voter lists already signed and filled by voters), became an effective instrument for falsifying

25 The Armenian word *barev* 'hello', which was the candidate's electoral motto, turned into the *barevolution* ('hello-revolution') slogan during mass protest post-electoral rallies.

elections. This 'Western facade' allowed authorities to 'legally' use some 500,000 ballots of migrants, with this number steadily increasing each year. Although the institution of elections in Armenia was an endemic acquisition, nevertheless, it is considered by Western analysts and politicians as a Western imposition. In any case, this institution had to be formed in a Western style and was monitored by Western observers. We saw how the Western model of elections encountered local models, especially the one of the village, where it was imposed from above (from the city) as a democratic institution, but led to the intensification of blood relations and to the decline of democracy. Despite these deplorable conclusions, new civil trends and activities, which became appreciable in the summer of 2013, when this chapter had already been submitted, give hope that we will see the long expected return to the fair and free nature of the precedent which gave rise to the present day deficient institution of elections.

References

Abrahamian, L., 1990a. Chaos and Cosmos in the Structure of Mass Popular Demonstrations: The Karabakh Movement in the Eyes of an Ethnographer. *Soviet Anthropology and Archeology*, 29(2), pp.70–86.

Abrahamian, L., 1990b. The Karabagh Movement as Viewed by an Anthropologist. *The Armenian Review*, 43(2–3), pp.67–80.

Abrahamian, L., 1993–94. Secret Police as a Secret Society: Faith and Fear in the Former USSR. *Anthropology and Archeology of Eurasia*, 32(3), pp.12–31.

Abrahamian, L., 1999. Typology of Aggressiveness and National Violence in the Former USSR. In: T. Allen and J. Eade, eds, 1999. *Divided Europeans: Understanding Ethnicities in Conflict*. The Hague: Kluwer Law International, pp.59–75.

Abrahamian, L., 2001. Civil Society Born in the Square: The Karabagh Movement in Perspective. In: L. Chorbajian, ed., 2001. *The Making of Nagorno-Karabagh: From Secession to Republic*. Basingstoke: Palgrave, pp.116–34.

Abrahamian, L., 2006. *Armenian Identity in a Changing World.* Costa Mesa: Mazda Publishers.

Abrahamian, L., 2008. Globalizatsiia po-derevenski: Armianskii variant [Globalization in a Village Way: An Armenian Version]. In: A. A. Kasianova, ed., 2008. *Sel'skie metamorfozy [Rural Metamorphoses].* Krasnodar: Dedkoff, pp.41–74.

Abrahamian, L. and Shagoyan, G., 2011–12. From Carnival Civil Society toward a Real Civil Society: Democracy Trends in Post-Soviet Armenia. *Anthropology and Archeology of Eurasia*, 50(3), pp.11–50.

Adonts, N. 1948. *Patmakan usumnasirut'yunner.* Paris: A. Ghukasean hrat.
Concort 2003. Decision of the Constitutional Court of the Republic of Armenia, 2003/412. Available at <http://www.concourt.am/armenian/decisions/common/2003/sdv-412.htm> [Accessed on 21 June 2013]

Council of Europe, 2005. The Process of Constitutional Reforms in Armenia. Resolution 1458/4.

Dzorakape boykotum e [Dzorakap Is Boycotting], 2003. Available at <http://www.a1plus.am/am/politics/2003/05/25/3433> [Accessed on 24 May 2013].

Hakobyan, T., 2013. *Worn out Armenia.* Available at <http://civilnet.am> [Accessed on 3 August 2013].

Hovhannisyan, A., 1957. *Drvagner hay azatagrakan mtk'i patmut'yan [Essays on the History of Armenian Liberation Thought].* Yerevan: HSSH GA hrat.

Ishkanian, A., 2008. *Democracy Building and Civil Society in Post-Soviet Armenia.* London and New York: Routledge.

Kharatyan, H. ed., 2003. *Artagaghte Hayastanits [Emigration from Armenia].* Yerevan: Zeytun.

Lying Numbers. 2013. Numbers Are Speaking. Available at <http://civilnet.am> [Accessed 22 February 2013].

Malkasian, M., 1996. *'Gha-ra-bagh!': The Emergence of the National Democratic Movement in Armenia.* Detroit and London: Wayne University Press.

Marutyan, H., 2009. *Iconography of Armenian Identity, Vol.1: The Memory of Genocide and the Karabagh Movement.* Yerevan: 'Gitutyun' Publishing House.

Marutyan, H., 2013. Gharabaghyan sharzhman kam hajkakan heghap'okhut'yan (1988–1990) himnakan ar'andznahatkut'yunnere [The Main Characteristics of the Gharabagh Movement or Armenian Revolution (1988–1990)]. In: H. Galstyan, ed. 2013. *Chugharkvac namakner [Unmailed Letters].* Yerevan: Gasprint. pp. 9–17.

Petrosyan, D., 1999. K itogam parlamentskikh vyborov v Armenii [On the Results of the Parliamentary Elections in Armenia], [on-line] Available at <www.ca-c.org/journal/cac-05–1999/st_03_dpetrosjan.shtml> [Accessed 6 April 2013].

Poghpatyan, T., 2013. : *Ushkhorhrdayin ev etkhorhrdayin sharzhumnere Hayastanum (entrut'yunnere azgagrageti tesankyunits)* [Late-Soviet and Post-Soviet Protest Movements in Armenia (Elections from Anthropological Perspective)]. M. A. Yerevan State University.

Sahakyan, V., 2002. *Hamaynk'i ev hamaynakanut'yan drsevorumnere ev zargatsman mitumnere Hayastanum (sotsiologiakan verlutzut'yun)* [*Manifestations and Trends of Communes and Communalism in Armenia* (A Sociological Analysis)]. PhD. Yerevan State University.

Smirnov, V., 2008. *Afery na vyborakh [Fraud During Elections].* Moscow: Algoritm.

Suleymanyan, A., 2013. *Mathematics and Geography of the Presidential Elections in Armenia,* [on-line] Available at: <http://www.radiovan.fm/matematika-i-geografiya-prezidentskix-vyborov-armenii-2013> [Accessed on 21 June 2013].

To Understand the Mechanism in Order to Fight, 2013. Available at <http://civilnet.am> [Accessed 22 February 2013].

Zhamakochyan, A. and Gyulkhandanyan, E., 2009. *Entrakan khtchankar: Azgayin zhoghov 2007 [Electoral Mosaics: National Assembly 2007].* Yerevan: Zangak.

Chapter 13
Capitalizing on Aid: Post-war Development and State-building in Georgia

Elizabeth Cullen Dunn and Austin Cowley

In recent years, the United Nations (UN) has begun to organise the international system according to a new principle: 'Sovereignty as Responsibility'. During the Cold War, it was assumed that nation-states had inviolable power over what happened within their borders. Under the principle of what Michael Barnett (2010) calls 'juridical sovereignty', other nation-states could not intervene in the domestic affairs of a country, even if a national government was violating the human rights of its own citizens. Today, however, the United Nations has advanced a new principle, one that Barnett says is based on 'empirical sovereignty', or the duty of a nation-state to protect the welfare and human rights of the people on its territory (see also Benhabib, 2004; Etzioni 2006, p.71). 'Sovereignty as Responsibility' dictates that when a state cannot provide for the welfare of its own population, the international community can and must intervene. As Francis Deng, the author of the 'Sovereignty as Responsibility' doctrine, wrote: 'A government that allows its citizens to suffer in a vacuum of responsibility for moral leadership cannot claim sovereignty in an effort to keep the outside world from stepping in to offer protection and assistance' (1996, p.33).

This new principle of international relations has driven a profound shift in the international community, particularly in the domain of humanitarian and development assistance. Foreign donor nations now demand the right to intervene in situations where they feel the local nation-state is unwilling – or more often, institutionally incapable of providing for its own citizenry. Aid to victims of conflict or disaster has become a particularly frequent point of entry for foreign donor nations (Pandolfi, 2003). Today, rather than just funding non-governmental organisations (NGOs) to hand out emergency aid to people displaced by conflict or disaster – as has been common practice since World War II – Western donors are increasingly attempting to alleviate the root causes of displacement by using humanitarian and development aid to 'strengthen' nation-states and 'build capacity' to govern (Weiss, 2013, p.151). In doing so, Western donor countries have established a larger system of patronage, one in which humanitarian funding is not just disaster relief but also a blueprint for the nation-state on how to govern properly. In a profound way, then, humanitarianism and state building have become linked, as the transformation of the nation-state becomes a central goal of humanitarian intervention, as increasing amounts of donor money are routed through central governments rather than through international NGOs, and as institutional reform is seen as a more important goal than the direct provision of services to victims of catastrophe. This, in turn, has profoundly reshaped the relationship between citizen and state.

In this chapter, we use the case of international aid to Georgia after the 2008 war with Russia to examine the ways that the combination of a large influx of humanitarian actors and a flood of funding for humanitarian relief combine to reshape the relationship between a state and its citizens. We argue that rather than promoting democracy and reducing the causes of conflict, as Deng hoped such intervention might accomplish, humanitarian funding is often co-opted by local nation-states to consolidate power. As we show here, this consolidation is often authoritarian: money for relief and for building the capacity of the state to care for its people is often re-routed in ways that feed the growth of police and security services, make citizens suspicious of one another and profoundly dependent on political officials, impede the development of other political parties, and drive remilitarisation in ways that make renewed conflict more, rather than less, likely. Despite the best intentions of donors, promoting sovereignty as responsibility is often a prelude to humanitarianism as authoritarian rule.

Background

In August 2008, a short but brutal war between the Republic of Georgia and Russia broke out in the territory of South Ossetia, a breakaway province of Georgia. The reasons for the conflict were complex, and remain in dispute: while Russia and South Ossetia both claim that Georgia attacked first in an attempt to regain control over the province, Georgia alleges that Russia attacked in order to occupy South Ossetia and gain a military foothold on the south slope of the Caucasus mountains, a barrier which had historically constrained Russia's ability to control its southern periphery (see Tagliavini, 2009; Asmus, 2010). Whatever the causes of the war, it had an undeniable result: 26,000 people, mostly ethnic Georgians, were ethnically cleansed from South Ossetia and have become internally displaced people (IDP).

In the wake of the war, Western donors pledged more than $4.5 billion to Georgia for post-war reconstruction. Some of these funds have gone to the direct provision of aid by donor governments, and some have gone to contracting international NGOs to provide aid to the war-affected population. Other funds have been routed through the UN agencies, which both directly provide services, and also work to build the capacity of the Georgian government to provide services. Comparatively little money, however, has been spent directly helping people affected by the war directly. In fact, only $450 million – roughly 10 per cent of the total amount pledged – has actually gone to assistance programmes for IDPs (World Bank, 2008). Rather, the overwhelming majority of post-war funding has been used for indirect assistance to 'securitising' the country. This has entailed funding government agencies, 'advising' government ministries on policy, training government officials in bureaucratic practices, financing large-scale economic development and infrastructure projects, and beefing up the military, the police, and the state security services. This means that while the Russian military continues to occupy South Ossetia, and while the Russian government *de facto* controls the ostensibly independent South Ossetian state, the Georgian government has become subject to another form of control by outside forces. Subject to Euro-American standards of sovereignty, it is ostensibly compelled to adopt the norms, practices, and values of Euro-American governance.

President Mikheil Saakashvili (2004–2013) seemed to be an ardent supporter of Western liberal democracy, and quite willing to adopt the forms and practices of 'transparent' governance (see Lilli Di Puppo in this volume). He stood as a strong contrast to his predecessor, Eduard Shevardnadze (1995–2003), who had allowed the government and the police force to become corrupt (see Barbara Christophe in this volume), and who had done little to quell an entrenched and well-functioning mafia that could reach from Moscow to village neighbourhoods effortlessly. While the country had endured the worst poverty and violence throughout this period – a time when the state had collapsed so badly that some of the most basic necessities of life such as heating in winter, food safety, and electricity were in dire shortage – it was growing tired and restless towards the intractable Shevardnadze regime that appeared intent on retaining its wealth and power at the cost of national well-being.

By 2002, the political climate in Georgia had begun to shift dramatically as hopes for a regime change seemed imminent (Mitchell, 2009). In the midst of the political fervour, Saakashvili emerged as a key voice to the opposition against Shevardnadze. Saakashvili, who had been educated in France and then who had studied law at Columbia University in New York City, proclaimed himself a democrat. His charisma, along with his promises of realigning Georgia with the West, swept him into office. In the 2003 parliamentary elections, Saakashvili's United National Movement (UNM) was initially projected to win a 26 per cent majority over the pro-government and other opposition parties, yet official results declared a victory for the Shevardnadze regime. The tide quickly turned, however, as, over the next two weeks, protests near the Georgian Parliament building on Rustaveli Avenue reached boiling point (De Waal, 2010). When Shevardnadze attempted to assemble the new parliament to legitimise the recent election, Saakashvili stormed the building with his supporters. Holding a single rose, he entered the parliamentary chamber yelling for Shevardnadze to resign. Security forces rushed the president out of the building as Saakashvili took the podium and drank from Shevardnadze's teacup, which had been left behind on a podium. Although provisional elections would have to be held later, the message was clear: Georgia had its new leader.

Saakashvili immediately moved to establish his credentials as a Western-style reformer by appearing to adopt Western norms of governance. In a highly visible and symbolic move, he purged the notoriously corrupt police force, firing more than 16,000 officers, and established strong criminal sanctions for acts of corruption (BBC, 2013). He prosecuted high-ranking state officials, including the former head of the state chancellery, for corruption, and threw them in prison. As a symbol of openness and transparency, Saakashvili began to build police stations with glass walls all over the country. The World Bank named Georgia as one of the most rapidly reforming countries in 2006 and 2008, and Saakashvili quickly became the poster child for the Bush administration's democratisation programmes. Standing in Tbilisi's newly renamed Freedom Square, George W. Bush declared that Georgia had become a 'beacon of democracy' (Daniel, 2005).

But Saakashvili's commitment to democratisation was at odds with another imperative: that of building a strong state on a unified territory. During his inauguration, Saakashvili made his intentions clear: 'At the grave of King David we must all say: Georgia will be united, strong, will restore its wholeness and become a united, strong state' (De Waal, 2010, p.194). That his speech occurred at the grave of the tenth century king who ruled Georgia during its 'Golden Age' of expansion (Suny, 1994) is no coincidence. Saakashvili's vision of a modern, unified Georgia was part of his greater aspiration as a state-builder. Indeed, he often compared himself to King David the Builder, Mustafa Atatürk, and Charles de Gaulle).

In 2004, he began to reclaim national unity by rolling tanks into another breakaway province, Adjara. He met little resistance from its *de facto* leader, Aslan Abashidze, who quickly decamped to Moscow. But while Saakashvili's vision to rebuild Georgia started auspiciously, the growth of his political regime was nonetheless troubling. As it turned out, the broader notion of change and progress meant to eventually encompass a soon-reunited country were translated into state-building and infrastructure development at the cost of political freedoms and social equality (De Waal, 2010). Because the police force had been extensively reformed, organised crime was crippled, and daily life became far easier to navigate for most people (Light, 2012), yet these forms of violence did not vanish altogether but rather diffused upwards into increasingly powerful government bodies such as the Ministry of the Interior.

In 2008, Saakashvili appears to have made another gamble to regain territory. Although the Saakashvili government still maintains that the Russian forces the began moving through the Roki Tunnel under the Caucasus Mountains were the first to begin the attack on South Ossetia, international observers believe it was Saakashvili who sprang the attack on Tskhinvali, the South Ossetian capital, in an attempt to take the territory before the Russians could intervene. It was a terrible miscalculation: the Russian 58th Army, which had been poised at the northern end of the tunnel inside Russia, quickly moved into South Ossetia and began a counterattack (McDermott, 2009). Within five days, the Georgian army had been defeated and more than 127,000 people were displaced. The streets of Tbilisi were overrun with people. Hospitals, schools, and other public buildings were shut down to house the influx. Many kindergartens were shut down for the remainder of 2008 to serve as temporary shelters. Entire families shared a single bed; the ill and the elderly were forced to lie on cardboard because there were no mattresses; toilets overflowed with human waste; and the atmosphere was characterised by panic and uncertainty about the future. The conflict in Georgia had become a full-blown humanitarian crisis.

Aid agencies, led by the United Nations High Commission for Refugees (UNHCR) scaled up their operations. The International Committee of the Red Cross (ICRC) and Médecins Sans Frontières (MSF) expanded their reach into the areas of conflict and military control in South Ossetia. Although most of the international community was too preoccupied with the Olympic Games in Beijing to comprehend the initial extent of the war's damage, French President, Nicolas Sarkozy, and US Secretary of State, Condoleezza Rice, flew into the country soon afterwards to negotiate peace treaties between Russia and Georgia. On 13 August 2008, the two countries agreed to a ceasefire. The war, brief but brutal, was officially over, but its aftermath would have lasting implications for the people who were not allowed to return to their homes in South Ossetia.

Key Actors: The Development–Security Nexus

In the wake of the war, a collection of different aid agencies rushed to provide humanitarian relief to the thousands of people fleeing the violence in South Ossetia. Even the international community met in Brussels to fund the 'Flash Appeal', or the document that organised aid by moving money from donors to contracting NGOs, organisations including the UNHCR, World Food Program (WFP), United State Agency of International Development (USAID), CARE International and even the United States Navy quickly began to provide immediate aid in the form of food, clothing, medical supplies and hygiene kits. While organisations like the Red Cross and MSF were well prepared for such a disaster, others were haphazardly opportunistic. As an official from the World Health Organisation (WHO) told one of us (Dunne): 'Some of the partners [international NGOs and donor agencies] were calling us from the airport the night before the Flash Appeal was due, saying "we want in". They didn't know Georgia, didn't know the situation, didn't know what anybody else was doing. They just cut and pasted some old projects together. They literally just took out the words "Indonesia" or "Congo", and put in "Georgia". Some of the projects were total bullshit.'

The money that flowed through the Flash Appeal was non-trivial: over $109,311,307 was raised in the first round of funding (United Nations, 2008). This enormous sum of money, meant to fund only 7.5 months of aid, was justified in the language of emergency. This temporal framing, which defines most humanitarian action, is a short-but-intense slice of time in which action must be taken quickly and within which goods and people must move rapidly across space to preserve life (Calhoun, 2008, p.76). Because the humanitarian imperative to 'do something' to alleviate suffering demands that something be done now, humanitarianism operates in a near-constant temporality of emergency (Calhoun 2008, p.76; Redfield, 2005; 2013, p.32). This is exacerbated by the fact that aid does not come in the form of open-ended long-term streams of funding, but in the form of the project, a time-limited plan for action that competes with other projects for attention and money from donors. Because the temporality of emergency attracts donor funding much more than long-term assistance plans do, aid agencies almost all move from emergency to emergency, funding their organisations by chasing projects that arise in response to crisis (Weiss, 2013). This is a chaotic and *ad hoc* process (Dunn, 2012), but one that is also extremely lucrative, as the 96 participating agencies in the Georgian post-war Flash Appeal quickly found out.

As the money that was funneled through the Flash Appeal began to dry up, many of the NGOs active in post-war Georgia attempted to call forth more funding by emphasising the conflict-affected population's need for long-term development as well as emergency assistance. World Vision, for example, gave this account of its activity: 'World Vision Georgia commenced its emergency response from the very outset of the conflict to meet the needs of thousands of Internally Displaced Persons (IDPs). World Vision began by providing emergency assistance to the conflict-affected population and then slowly switched to the recovery phase in 2009 by focusing on social and economic aspects of the affected groups.'

As relief shifted to reconstruction, international donors, mainly Western Europe and the United States, pledged over $4.5 billion.[1] Following the money stream, international aid agencies transitioned from humanitarian assistance to longer-term development strategies. Humanitarianism, working within a perceived state of emergency (Redfield, 2008), had performed a kind of triage to provide relief in the field. Development, on the other hand, was aimed towards longer-term goals, sometimes loftier goals such as to 'eradicate extreme poverty and hunger', 'promote gender equality and empower women', and 'ensure environmental sustainability' (Millennium Development Goals, 2015). Although these missions implied very different organisational capacities than the provision of emergency aid did, most aid agencies conceived of the transition as a seamless process.

The mission statement from CARE International in the Caucasus, an aid agency that received $3 million from the Norwegian government to carry out a project to benefit the IDPs, illustrates the shift: 'Bridging the gap between humanitarian relief and development work, CARE started the three-year programme, Stabilisation & Integration of IDPs into Mainstream Georgian Society .... The programme aims not only at economic development of the IDP settlements, but also at creating viable socio-economic ties between IDPs and the host communities. It moves from providing aid to the displaced people to creating conditions for development and integration of their communities' (CARE, 2010).

The key notion linking humanitarian aid and development was security. Although the immediate problem was clearly military security – the Russians were less than a kilometre away from some of the IDP camps – the aid agencies quickly moved from dealing with geopolitical security issues to dealing with

1 The United States, which was the leading donor, gave a total of $135 million in emergency aid through two Flash Appeal mechanisms, and gave over $1 billion in total aid in the wake of the war (see Nicolls, 2010).

human security on the local level. Using neoliberal ideas about individuals and markets, they promised to provide the IDPs with day to day economic security. Many of the projects that popped up during the post-war reconstruction were aimed at creating jobs or at giving IDPs start-up capital to start businesses. The logic behind the schemes was often to 'generate income' in IDP camps and collective centres, as a way to transform these places from temporary shelters into long-term housing arrangements with a sustainable market. Given the relative poverty and social disintegration in these places, such logic demonstrated the unwavering faith development agencies put into the notion of capital investments at any scale (Willis, 2005). As in other development projects, the notion was that somehow, the beneficiaries could only find security by reducing their dependence on international donors and/or the state and entering into the market on their own (Roy, 2010). With high unemployment, a glut of low-value agricultural products on the local market and almost no manufacturing employment, though, these aid projects quickly failed. Despite hundreds of thousands or even millions of dollars spent on them, they often benefited only a handful of IDPs, and many of the businesses those IDPs started failed.

In response, the NGOs came to try and provide other, more nebulous forms of security, typically under the banner of 'conflict resolution', a placeholder term which covers the collection of projects that do not fit as neatly under the rubric of economic development. From 'women's peacebuilding' seminars, which promised that poor Georgian women could somehow create security by becoming friendly with poor Ossetian women, to 'psychosocial aid' programmes for children, which promised them emotional security by offering them art therapy, the NGOs argued that 'creating the conditions for development and integration' was the key to a the long-term strategy of securitisation through socio-economic stability.

But these claims weren't as strong or as self-evident as the NGOs believed them to be. Although a substantial proportion of the emergency humanitarian aid funding was routed through international NGOs, most of the $4.5 billion for long-term development and reconstruction was sent to another recipient: the Georgian government, which had very obviously become a client state and a geopolitical tool of Western governments, especially the United States. In important ways, the project of security had, at least for Western donors, become inextricably linked to state building.

New Power Geometries

Although new power assemblages between the Georgian government, Western donors, aid organisations, and the private sector had been emerging since Saakashvili's election in 2004 (Schueth, 2011), the enormous influx of aid dollars changed the practices and logics of governance in unexpected ways. In some cases, international bodies took over certain state functions. In other areas, though, donor funding was supposed to help the Georgian government to 'increase capacity' to govern by itself. For instance, because the Ministry of Refugee and Accommodations (MRA) was underfunded, lacked solid leadership, and had very little authority under Georgian law, the task of managing the future and well-being of displaced populations was largely taken on by the UNHCR and a collection of other NGOs including the Danish and Norwegian Refugee Councils. At the same moment, however, large-scale programmes were launched to 'build capacity' at the MRA so that it could take the functions of governing IDPs back. The USAID, for example, launched a 'full-scale' project to reorganise the MRA and implement Western-style procedures for human resource management, fiscal management, and other bureaucratic tasks. With the help of the Danish Refugee Council (DRC), who had a representative working full time at the MRA, the USAID also created a new database system to create aggregate statistics and track individual IDP cases, as well as a new reception centre where individual IDPs who were coming to plead for resources could be handled. The project became so large that eventually the European Union pledged an additional €50 million, and the project was transferred from the USAID to the DRC. Likewise, under the heading 'National Administrative Framework Provides Better Protection', the UNHCR provided over $858,931 in unspecified projects aimed at assisting the Georgian government in changing the national legal framework and the national administrative framework (UNHCR, 2011, p.290).

But not all aid to the Georgian government was aimed at helping displaced people, even indirectly. Over $678 million of the $2.5 billion given by international donors for public sector support flowed to the Georgian government in the form of direct budget support – money sent not to the intended beneficiaries, but to the national government (Shatirishvili, 2010, p.7). The United States, for example, provided $250 million of 'cash transfer assistance' to the Georgian government. This was a direct transfer of money to the government, which was meant primarily to stabilise the Georgian economy and 'mitigate fiscal shortfalls', primarily by ensuring that the Georgian government could continue to pay wages for government employees as well as pensions and other social subsidies (Shatirishvili, 2010, p.7). The agreement for this cash transfer, which was signed by Georgian Minister of Finance Nika Gilauri (2007–2009), who explicitly stated that the money could not be used for surveillance equipment, or to support the police, the military, or the paramilitary forces (US Department of State, 2008).

There is no indication that money from the cash account funded by the US government – or any other bilateral aid from Western donors – went directly to fund the police and the military. Yet, even though the government claimed to be unable to pay teachers' salaries and retirees' pensions, the military budget doubled between the war's end in August 2008 and 1 January 2009, reaching $1.625 billion, or more than one-third of all government spending. The budget of the Ministry of the Interior, the powerful agency in charge of Georgia's intelligence community, grew at a similar rate, reaching $323.4 million by 2011 (Corso, 2010). Clearly, notwithstanding signed contracts, the influx of foreign aid in the wake of the war was being used to grow the police and military apparatus. A focus on rebuilding the intelligence services and the military after a war might be expected – after all, the Georgians had been so resoundingly defeated that they had lost millions of dollars' worth of military equipment. But there were soon powerful reasons to suspect that the military and the State Security Service (*ushishroeba*) were being used not just against the Russian forces occupying South Ossetia, but against Georgian citizens – among them the very IDPs who foreign humanitarian aid was supposed to help.

Building 'Security' in the Camp

With the massive influx of aid, Saakashvili seized the moment, and used the resources available to him to increase his grip on power. Not only content to focus on weakening opposition parties and intellectual dissidents – as he had done from 2003 to 2007 – he used post-war humanitarian aid to begin tightening his control over non-elite populations in regions outside the capital. The IDPs, easily accessible in the new settlements, were soon caught up in a rising tide of authoritarianism funded with humanitarian dollars.

In the Tsmindatsqali settlement, close to the city of Gori, the rise of political oppression became overt in the spring of 2010, as the IDPs struggled to deal with the newly imposed cost of power. From the time they had moved into the new cottage settlements, gas and electricity had been provided free of charge in the urban settlements. Heaters were an absolute necessity. In addition to the travails of a cold winter, the IDPs also had to contend with the fact that their cottages had been built with wet materials, which left gaping cracks between walls and floors that let cold air rush in. The floors of the cottages, which were made of unvarnished planks over bare earth, were built with uncured wood, which shrank as it dried and left gaps between the boards where freezing air and pooling water could enter living spaces. To combat the cold, the IDPs ran gas heaters at full blast, and plugged electric heaters in the bedrooms that consumed power at an astonishing rate.

From the time they had moved into the settlements in January 2009 until late January 2010, the government had paid all the utility bills in the camp. It was a shock, then, when the power company cut off gas and electricity in late January. In the dead of winter, with no light, no heat, and no way to cook food, the situation in the settlements became dire. As Khatuna Mirashvili,[2] an IDP from the village of Eredvi, put it: 'It was a terrible, terrible winter. We were so cold, and we didn't even have a woodstove to get heat with. My daughter in law was seven months pregnant, and because she was freezing day after day, she caught a virus. She had such a high fever! The cold and the virus killed the baby, our baby. It was born too early, and it died right away. If only we'd been home, in Eredvi, we would have a baby now.'

2 All names in this chapter have been anonymized.

The power cuts were not only logistically challenging, but emotionally humiliating. As Dato Shalikashvili, an IDP from Tamarasheni, told us: 'How could they cut off the electricity and the gas in the middle of winter? They made us these terrible gas heaters; they hardly work, and now they cut off the gas? What is this government doing? When the electricity was cut, we all had bills of 600–800 lari [Georgian lari, GEL, around $340–460]. Nobody was told we would have to pay for gas and electricity after January, so when we got the bills, it was a shock. Some people still don't have power. What was worse, they cut the power right on the Old New Year! We could see the streetlights burning outside, but inside, we had no light. It was so humiliating, so belittling to us! We aren't Megrelebi [the first wave of IDPs], we aren't aggressive people, and we have some culture. We have doctors, and lawyers and engineers among us. But this was a provocation, cutting off the power.' Shalikashvili added a comment showing just how much pressure the electricity shortage caused, both emotionally and logistically: '*Damtrgunevelia*', he said. 'It's oppressive.'

In Tsmindatsqali, a small group of IDPs decided to respond to what they saw as government provocation, and to take political action to alleviate the pressure of the cold and the damp. Gathering together, they went to the East–West highway, which passed the far end of the settlement. The highway was Georgia's single artery: as the Russians had demonstrated during the war, blockading the highway that cut the country in two, isolating the capital from the rest of the country. For the IDPs to block the highway, then, was no mere attempt to 'have their voices heard', no mere symbolic demonstration of fear or ire. It was an intense political threat, one that threatened to cut Tbilisi off from the entire Western half of Georgia.

Shoulder to shoulder, the IDPs blocked the road with their bodies. Traffic was stopped, and the buses and *marshrutka* (minibus) that were the main form of transport between the regions and the capital began to pile up behind the blockade. The IDPs did not have long to wait for a response from the government: within an hour, police and militia – in tanks, with soldiers armed with M4 carbines – came to break up the protests. Soon, an official from the power company came, bringing bad news. As Shalikashvili recalls, the man from the power company refused to be swayed by the protest: 'Your power was being paid for by a foreign donor. But now the donor is gone, and you'll have to pay for this yourselves. You have to pay what you owe, or we're not turning the heat on.'

Discouraged and cold, surrounded by the threat of armed violence, the unarmed IDPs began to break up and go back to their cold, dark cottages. Some hoped to plan another action to demand that the government pay the arrears and turn the power back on. But the government was firm in its resolve to break what it saw as the IDPs' dependence on humanitarian aid and the state.

Neoliberal policy was not the worst form of oppression for the IDPs, however. It was followed up by a form of pressure that was much more overt. Late on the night of the protests, and for several days thereafter, unnamed men from an unnamed agency began visiting the settlement, going house by house to each family. One of the IDPs referred to them as *Sonderkommando*, comparing them to

Jews who acted alongside Nazi guards in Nazi Germany: 'We didn't know them. But they knew us. The *Sonderkommandos* came to each house, and they knew what each one of us had. If we were getting social welfare payments or IDP status payments, they knew it. If one of us had a government job, in the police or in the *ushishroeba*, they knew it.'

At each house, the political operatives made it clear: if anyone in the family joined another protest, the family would find itself suddenly 'too rich' to receive welfare payments. People with state jobs – which meant virtually anyone who was employed – would lose their jobs immediately, should anyone in the family show up at another *aktsia*. Political activity, it was clear, would deprive the IDPs of their only sources of income, leaving them destitute. Authoritarian political pressure was thus applied in a calculated manner, in the form of concrete threats to the reproduction of physical life. The threat of 'letting them die' was not used as a means of excluding IDPs, then, but of bringing them more tightly into the web of political control, of rendering them political, in and through their depoliticisation. Humanitarian power, moving through the channels of rising authoritarianism, thus rendered displaced people not as active citizens, but as silent subjects.

The dramatic and pointed visits by political operatives had an immediate effect on the IDPs' solidarity with one another. State pressure opened the rifts already apparent in the community, turning them into social fault lines in the settlements. Rather than seeing the community leaders, or *mamasakhlisebi*, as the benevolent figures that the NGOs believed them to be, people in the settlements began to whisper that they functioned in fact as informers and state enforcers, just as the *mamasakhlisebi* who had occupied every apartment block and village during the communist period did: 'They watch us and tell the government what we are doing', said one woman. Other IDPs also employed by the government were soon suspected of being spies. 'Watch out for Mariami', a friend told me, warning me about a neighbour's daughter, who worked for the Eredvi municipal government in exile, 'She reports her mother's gossip to the government. She tells them what we think.' Rumours circulated of old-style Stalinist denunciations. A friend told me that the poorest of the IDPs were being paid by the government for informing on their neighbours. 'It's a pittance they're paid, only enough money for a pack of cigarettes. But for such little money, they're willing to sell their neighbours.' Other IDPs believed that the *ushishroeba*, Saakashvili's state intelligence agency, was tapping their telephones, and began carefully monitoring every word they said.

Fear of the *ushishroeba* became even more profound in the run-up to the 2012 parliamentary elections, in which Saakashvili's government was being challenged by the billionaire oligarch, Bidzina Ivanishvili. In the settlements, the IDPs believed that their political loyalty to the Saakashvili regime was being constantly monitored. Although many might have had good reason to oppose Saakashvili – who, it turned out, started the war with Russia that led to the loss of their homes – few were willing to say so openly. Most were afraid to talk politics at all. When representatives from Ivanishvili's Georgian Dream party came to the camp, some of the IDPs were so concerned about the appearance of being disloyal to Saakashvili that they chased the visitors out of the camp.

They had reason to fear the *ushishroeba*, which often struck in unpredictable ways against individuals. Aleko Mentashvili, for example, had attempted to support his family by farming. But with only a very small plot in a nearby field, and a yard so small that his beehives and pigsty touched the walls of the cottage, he could not make ends meet. He felt incredibly lucky when he was hired as a forester, managing nearby woods. One day, two men came to him, and offered him a small bribe – 60 GEL, or about $30 according to his wife – to allow them to cut firewood illegally. Aleko, whose children had no winter coats and whose wife was wearing sodden carpet slippers outside in the snow and mud, took the bribe. But then the whole scene was quickly revealed to be a ruse: the men were agents from the Ministry of the Interior, the offer of a bribe was a sting, and Aleko Mentashvili was arrested on charges of corruption. He was found guilty and sent to Gldani prison for a three year term.

In 2012, in the lead up to the presidential elections, a series of videos were released documenting widespread abuses in the Gldani prison. The Georgian prison system was well-known to be terrible, with extreme overcrowding, dangerously dilapidated facilities, short rations, and hyper-endemic tuberculosis. But Gldani prison, in particular, was soon revealed to be far worse. In a series of videos leaked to television channels by a former prison officer, prison staff were shown verbally abusing inmates and spitting on them, beating them with police batons, and, in an act that shocked the Georgian polity, raping them with broom handles (Fairbanks, 2012).

The effects of increased activity by the *ushishroeba* were thus profound and pervasive. They isolated the IDPs from the surrounding community, limited their freedom of speech, and made them so suspicious of one another that any form of organising was soon made impossible. They put the IDPs in fear for their livelihoods, bodily integrity, and their very lives. By making it possible for the Saakashvili administration to fund the Ministry of the Interior at such a high level, the money donated to help the IDPs was turned against them, in ways that impeded their ability to re-join Georgian society, economy, and politics.

Conclusion

Humanitarian and development aid are aimed at not only at the preservation of biological life, but at the creation of 'human security,' or a mode of life which ensures a basic income, enough food to eat, a clean environment, and the upholding of human and political rights. Aimed at protecting individuals rather than nation-states, humanitarian aid is also often aimed at providing 'security' in Michel Foucault's (2009) sense of that term: a form of pastoral care which evokes the productive capacities of the population to make individuals healthier and more affluent, more entrepreneurial, better spouses and parents, and so on. For donor governments and international humanitarian agencies, then, state building is a tool for creating a welfare state, one with the capacity to ensure the well-being and productivity of its displaced population.

The Saakashvili government, however, transformed 'security' in the sense of 'the provision of welfare' into another form of security: one based not on welfare but on penal means. As money meant to support the displaced population was channeled into the Ministry of Internal Affairs, 'security' came to mean rooting out crime, corruption, dissidence, and even potential political opposition. The camp was transformed from a site of service delivery for needy people into a locus of suspicion that required surveillance and intervention by state institutions (see Simon, 2007). This was a phenomenon that exceeded the question of internally displaced people: even before the war, the Saakashvili regime was widely engaged in 'governing through crime', or the act of 'governing through a relentless focus on criminal justice, a concentration on the discourse of crime', and the solving of policy problems in unrelated spheres through criminal justice logics (Slade 2012, pp.51–2, see also Simon, 2007). As the Ministry of Interior began to take extra-legal measures, like torture, in order to govern, the state soon began to govern through crime in a double sense: the state committed crimes and the state managed others by suspecting them of criminality.

As Jonathan Simon points out, this is not entirely unusual: 'History is replete with political regimes that mobilise around crime, use criminal law to cover up the asymmetrical effects of power, bolster the elimination of political dissent, and terrorise and deter organised resistance by systematically exploited classes' (2007, p.14).

What is new is the funding of such authoritarianism through such a massive influx of humanitarian dollars.[3] In the aftermath of the Russo–Georgian war, the government found both another problem to govern through crime, and a massive source of funding to fuel the government of the wider society through penal means. Far from fostering democracy, humanitarian aid to Georgia eroded democratic capacity in the state and among its beneficiaries by destroying social trust and capital.

In the 2012 elections, the Saakashvili government was ousted by a new political party, Georgian Dream, largely because of political protests over the state's move towards governing through penal means. Protesters objected not only to the graphic forms of torture in the prisons, but to the more widespread criminalisation of dissent (Slade, 2012). When Saakashvili acknowledged defeat, it was widely hailed as evidence that Georgia had finally become a democratic country. 'Democracy works in a way that the Georgian people make decisions by majority', said Saakashvili, handing power to his rival, Bidzina Ivanishvili (Harding, 2012). 'Saakashvili's party loses as Georgian democracy takes step forward', cried the Christian Science Monitor, echoing other Western newspapers' coverage of the event (Rimple, 2012).

3 But see Weizman, 2011: Chapter 1 on a similar case in Ethiopia.

But was the state more democratic? Although the players had changed as Ivanishvili took power, the principle of state governance through crime appeared to have become firmly entrenched. In a move that was both tactical and symbolic, one of the first new prisoners after the election was Vano Merabishvili, the head of the Interior Ministry under Saakashvili. Meanwhile, the IDPs in Tsmindatsqali, who soon found projects drying up as aid money ran out, were left largely to make do.

References

Asmus, R., 2010. *The Little War that Shook the World: Georgia, Russia and the Future of the West*. New York: Palgrave MacMillan.

Barnett, M., 2010. *The International Humanitarian Order*. London: Routledge.

Benhabib, S., 2004. Negotiating Republican Self-Determination and Cosmopolitan Norms. Lecture delivered at University of California at Berkeley. Available at <http://tannerlectures.utah.edu/_documents/a-to-z/b/benhabib_2005.pdf> [Accessed 15 November 2013].

Calhoun, C., 2008. The Imperative to Reduce Suffering: Charity, Progress and Emergencies in the Field of Humanitarian Action. In: M. Barnett and T. Weiss, eds, *Humanitarianism in Question: Politics, Power, Ethics*. Ithaca: Cornell University Press, pp.73–98.

CARE, 2010. South Caucasus Fact Sheet 2010. Available at <http://www.care.org/south-caucasus-fact-sheet-2010> [Accessed 21 February 2014]

Corso, M., 2010. Georgia: 2011 Budget is Big on Bucks, Small on Public Details. *EurasiaNet*, 10 December. Available at <http://www.eurasianet.org/node/62604> [Accessed 15 November 2013].

Daniel, C., 2005. Bush Backs Georgia as 'Beacon of Democracy'. *Financial Times*, London, 10 May. Available at <www.ft.com/cms/s/0/3cc8ba4e-c128-11d9-943f-00000e2511c8.html#axzz2gsM6OUfi> [Accessed 15 November 2013].

Deng, F., 1996. *Sovereignty as Responsibility: Conflict Management in Africa*. Washington: Brookings Institution Press.

De Waal, T., 2010. *The Caucasus: An Introduction*. New York: Oxford University Press.

Dunn, E., 2012. The Chaos of Humanitarianism: Adhocracy in the Republic of Georgia. *Humanity* 3(1). Available at <http://www.humanityjournal.org/humanity-volume-3–issue-1/chaos-humanitarian-aid-adhocracy-republic-georgia> [Accessed 15 November 2013].

Etzioni, A., 2006. Sovereignty as Responsibility. *Orbis* 50(1), pp.71–85.

Fairbanks Jr., C. H., 2012. Georgia's Prison Rape Scandal – and What It Says About the Rose Revolution. *The Atlantic*. Available at <http://www.theatlantic.com/international/ archive/2012/09/georgias-prison-rape-scandal-and-what-it-says-about-therose-revolution/262720/> [Accessed 15 November 2013].

Light, M., 2012. Georgian Police Reforms in Comparative Perspective. *The Caucasus Research Resource Centers (CRRC) 20th Works-in-Progress Talk.*

Mitchell, L., 2009. *Uncertain Democracy: U.S. Foreign Policy and Georgia's Rose Revolution.* Philadelphia: University of Pennsylvania Press.

McDermott, Roger N., 2009. Russia's Conventional Armed Forces and the Georgian War. *Parameters* 65–80. Available at <http://strategicstudiesinstitute.army.mil /pubs/parameters/Articles/09spring/mcdermott.pdf> [Accessed 15 November 2013].

Pandolfi, M., 2003. Contract of Mutual (In)Difference: Governance and the Humanitarian Apparatus in Contemporary Albania and Kosovo. *Indiana Journal of Global Legal Studies* 10(1): 369–81.

Redfield, P., 2005. Doctors, Borders, and Life in Crisis. *American Ethnologist* 20(3): 320–61.

Redfield, P., 2008. Sacrifice, Triage, and Global Humanitarianism. In: M. Barnett and T. Weiss, eds, *Humanitarianism in Question: Politics, Power, Ethics.* Ithaca: Cornell University Press, pp.196–214.

Redfield, P., 2013. *Life in Crisis: The Ethical Journey of Doctors Without Borders.* Berkeley: University of California Press.

Roy, A., 2010. *Poverty Capital: Microfinance and the Making of Development.* New York and London: Routledge.

Schueth, S., 2010. State Assemblage in the Republic of Georgia [Dissertation]. University of Minnesota.

Shatirishvili, M., 2010. Efficiency Analysis of USG Cash Transfer Assistance Program. Available at <http://www.state.gov/documents/organization/193590.pdf> [Accessed 15 November 2013].

Slade, G., 2012. 'Georgia's War on Crime: Creating Security in a Post-Revolutionary Context. *European Security* 21(1), pp.37–56.

Simon, J., 2007. *Governing Through Crime: How the War on Crime Transformed American Democracy and Created a Culture of Fear.* London: Oxford.

Suny, R. G., 1994. *The Making of the Georgian Nation.* Bloomington and Indianapolis: Indiana University Press.

Tagliavini, H. et. al., 2009. *Report of the Independent International Fact Finding Mission on the Conflict in Georgia.* Brussels: Council of the European Union. Available at <http://www.ceiig.ch> [Accessed 15 November 2013].

United Nations, 2008. Georgia: Summary of Joint Needs Assessment Findings. Available at <http://www.reliefweb.int/rw/rwb.nsf/db900SID/MUMA-7KP5DR?OpenDocument> [Accessed 15 November 2013].

United Nations High Commission for Refugees, 2011. *UNHCR Global Report.* Available at <http://www.unhcr.org/4fc880b9b.pdf> [Accessed 15 November 2013].

United States Department of State, 2008. *Cash Transfer Grant Agreement.* Available at <http://www.state.gov/documents/organization/120560.pdf> [Accessed 15 November 2013].

Weiss, T., 2013. *Humanitarian Business.* New York: Polity.

Willis, K., 2005. *Theories and Practices of Development*. London and New York: Routledge.

World Bank, 2008. *Joint World Bank – European Commission Press Release: International Donors Pledge – US$4.5 billion (€3.4 billion) in Post-Conflict Support to Georgia*. Available at <http://web.worldbank.org/WBSITE/EXTERNAL/NEWS/0,contentMDK: 21949175~pagePK:34370~piPK:34424~theSitePK:4607,00.html> [Accessed 15 November 2013].

Chapter 14

A Guest or a Client? Community-based Tourism in Armenia between Industry and Hospitality[1]

Gayane Shagoyan

In the anthropology of tourism, together with questions of the economical or cultural influences of tourism on local communities (see Smith, 1989), different understandings of the definition of the 'tourist' often appear in the focus of researchers (Graburn and Barthel-Bouchier, 2001). Depending on these definitions, both the tourist industry and local services can be perceived in various ways. In the following chapter, I will try to discuss the perception of who the 'tourist' actually is from the point of view of the hosts rather than polemicise with existing concepts. As McCabe noted 'the word "tourist" is not an ossified, megalithic container of "primordial meaning" but a precise concept, an ideological, moral and political construct used to achieve interactional goals' (2005, p.96). I will discuss how the hosts try to insert new models of relations into traditional schemes or 'rewrite' themselves to adapt to a new situation, with the appearance of tourists and the tourist industry. By hosts I do not mean professional service industry workers, but residents of two Armenian villages who have unintentionally become involved with the tourist industry, occupying the niche of so called 'community-based tourism' (CBT). The chapter is based on interviews and observations and some autobiographical experience as well, as I was both the coordinator of a number of international projects (starting as an expert anthropologist) aimed at the development of CBT, and an observer and participant in some processes. The material presented concerns the villages of Gosh and Tatev. The first is located in the north-east of Armenia, relatively close to Yerevan (127 km), seven kilometres from the arterial highway; the second is located in the south-west of Armenia, at some distance from Yerevan (250 km), 33 kilometres from the arterial highway.

The villages of Gosh and Tatev were chosen while taking into account a number of factors: firstly, there are well known medieval architectural complexes within the territory (Gosh) and in the neighbourhood (Tatev); due to this the villages became attractive to tourists and were included in standard tourist packages. Secondly,

1 The chapter was prepared within the framework of the project 'Globalization Processes in the Contemporary Armenian Village', which was sponsored by the John D. and Katherine T. MacArthur Foundation (Grant no. 06–86346–000–GSS).

the villages were included in the projects of some international organisations. For example, within a programme of the Project 'Harmony', 330 schools in Armenia got access to the internet and gained computer classes.[2] Another example is the World Bank's regional project, 'Transcaucasian Tourist Initiative' (2002–2005); within this project tourist information centres were built in the two villages[3] and some activities were initiated for the development of CBT.

The concept of the 'tour' was first introduced in the 1750s; the term 'tourist' then soon became accepted for denoting the participants of such entertaining and educational journeys (Jafari, 2000). In the anthropology of tourism of the late 1980s (for example Greenwood, 1989; MacCannell, 1989), the estimation of the latter's influence on the local social-cultural processes in settlements that accepted tourists was labelled as 'coca-colonisation' meaning both the processes of Westernisation (especially that of Americanisation) and neocolonialism, since the West is considered to continue to take from the 'rest of the world' what it wants while undermining the solidarity and traditions of local communities (Rapport and Overing, 2000, pp.353–56; Nash 1989; MacCannell, 1989, pp.37–52). However, in the tourist industry this assumption can also be reversed. Tourism began to develop and to be maintained by many international organisations purely as an instrument of aid; the successful West helping the poor East. While the expectations from tourism discussed in the 1960s turned out to be not so high; the 'sun, sand and friendly people' turned out to be deficient resources for enriching third world peoples since the European tourists needed the hotels, restaurants and transportation they were accustomed to, so that the greater part of the profit was returned to the first world countries. This enriched international corporations which supplied the corresponding conveniences leaving the profit remnants in the hands of local elites and thus promoting property polarisation in the local communities (Rapport and Overing, 2000, pp.354–55). However, faith in the 'tourist miracle' reoccurs each time a novel tourist product or an unknown exotic location off the beaten track appears on the international market. This also happened in the case of the fall of the iron curtain and the discovery of many little known places in countries of the former Soviet Union. Here, it was less the first world countries that began to show interest in international tourism, but more the countries of the former socialist sector who found themselves in the 'open world of the capitalist

2 The aim of this programme (2002–2007) was to allow internet access for the majority of Armenian schools. For schools of remote and hard to reach settlements, a movable internet centre was planned. Since a great deal of computerised schools are regional and, in particular, rural, the situation in the schools of our two villages can be considered typical for Armenian rural schools.

3 The villages also found themselves in this project as a result of their cultural monuments. In addition, the high poverty rates were taken into consideration, as well as the involvement of both villages in other projects of the World Bank. The construction of the tourist information centres was backed by the Swiss Agency for Development and Cooperation (SDC).

market'. Obviously the formula of the tourist industry, 'much profit from little investment', turned out to be a very attractive one. I will not discuss here the real economic results of tourism – these estimations are of interest for us only in the perspective of social discourse. However, in present day Armenia, the Department of Tourism, which falls within the structure of the Ministry of Trade and Economic Development, began to report figures related to tourism with increasing frequency together with activities related to the economic upturn within the country. In other words, the increase in the number of tourists became an indicator of the country's flourishing and integration into the Western world.

The 'Exoduses' of Tourists into Armenia

Besides the pan-Caucasian tourist rush, there were some special expectations for Armenia, since serious resources were also present here in the form of the Armenian Diaspora, which was three times as big as the population of the republic.[4] In addition, it was considered that tourism might decrease the rate of emigration, a serious problem in post-Soviet Armenia, by inculcating a feeling of pride towards the place of one's habitation, development of local artisan traditions and, most importantly, by creating a labour market.[5] Thus tourism was declared to be one of the priorities in the republic's development. When tracing 'texts of power' (texts produced by state authorities), one can find such statements in the speeches of all the *marzpet*s (governors) and mayors of different cities and towns. Many authority representatives dream of making their 'patrimony' a tourism centre.[6] Tourist information centres started to open in bigger and smaller cities in Armenia and even in some villages. In 2001 a closed joint-stock company was founded: the Armenian Agency of Tourism Development (AATD). Its main function is marketing and promoting the tourist potential of Armenia: participation in international exhibitions, producing and publishing promotional and informational materials, organisation of tours for foreign journalists and tourist operators, and the organisation of traditional festivals (Tourism, 2007).

---

4 It is noteworthy that one of the collections of papers issued by the Caucasus Mass Media Institute and the German Heinrich Böll Foundation on the countries of South Caucasus was entitled 'Diaspora, Oil and Roses: What Makes the Countries of the South Caucasus Tick' (Haindrava and Iskandaryan, 2005): 'The "key words" *diaspora*, *oil*, and *roses* in the title reflect the most common notions of the factors at the heart of the development of South Caucasus countries: Armenia receives aid from her wide diaspora, Azerbaijan earns on the oil project, and Georgia made a gigantic step forward due to the "rose revolution"' (2005, p.3).

5 On the economic 'pros' and 'cons' of tourism, see Harrison, 1992.

6 On the urban tourism discourse in Gyumri (formerly Leninakan), see Shagoyan, 2007b.

The date of the agency's opening was not purely accidental. In 2001 a great flow of tourists was anticipated in the Republic, as a consequence of the celebration of the 1700th anniversary of Armenia's adoption of Christianity. The importance of the event was greatly anticipated, so that the construction of the new Cathedral of St Gregory the Illuminator in Yerevan was not only timed for this date, but the symbolic number 1700 figured architecturally: the cathedral was planned to seat just 1700 people.

The beginning of the 'tourist rush' in the Republic is related to this event. Of course, there was tourism during Soviet times, too, but the Soviet-planned economy did not always accommodate real tourist demand. The two settlements involved in our research project, Gosh and Tatev, have been known as tourist destinations since Soviet times, tourism, however, sharply declined during the period of military operations in Nagorno-Karabakh and the ensuing political instability, and economic and energy crisis (1991-1995).

The situation abruptly changes by 2001, when the gross revenue of the tourist industry made up nearly $164 million with 75 percent accounting for international tourism. The spread also widened – tourists from eighty countries visited Armenia in 2001 (Tourism, 2003). However, it should be taken into consideration that the variety of countries does not yet mean an ethnic variety of tourists: naturally, the greater part consisted of Armenians. Actually, regardless of cultural monuments and tourist services in the Republic, it would, in any case, be visited by tourists suffering from nostalgia for a historical or symbolic fatherland characterised as a kind of tourist pilgrimage.

One of the main peculiarities of pilgrimage is that pilgrims usually have much less demands concerning the level and quality of service, food and accommodation. Just such a type of tourist suffering from nostalgia for their fatherland drove the creation of a special service which was accordingly oriented towards constructing the 'traditional', which could be termed 'Armenian' or representing a 'kind of Armenian'. In contrast to more general tourism, where the local culture is devalued as a result of its commercialisation or, to follow Greenwood, becomes a 'trinketised' version of the native way of life (Rapport and Overing, 2000, p.356), the preparation for the reception of pilgrim tourists in 2001 was in line with a national revival, ideas of regaining Christian values, of the nation's integration, and of the unification of its two halves, the motherland and the diaspora, and so on. Therefore the emphasis was on 'spiritualising' tourism rather than commercialising local culture. As a result of its 'entertainment' connotation, tourism was often substituted for the term 'pilgrimage', although the visitors, of course, were not pilgrims in the strictest sense of the word.

In the anthropology of tourism, the latter is often compared with religion (see tourism as a new form of religion, and pilgrimage as religious tourism, for example in Khristov, 2003; Clift and Clift, 1996, pp.58–9; Smith, 1992; Graburn, 1982), which is usually based on its conceptualisation as a globalised process. However, as we have already noticed, in Armenia, tourism, together with a widening of the infrastructures needed (for example roads and hotels), came through a religious event. Apart from working out itineraries for visiting monuments of Christian cult architecture, there were also plans to accommodate the pilgrim-tourists in the neighbourhoods around these monuments (the project of accommodating the pilgrim-tourists in the houses of ordinary villagers acquired the name *hogetun* – literally 'spiritual house').

In Armenia, as well as in other South Caucasian countries, many cultural monuments are located close to or within villages, so that tourists who are visiting somehow find themselves in a rural environment. The celebration of the 1700th anniversary of conversion to Christianity gave rise to the engineering of the tourist trend of CBT,[7] which became an alternative 'magic wand' within the tourism discourse (Galyan, 2003). The development of this trend is considered as allowing a more or less even distribution of the profit from tourism in local communities, as well as interesting the people in guarding and caring for the monuments of culture and nature by developing a special affordable and ecologically safe infrastructure of ethno-tourism.[8] Thus, CBT becomes an intermediary niche between the tourist industry and local hospitality: rural residents are involved in the tourist industry but do not have to change their everyday lives and turn into professional hotel staff. Correspondingly, village residents are tasked with two incompatible ideals: to not change their daily lives in order to provide an authentic experience for the tourists, and, on the other hand, to provide conditions fitting European and American living standards. And here some problems arise concerning 'what is good for the tourist' from the point of view of a rural resident and of the tourist industry. So, the traditional forms of interrelations with the others (aliens) have to be reconsidered: for example, hospitality, which in its turn influences the forming of new daily practices. Below, I will outline the situation as of 2006 through the example of two villages, which already had some experience of involvement in the tourist industry.

7 One may find this trend in the tourist literature under different names. The German organisation InWEnt prefers to appeal to a notion of the CBT which includes ecological, agrarian, rural, ethnic and cultural tourism, souvenirs, and crafts (Häusler and Strasdas, 2003, pp.10–13, see also Godde, 1998, pp.10–12). Sometimes notions of cultural and ethnographic tourism are considered synonyms (Walle, 1998, pp.126–50): 'An essential difference between "communal tourism" and "ethnographic tourism" is that in the first case the tourist product is formed in such a way that the community itself is involved in its planning and realisation and correspondingly it gets the profit from the tourist product' (Saryan, 2005, p.7).

8 CBT was declared as one of the trends in tourism development in the Caucasus and a regional forum dedicated to its problems was held in December 2005 in Tzaghkadzor (Armenia) at the level of deputy ministers of corresponding departments in Armenia and Georgia. The private sector and interested non-governmental organisations (NGOs) also participated in this forum, which was initiated by the World Bank.

Who Are the Tourists?

According to the wording of the World Tourism Organisation (WTO), tourism 'comprises the activities of persons traveling to and staying in places outside their usual environment for not more than one consecutive year for leisure, business and other purposes' (Recommendations, 1994, p.5). The necessity of defining a 'tourist' is not only about the need for a clear understanding of the phenomenon, but also important for conducting tourism statistics. A similar definition is given by the Armenian authorities. An officer in charge of tourism defined international tourists as 'foreign citizens who stay in Armenia for at least a night, but who live here for no more than for a year'.[9] As we see from these definitions, the motivation of the visitors is not so important. Even the point stating that tourists 'should not engage in commercial activity', is conditional: although in the list of tourism types one can usually find commercial or business tourism, as well as foreigners sent to Armenia on a business mission. All of these visitors are nevertheless perceived as tourists. Let us note that the English word 'to travel' is etymologically related with the French *travail* – with work and activity (Rapport and Overing, 2000, p.353). Thus, almost all the travellers crossing the boundary are classified as 'tourists'. However, in anthropology tourists are often opposed to 'travellers'. The latter are ascribed with a nobler role that allows them to be in contact with the authentic culture, to get to know it on a deeper level, while tourists have a derisive label connoted with 'inauthentic' experiences. It is considered that travellers are active, while tourists are passive, that is why the tourists are usually kept away from the real situation (Rapport and Overing, 2000, p.353). In the definitions of anthropologists, the idea of 'leisure' and 'rest' is also usually stressed, which is thought to be the main aim of tourism. Thus, Smith defines the tourist as a 'temporarily leisured person who voluntarily visits a place away from home for the purpose of experiencing a change' (1989, p.1). In the villages where I did my research, the local population had a stereotyped image of the 'alien tourist', whom one had to treat in a special way. This image was a result of their experience in communicating with tourists, travellers and foreigners who had come there with various purposes.

This experience is somewhat different in Gosh and in Tatev. In Gosh, the notion of what constitutes a tourist was mainly formed by the example of visitors to the monastery located in the centre of the village. Accordingly the tourist stream passes in full view of almost all the inhabitants (excluding those on the outskirts), and short-term visits by foreigners are in their own way integrated into local life: tourists might stay casually, ask for an overnight stay, ask for food, water, take a look at a detail of everyday life that interests them, and so on. In Tatev, the monastery complex is located four hundred metres from the village and hardly anybody goes there, according to the monastery candle vendor who is a

9 Interview with Ara Petrosyan, Vice Minister at the Ministry of Economy of the Republic of Armenia, 2003.

go-between. Notions of tourists among the natives of Tatev are associated rather with volunteers from the 'Motherland and Culture' diaspora organisation, who for several years (since 1998) were reconstructing the village Church of St Minas and repairing the village school. This church is not so popular among travel agents, since as a rule they don't bring tourists here as they confine themselves only to the famous monastery complex outside the village. Unlike the polyethnic visitors to the Gosh monastery, who stayed in the village for a short time, the 20–25 foreign volunteers of Armenian descent, who had lived regularly in Tatev, influenced village life in a special way and also influenced notions about what tourists are. To assess the situation, apart from in-depth interviews at the schools in both villages, I asked pupils to write structured essays (with some binding questions) entitled 'Tourists in Our Village' during classes, and also to complete freer take-home essays on the same topic. In Tatev, I had an enhanced opportunity to trace the dynamics of notions on tourists, since I had conducted the first such essay writing in 2001 and the second one in 2006, while in Gosh I have only the essays written in 2006.

So, for the natives of Gosh a tourist is any visitor to the Gosh monastery complex who is not a village resident. Within the already mentioned 'Transcaucasian Tourist Initiative' project, local residents were asked to conduct statistics on the tourists visiting the village without additional instructions regarding who should be considered a tourist. This task was entrusted to the market vendors, who were selling souvenirs in the neighbourhood of the monastery. Not only foreigners were listed ('counted') as tourists here, but also any non-local visitor to the monastery ranging from Yerevan residents to schoolchildren from neighbouring towns and villages, who regularly visit the monastery for excursions.

In Tatev, the tourist statistics were provided by a monastery employee who sold candles. He defined as a tourist, any person who crossed the threshold of the monastery, including residents of Tatev. However, he followed some 'restrictions'. When counting 'tourists and residents of Tatev' this 'statistician' took into account the purposes of the visit. If local people accompanied non-local tourists, they were classified as tourists, but if they came alone, for example, to light a candle or to offer a sacrifice, they were not 'counted'. The residents of other Armenian settlements (non-Tatevian), who came to the monastery to offer sacrifices, were nevertheless marked as tourists. So, for a tourist the most important characteristic is his or her 'alienness', only then is this followed by the recreational and/or cognitive purpose of the visit. It is interesting that depending on whether the tourists stayed overnight in the village or visited for a couple of hours, the Tatev 'statistician' classified them into two categories: he considered as 'tourists' those who visited the monastery without staying overnight, while for those who spent some nights there he chose the name *zbosashrjik*, the Armenian word for 'tourist', which only relatively recently became current in speech practice; in Armenian the Russian word *turist* was usually used.

Other residents of Tatev understand 'tourists' as somewhat different people. Of course, they are also those who visit the monastery, but villagers have little contact with them. Residents partly remember how during the Soviet times tourists came on big buses to observe the monastery and are sure that any foreigner should be classified as a 'tourist'. Correspondingly, the volunteers from the 'Motherland and Culture' organisation, who appeared in the village in 1998, were classed as tourists as a result of their foreigner status. Since the first group of volunteers was mainly represented by Americans, the natives formed a specific chain of associations: tourists are foreigners, foreigners are Americans, and hence tourists are Americans. During interviews one could hear: 'Yes, here came the French Americans, the German Americans, the Lebanese Americans, Iranian Americans – they were all Armenians'. Children were crying 'Americans, Americans' to tease the tourists. Local beggars (mainly children), who show up and vanish when the 'tourists' are gone (begging is not done among their own people, including local Armenian tourists), usually address them: *Amerikatsi, amerikatsi, davai money!* ('American, American [in Armenian], give [in Russian] money').

Interestingly, the culture of the post-Soviet penury/begging addressed to the aliens in the community differs between Yerevan and what happens in the other villages. While one meets old men and women begging in Yerevan much more often (Abrahamian 2001, pp.407–08), aged people in villages rarely live by begging:[10] especially, they would not beg from foreigners. However, children are forgiven for such behaviour, which is considered as children's games or an infantile inability to behave oneself. In Tatev, this was also encouraged by volunteers who often gave presents to the children – toys, markers, felt-tip pens (which were a rarity in those days in Armenia), foreign hairpins and other surprises. Soon some of the aged people especially, began to invite the volunteers into their houses hoping to gain some 'Western goods'. In connection with this, an attitude was formed to evaluate native behaviour regarding the 'tourist-Americans'; it reproached them for befriending foreigners for mercenary ends contrasting this behaviour with disinterested relations and friendship with 'tourists', and the good manners of children who don't accept from or at least don't beg the foreigners for presents. However, the appearance of 'beggar children' at the same time as the tourists is not purely a Tatev phenomenon resulting from the volunteers' temporary residence in the village. One can see a similar behaviour in Gosh, where some children from problem families who lived close to the monastery would beg tourists for money, but would never appeal to the locals and, moreover, as in Tatev, they would try to do this without being noticed by the native residents.[11] In the Armenian

10 In Tatev, some cases were reported where middle-aged drunken men (never women) begged tourists for money; they addressed them exclusively in Russian, the only foreign language they knew. However, even though drunk, they kept a vigilant watch over not being spotted at this occupation by their co-villagers.

11 In other villages, which are not visited by tourists, but which have marginally problematic families, children go begging to a neighbouring town or village They never beg in their own villages where people are ready to give them something to eat, but prefer to 'beg' from others (Shagoyan, 2007a, pp.352–59).

community, the traditional institution of mutual assistance regarded the formation of a class of beggars as inconceivable; the community usually undertook to provide its members with the minimum for living.[12] The presence of beggars is a result of the absence of communal management; this is a strictly urbanised (partly global) phenomenon, which supposes the presence of 'aliens' from whom one might beg. These aliens are presented in the person of the tourists. The irony is that usually the authorities try to isolate tourists so that beggars would not bother them (Rapport and Overing, 2000, p.355); while in our two villages beggars appear only coupled with foreigners, who brought together with 'the good things of civilisation' also its 'undesirable topics'.

'The Ones Who Gaze'

In the anthropology of tourism, usually more attention is paid to the study of tourists themselves (Graburn and Barthel-Bouchier 2001, p.147–58) and of their behaviour and of changes they undergo, rather than to their influence on local cultures. In anthropological literature, together with different types of tourists, the problem of the 'tourist gaze' is discussed in detail (Urry, 1992a, 1992b, 2002); this concept stresses first of all the idea of a superficial (only visual) perception of other cultures, without going deep into the essence and peculiarities. Although residents of our two villages also marked out the image of the 'gazing' tourists, their assessment of this 'gaze' somewhat differs from the academic interpretation. For the residents of Gosh and Tatev, tourists are indeed the people whose mission is firstly to 'see' and 'observe', which at the same time supposes 'to understand' and 'to learn' (to see in the meaning 'to understand'). And, if tourists 'don't gaze', they would be classified as 'wrong tourists', or the situation would be considered a 'wrong' one, such as would be the case if the cars heading for the monastery could not get there because of a bad road. This unfortunate circumstance was mentioned in almost all the essays of the Tatev pupils. For native residents, to observe the tourists confining themselves only to a visit to a natural monument, such as the Devil's Bridge (there is a road to this place which the owners of foreign brands of cars are not afraid to drive), and not to see the monastery, is something equivalent to sacrilege.

The tourists who 'gaze' are usually 'armed' with advanced Western ocular instruments – cameras, camcorders and spectacles. The latter served for the natives, for example, as a distinguishing mark for spotting female tourists, since the village girls avoid wearing glasses as they are considered to be evidence of

12 Seeing beggars in Yerevan is the main shock for some Armenians of the diaspora (for example, Syrian Armenians), who would never tolerate begging among Armenians. The community of the diaspora, as a rule, takes the responsibility for supporting such problem families. I would like to thank anthropologists Zaruhi Hambardzumyan and Yulia Antonyan for this observation.

a physical defect. Stories related to glasses often go back to one or other source of information. So, the elder generation is convinced that eyesight worsens as a result of too much watching of TV. Earlier it was reading that was considered to be a threat to eyesight: while the present generation speculates that in cities many young people wear glasses in contrast to the village youth because they work too much in front of computers. So, wearing glasses, on the one hand, tells of an impairment (bad eyes), which is why many parents don't encourage their daughters to wear glasses. On the other hand, this is an indication of being 'informed', of 'better knowledge'. This accessory also reveals in the 'gazing' tourists, an image of 'learning' and 'researching' tourists. No wonder that people listed among the tourists include also the ethnographers and folklorists who conducted field work there. Interestingly, in anthropological literature the discourse is on how and to what extent anthropologists and tourists differ from each other or, on the contrary, are similar (Clifford, 1997, pp.17–104; van den Abbeele, 1980, pp.2–14; Crick 1985; pp.307–44, 1995, pp.205–33; Galani-Moutafi, 2000), while from the perspective of the receiving side, the local residents, these two categories join into one to create an image of an inquisitive tourist, who is interested in information on the local monuments, nature, mode of life, folk songs, and so on. More than that, the tourists' 'contagious gaze' opens the 'inner' vision of the natives, and they start to notice what they didn't see before, what they didn't pay attention to. Many began to take an interest in the history, the ethnography and the flora and fauna of their native region, in order to be able to satisfy the curiosity of tourists – in case they asked questions. A graphic example of such an attitude was a compact disc issued by the 'Tatev Foundation', which sponsored the initiative of a Tatev native woman to create an 'informative CD' on Tatev, on which were not only items about the village, monastery, Devil Bridge, school and other institutions of the village which were more or less known and available for the villagers, but also the ethnographic descriptions of the compiler's late grandfather, some statistical data on the village based on parish books since 1914, the ethnological studies of the Institute of Archaeology and Ethnography, a photo gallery and, finally, a video showing a landscape, the monastic complex and a Tatev wedding. Thus the tourists' sightseeing determined the attempt to look at oneself from outside and make one's gaze comprehensible for aliens – the text on the CD was translated into English; this was done with the help of an American volunteer from the Peace Corps who had worked in Tatev at that time. This is a good example of how globalisation mechanisms (international organisations, digital technologies, internet, and the international market) promote the 'globalisation' process. It is the new visual-informative technologies that the village tries to use in order to get into the 'big world'. And to do so, it mainly focuses on the tourist target group.

Almost every Tatev and Gosh dweller marks out their 'own' sights which, according to his or her opinion, are deserving of the tourists' eye. Many of my interlocutors presented their 'copyright' itineraries, along which they were ready to organise a guided tour for foreigners. One such itinerary in the Tatev and another one in the Gosh environs, were registered in a special handbook on pedestrian tourism published in 2004 in Armenian and English (Bachmann and Tufenkian, 2004). It should be noted that quite a few tourists had already followed this handbook to reach on their own the villages noted there. Thus, they were able to ask local 'guides' to lead them along the marked paths, thereby avoiding the brokerage of any tourist agencies: escaping the agencies' globalisation services.

While tourists are busy sightseeing, the local population examine tourists no less intently, summarising a number of characteristics of these 'aliens' that reveal an 'average globalised citizen of the world': apart from the spectacles, it is the blue jeans, the sneakers and finally the specific nationalities' skin which 'is notable for unhealthy colour and wrinkles'.[13]

Foreigners also notice the 'gazing aborigines' and try to interpret and explain in their manner this keen look, since their etiquette does not allow long gazing openly: after a somewhat lingering glance it would invariably be followed by a smile and/or winking sometimes with the complimentary address 'hi'; these are attempts to soften the alien's 'invasion' into private space. Armenian non-verbal behaviour, which does not really presuppose[14] 'restrictions' on the duration of observing each other, became an object of a kind of self-reflection due to American etiquette, while one's own etiquette is usually a sphere of behaviour one is less aware of: the American woman noted that we look at her with a somewhat lingering glance, that our glance is very long. So, she asked us whether everything was OK with her. And, when the translator explained to her that people look at her in this manner because they like her very much, she began to thank them for receiving her so favourably. But people didn't receive her at all, they just gazed. Well, this was what the translator said: who tried to save the situation. She said that in America, nobody looks at each other; people are indifferent towards each other. 'In our country', she says, 'you can walk in whatever manner you wish, sit right on the ground, do what you want, nobody would look at you, but here, when we walk in a group along the city streets, step into a shop or just walk, everybody gazes at us' (field material, Gosh, 2006).

Thus, although the image of the 'gazing' tourist is a metaphor for superficial perception in anthropological literature, for the native populace the 'gazing ones', on the contrary, were notable for a penetrating glance that helped the natives to see themselves better and try to present themselves to the outer world in respect of this 'gaze'. More than that, the 'gazing ones' become the best instrument for spreading information about the village, a kind of advertisement: 'Yes, very many people visit us. Tourists come to take shots, to study. They praise the village, they like it, they admire the village as a rule. And it is good that they come, photograph, study, and then they demonstrate all this. Take the fact that they start to show our Tatev

13 From the materials of a focus group with high school students in Tatev, 2001.

14 A lingering glance needs to be interpreted. It presupposes certain behaviour in response (for example, a sneer, amazement, and so on). It may also need to be restricted and the gender and age characteristics of the ones gazing (for example, a young girl would not linger looking at a young strange man) may need to be taken into consideration.

on the 'Vesti' [Russia 24] programme: this happened due to them, it was them who told people about us and provoked interest' (field material, Tatev, 2006).

So, the 'shallow' gazing tourist, who became a target for many scholarly discussions, turns into an additional ocular device for the villagers, which widens not only the tourist's vision, but also the villagers' vision of themselves. To get into the tourist industry the local residents rediscover and reconsider themselves.

'The Ones Who Smile'

One of my American acquaintances measured the level of civilisation of the South Caucasian peoples according to the length of the glance directed towards her. Accordingly, the 'less gazing' ones, as more approaching European culture, were classed in a 'more civilised' category. However, while for the bearers of Western cultures gazing is considered to be a violation of private borders (with a negative assessment), the native population considers the 'American smile' an instance of such a violation (mainly with a positive assessment). This smile has been discussed in literature more than once and was named 'institutional' by Baudrillard (2006, pp.205–06), since in reality it does not express a true emotion but is an unshakeable part of a consumer society service, which tries to introduce the 'smile' into the native tourist industry as well. In contrast to the Armenian capital, where the 'smile' is introduced with more or less success, in villages the accessible 'smile' meets with some difficulties. As a matter of fact, the village residents realised their 'gloomy' nature as a result of communication with foreigners irrespective of the service purpose: 'We also have another habit: we are very gloomy. Well, Arzumanyan recently returned from America. The first day of her arrival she was standing near the school and saw me approaching, and she began to smile, so I also smiled in response. She said: "At last! You are right: one has to smile. In that damned America people smile at each other, regardless of their mood, of the level of their acquaintance. What hinders you to smile here, too? It's so nice, isn't it?" And really, I also thought it over and understood that we seldom smile. Although I don't like the American smile, it is artificial, it is feigned. The moment you pass, they would forget you immediately and when meeting you the next time they will not even remember that they had smiled at you so widely and amiably. It is just a form of theirs' (field material, Tatev, 2006).

At the same time, the 'artificiality' of the emotional display gave rise to its own mythology, the 'smile' began to be treated as a psychological weapon of American missionaries: A villager relayed to me that a missionary had said to him: 'Brother Armen, regardless of what problems we have, whether we have money or not, we always smile. Thanks to this smile, we penetrate deeper into people's psychology. And because of our smile people believe more in themselves, become more self-confident, know that we are nearby and will help them' (field material, Tatev, 2006).

Despite this awareness of the 'etiquette' nature of the smile, the latter has certain limits in the rural service destined for foreign tourists. While the woman from Tatev that had visited the US tries to introduce smiling among her colleagues, the school teachers, she absolutely does not see to it that her young daughters follow this rule, although they communicate with tourists more often than others, since their family offers the tourists a Bed and Breakfast service. More than that, the excessive courtesy of unmarried girls towards a stranger would be at variance with the native norms of etiquette and would look like a demonstration of 'accessibility' in the eyes of the others. It was in this way that the natives saw the smiles of female volunteers and denounced their 'liberty of behaviour' as inadmissible. During fieldwork I witnessed the accentuated restraint that girls showed when meeting foreigners for the first time. It was even a slight disregard, which gave way to smiling and affability after some communication and closer relations, when a 'foreigner' had already passed from the category of 'stranger' into the category of 'guest and friend'. So, it was not the institutional demonstration of the '*sign* of human affection' (Baudrillard, 2006, p.205) but the warmth of friendship and/or hospitality. It has to be said that not all the foreigners were honoured with such treatment from the girls, whose families offered tourists lodging for the night, but only those who succeeded in traversing the borderline between 'lodger' and 'guest'. One might think that it is only members of the families that offer lodging for the night who make this invisible differentiation between 'lodgers' and 'guests', and one may guess that an indicator for such a division could be the hosts' smile rather than the lodgers' payment.

'Have Gone through the Experience'

The 'perfunctorily gazing' tourists are opposed to another type of travellers, who go through a relatively deep experience of familiarising themselves with a new culture by participating in one or other activity (Perkins and Thorns, 2001, pp.185–204). However, any passage, even the most passive journey, has an influence on the traveller in one way or another and enriches his or her life experience. It is no mere chance that Arnold van Gennep treats the experience of travellers in the context of a 'rite de passage', considering the tourists, merchants and pilgrims, who leave their homes and move away from the familiar milieu, as being able to be approximated to the initiates who find themselves in a liminal situation, when many norms of everyday life cease to function (1999, pp.29–42) and, following Victor Turner's terminology, one can say that a person passes into a condition of anti-structure, returning afterwards to their familiar world after an experience of renewal (Turner, 1969).[15]

15 On considering the tourist in the context of passing from structure to anti-structure, see also (Graburn, 1983; Rapport and Overing, 2000, pp.358–59).

Foreign volunteers, who for one reason or another find themselves in Tatev and Gosh, indeed have different experiences of being involved in native culture, as well as of having different levels of influence on the life of the local communes. Among the visitors, the volunteers from the organisation 'Motherland and Culture' attained the richest experience and probably had the most influence on native life, and not only because they first came to the village as early as 1998, which was still before the beginning of the tourist boom in 2001. In contrast to the ordinary tourists, who travel in search of attaining an experience of something differing from their own culture, the volunteers from the Armenian diaspora, together with performing purely organisational tasks, also had a personal aim – to 'find themselves', to assert their Armenian identity. This, by the way, also partly concerns the tourists (not only volunteers) from the Armenian diaspora.[16]

Volunteer-foreigners (of non-Armenian origin) from the 'Peace Corps' lived both in Tatev and Gosh. Their involvement in native culture usually took place within the framework of this organisation's mission, though in some cases they continued to correspond with the natives after returning home. As for the tourists, who stayed in the village for one or two days, their involvement in the life of the native commune took place at their own initiative. For example, a couple from France decided to participate in construction work on a village bridge. Being inspired by the extraordinary atmosphere of a 'labour festival', a tourist decided to make a proposal to his girlfriend and present her with a wedding ring during a conjoined supper with their Armenian hosts who commented thusly on the event: 'We stayed there for a long time and came back home very late. Mother made *tolma* [stuffed cabbage]. There were also some other people in our place; they prepared roasted meat. As is the custom among Armenians, we sat at the table; had wine and dinner together. Well, as is the custom, in Armenian manner, if guests come for a visit, how would you entertain them? We sat around the table, and then he said: "I want to do one thing. I like Armenia so much, especially your family …. One usually does such things in one's own family. It has already been five years that we are together. I want to present her with a wedding ring". And he took out the ring and presented it to her. This girl was so happy, she just shined. I also congratulated them: presented them with some souvenirs – two doves. They were very glad. Later we corresponded for a long time. I don't know whether they got married or not. In any case, the engagement took place in our house. Dad said: "I am your *kavor* [wedding sponsor]"' (field material, Gosh, 2006). Such topics lose their episodic nature, if we consider them in the context of liminal behaviour,

16 The Armenian tourists from the diaspora differ in showing more interest in history and cultural details. Thus, according to the candle vendor in the Tatev monastery, who often plays the role of a guide, they always ask many questions so that his narrative always differs from the one for the tourists of non-Armenian origin who listen to him in a less interested manner and ask the guide to cut his explanations to the minimum (field material, Tatev, 2006).

when one is allowed to do out of the ordinary things, for example, behave like a child, wear clothes of another rank, and so on.

They told us an example of 'liminal impersonality' in Gosh: the natives didn't recognise the Minister of Justice under the tourist 'uniform' (glasses, baseball cap, sneakers and rucksack). He modestly asked the natives to provide him with a guide to get to a lake not far from the village. The enigmatic friendship of the tourists with children becomes quite natural, if we take into account that the behaviour of a tourist is specified by a kind of childishness and frolicking, by an inversion between adults and children, which is characteristic of any 'festival'. In the observed villages, kids really were the first to get into communication with foreigners, so that they became mediators between the tourists and local adults. And the reason is not only the fact that at the peak of farming work, which coincides with the peak of the tourist season, the adults have no time to enjoy the festive company of the guests. Kids are no less involved in these works, but their schedule is freer and less rigid correlating with the 'anti-structural' improvisations of the tourists. Friendship with children added one more local generalisation to the image of the tourist. It was based on the native experience of communication: tourists like and respect children; they treat them more seriously, as equals. This friendship also gradually involves the native adults in the 'festival', which very often develops into a conjoined feast: 'It was my son, who befriended them [the volunteers] and invited them to visit our house for the first time. In general, a tradition was formed in the village to entertain the volunteers in natives' houses. Their work ended by five o'clock; then surely they would be invited to visit someone's house. Villagers usually entertained them with sweets and coffee, but we managed to invite them at dinner time and served a good spread. I made *tolma*, prepared salads. We had a very good time that day. There were two people among them who couldn't dance Armenian dances; we taught them, and they were very grateful. We also invited our neighbours, and they (the volunteers) were sitting with our family members too and were behaving like relatives' (field material, Tatev, 2001).

Villagers began to time the 'festive' elements of everyday life in Tatev with the visits of tourists. For example, the discotheques were organised solely during summertime, when there were both foreign tourists and summer residents in the village; the villagers, according to our informants, seldom go to disco clubs.

Creating 'events' and 'performances' where tourists could be involved became the task of the groups that organise the leisure time of tourists within the framework of the above mentioned 'Transcaucasian Tourist Initiative' project. Both in Gosh and Tatev they began to search for festivals in order to involve tourists, and attempted to reconstruct (following written descriptions) some traditional festivals (for example, the Meeting of the Lord, or *Trndez* in a popular version). In Tatev, the situation became even more complicated because the villages of the Syunik region (Tatev is one of them) are known for their 'atheism' and, in contrast to the northern and western regions of Armenia, almost all the traditional festivals had been eliminated here during the years of Soviet rule. However, the organisation of the non-existent festivals became at best the staging of performances at schools in the morning which did not reach the tourists. It seems that the artificial reproduction of a festival inevitably divides it into performers and spectators, which is convenient for any scenic performance but contradicts the spirit of a festival, in which everybody should be a participant (Abramian, 1983, pp.14–20).

The 'living' festivals that coincide with the tourist season, being a part of a family and not communal rites (see the *Vardavar* festival, which is traditionally observed in Gosh), also did not find a mechanism for involving tourists. This failed to happen, since in this case a commercialisation would have been needed – something inadmissible from the point of view of traditional culture.

The foreign volunteers also made attempts to involve people in their own festive world. Thus, in Gosh, they organised a kind of a picnic for the native residents on the occasion of the fourth of July, Independence Day, with a journey to a famous monastery in the neighbouring village of Haghartzin. This 'festive experience' gave the natives little knowledge of the ritual practice of the foreigners, for whom a festival (apart from a wedding) often boils down to a picnic, which in Armenian culture is a form of everyday, rather than festive, rest.

There was little involvement of the adult population of the above-mentioned villages in the world of volunteer-tourists. There were serious reasons for this. As we have already mentioned, the 'festive everyday' of the tourist coincided with the natives' 'labour everyday' and, despite the promised golden mountains that tourism seemed to bring them, the local population, realising that the profit from this business is actually small, took it as just an additional, side-line source of profit, a kind of not so serious activity. For the natives, tourism could provide only a little extra help for developing agriculture: at best a market where they could sell their agricultural surplus. As a matter of fact, even the retail trade near the monastery turned out to be the business of a select few, since it distracted from the habitual agricultural rhythm. Usually, villagers sold the harvest grown by themselves directly from their yards to wholesalers who came to the village to buy up the merchandise; or, they took the harvest to town and delivered it to the local dealers. Therefore, the search for a market is beyond the habitual model of behaviour of the main population of the village. As for the little surplus of agricultural goods, they are often delivered among the relatives who live in the city. That is, the extended social network comes out, in this case, as a serious competitor of commercial relations.

In Tatev, despite the attractive statistics on the flow of tourists (on average 20,000 people per year), a permament market near the monastery had still not been established. In Gosh, the market, which functioned in the beginning as a souvenir shop, later expanded into a number of competing clans of local traders. However, in general the native population was involved in this process to a lesser extent than the organisers of the vendor shop supposed. Villagers nevertheless, are united about the priority of agriculture in the development of the village: 'If tourism developed in the village at the expense of agriculture, the village would be lost. Tourism could only be a secondary business as an additional source of profit, not the main one' (field material, Tatev, 2001). Such an attitude is one more reason that communication with tourists falls rather into the sphere of a childish 'unserious' pastime. In addition to the unserious nature of the rural tourist industry, I think, it is regarded mainly as 'women's service'[17] – to cook, to keep the place clean. In such cases men feel somewhat offended, since their participation in this family business falls to entertaining the guest. But to 'entertain the guest' in one's home is only possible if one plays the role of the host (it is difficult to find some other application), which is practically impossible, if 'the host' is being paid for his hospitality. It was no wonder that it was the families that had no men of middle age (who are considered to carry the burden of providing the family with the main source of subsistence) that were involved in family tourist services in the village. The 'serious' tourist industry, or rather the business of professional firms, is mainly concentrated in Yerevan and is involved in the global world of commerce which is alien to the village.

In Tatev, the image of the tourist was later modelled according to the experience of communicating with the volunteers engaged in construction work; hence 'diligence' became one of the widespread characteristics of travellers. The Gosh schoolchildren, on the other hand, formed another image of the tourist that which was based on the activism and work of the members of the Yerevan youth ecological organisation 'Burg' ('Pyramid' in Armenian). These activists were equated with tourists; tourists are defenders of nature. The local schoolchildren learned these ideas and 'ecological behaviour' from them (field material, Gosh, 2006).

Thus communication between tourists and natives brought 'acculturation' on both sides. Actually, one could divide the foreigners perceived by the natives as tourists (in fact, they were not only tourists, but also volunteers, summer residents or specialists travelling on business) into the ones who 'gaze', and the ones who 'experience' it depending on whether they lived in the village or not. The natives, irrespective of their 'gazing' or 'communicating', adopted the new experience more eagerly, partly because they tried to get to know the tourists in order to use their financial resources (Cohen 1979, pp.197–202; Watson and Kopachevsky, 1994, pp.643–60), and partly because the 'tourists' were for them the bearers of the advanced, of the Western (and hence globalist) society.

Cultural differences in norms of etiquette (for example, Armenians would never blow their noses at the table); in fashion (for example, wearing shorts); in notions about pure and dirty; in male and female behaviour, however, gave rise to a certain intolerance towards the foreign among the natives, making the 'traditional national culture' more attractive for them. At the same time, it could be said that acquaintance with globalisation introduced by tourism gave rise to a kind of anti-globalism.

17 See the official estimation of the gender and age composition of the labour market of the tourist industry: 'In general women and young people are engaged in the sphere of tourism, since they are more subject to social changes' (Tourism, 2007).

Conclusion

Observing the life of the two Armenian communities for a period of several years, when tourist projects initiated by international organisations were being realised – these organisations trying to introduce the tourist industry into the local situation – one can say that such projects in general face the same problems as commercial tourism, though on a lower scale. In fact, we are not only dealing with an inclusion of tourism into a rural life context without commercial mechanisms being worked out (the low motivation and involvement of the rural residents in such a form of tourism is good evidence of this) but also with a transformation of the life of the families involved, into a kind of an 'authentic sham'. In contrast with the expectations of the tourist projects oriented towards CBT, the new category of the 'semi-friend', who would pay and befriend, never became a reality. In the process of communication between the tourists and local residents their relations line up in two directions: in the case that the tourist becomes a friend, he/she stops being 'commercial client' and moves into the group of 'our tourists' (who are the best friends of the children, ecologists and so on, in other words, they are notable and desired guests) with all the consequences (one can smile at them, discuss with them how to represent themselves to the world, celebrate family and community festivals, entertain them as guests, and so on). While in the case where relations stay formal and/or dissociated, the 'alien tourist' (who looks differently, speaks incomprehensibly, doesn't try to get into contact, doesn't follow local rules of hygiene and behaviour, dresses in the wrong way, smiles 'artificially', blows his/her nose in the wrong place, and so on) is perceived in general as a financial source and unintentionally gives birth to the plots characterised by commercialised urban practices. Thus, one may speak of multiplicity in the local perception of 'tourists': the image and principal characteristics of whom, in general, are based on personal experience and are only slightly influenced by official and/or commercial professional discourse.

References

Abrahamian, L., 2001. ' … Hiravi, bolor dzhbakhtut'yunneri skzbnaghbyurn aghk'atut'yunn' [' … Indeed, all Misfortunes are a Result of Poverty']. In: H. Kharatyan, ed., *Patmut'yunner aghk'atut'yan masin* [Stories about Poverty]. Yerevan: Zangak-97, pp.407–08.

Abramian, L., 1983. *Pervobytnyi prazdnik i mifologiia* [Primitive Festival and Mythology]. Yerevan: Izd. AN Arm. SSR.

Bachmann, C. and Tufenkian, J., 2004. *Adventure Armenia: Hiking and Rock Climbing*. Yerevan: Kanach Foundation.

Baudrillard, J., 2006. *Obshchestvo potrebleniia: Ego mify i struktury* [*Consumer Society: Myths and Structures*]. Moscow: Respublika, Kul'turnaia revoliutsiia.

Clifford, J., 1997. *Routes: Travel and Translation in the Late Twentieth Century.* Cambridge and London: Harvard University Press.

Clift, J. D. and Clift, W. B., 1996. *The Archetype of Pilgrimage: Outer Action with Inner Meaning.* New York: Paulist Press.

Cohen, E., 1979. A Phenomenology of Tourist Experiences. *Sociology* 13, pp.197–202.

Crick, M., 1985. 'Tracing' the Anthropological Self: Quizzical Reflections on Fieldwork, Tourism and the Ludic. *Social Analysis* 17, pp.307–44.

Crick, M., 1995. The Anthropologist as Tourist: An Identity in Question. In: M. Lanfant, J. Allcock, J. and E. Bruner, eds, *International Tourism: Identity and Change.* London: Sage, pp.205–33.

Galani-Moutafi, V., 2000. The Self and the Other: Traveller, Ethnographer, Tourist. *Annals of Tourism Research* 27(1), pp.203–24.

Galyan, Z. ed., 2003. *Turizm v gornykh regionakh: Vliianie na prirodnoe i kul'turnoe raznoobrazie* [*Tourism in Mountainous Regions: The Influence on Natural and Cultural Diversity*]. Yerevan: Lusakn.

Godde, P. ed., 1998. Community-based Mountain Tourism: Practices for Linking Conservation with Enterprise. Available at <http://www.mtnforum.org/content/community-based-mountain-tourism-practices-linking-conservation-enterprise-0> [Accessed on 28 February 2014].

Graburn, N. H. H., 1982. Tourism: The Sacred Journey. In: V. L. Smith, ed., 1989. *Hosts and Guests: The Anthropology of Tourism.* Philadelphia: University of Pennsylvania Press, pp.21–36.

Graburn, N. H. H., 1983. *To Pray, Pay and Play: The Cultural Structure of Japanese Domestic Tourism.* Aix-en-Provence: Centre des Hautes Études Touristiques.

Graburn, N. H. H. and Barthel-Bouchier, D., 2001. Relocating the Tourist. *International Sociology* 16(2), pp.147–58.

Greenwood, D., 1989. Culture by the Pound: An Anthropological Perspective on Tourism as Cultural Commoditization. In: V. L. Smith, ed., *Hosts and Guests: The Anthropology of Tourism.* Philadelphia: University of Pennsylvania Press, pp. 171–85.

Harrison, D., ed., 1992. Tourism and Less Developed Countries. London: Belhaven.

Häusler, N. and Strasdas, W., 2003. Training Manual for Community-based Tourism. Zschortau: InWEnt

Jafari, J. 2000. Fenomenologiia. V: Teoriia i praktika fizicheskoi kul'tury [Phenomenology of Tourism. In: Theory and Practice of Physical Culture]. Available at <http://lib.sportedu.ru/Press/tpfk/2000N8/p23–26.htm> [Accessed on 28.02.2014].

Khaindrava, I. and Iskandaryan, A., eds, 2005. *Diaspora, neft' i rozy: Chem zhivut strany Iuzhnogo Kavkaza?* [*Diaspora, Oil and Roses: What Makes the Countries of the South Caucasus Tick?*] Yerevan: Heinrich Böll Stiftung and Caucasus Media Institute.

Khristov, T. T., 2003. *Religioznyi turizm* [*Religious Tourism*]. Moscow: Academiia.

Llewellyn Watson, G. and Kopachevsky, J. P., 1994. Interpretations of Tourism as Commodity. *Annals of Tourism Research* 21(3), pp.643–60.

MacCannell, D., 1989. The Tourist: A New Theory of the Leisure Class. New York: Schoken.

McCabe, S., 2005. 'Who Is a Tourist?' A Critical Review. *Tourist Studies* 5(1), 85–106.

Nash, D. 1989. Tourism as a Form of Imperialism. In: Valene L. Smith, ed., *Hosts and Guests: The Anthropology of Tourism*. Philadelphia: University of Pennsylvania Press, pp. 37–52.

Perkins, H. C. and Thorns, D. C., 2001. Gazing or Performing? Reflections on Urry's Tourist Gaze in the Context of Contemporary Experience in the Antipodes. *International Sociology* 16(2), pp.185–204.

Rapport, N. and Overing, J., 2000. *Social and Cultural Anthropology: The Key Concepts*. London and New York: Routledge.

Recommendations on Tourism Statistics. 1994. Statistical Papers Series, M, No. 83. United Nations Department for Economic and Social Information and Policy Analysis Statistical Division and World Tourism Organization. Available at <http://unstats.un.org/unsd/publication/Seriesm/SeriesM_83e.pdf> [Accessed on 28 February 2014].

Saryan, M. A., 2005. Etno- ili obshchinnyi turizm v Armenii: problemy i perspektivy [Ethno- or Community-based Tourism in Armenia: Problems and Perspectives] [BA thesis]. Rossiisko-Armianskii (Slavianskii) gosudarstvennyi universitet. Fakul'tet sotsial'no-kul'turnogo servisa i turizma. Yerevan.

Shagoyan, G., 2007a. Hmi chunenaluts ed aghjike shat e charatsel [Because of Poverty This Girl Has Been Embittered]. In: H. Kharatyan and H. Marutyan, eds, *Patmut'yunner aghk'atut'yan masin* [*Stories about Poverty*], vol. 2. Yerevan: Hazarashen, pp.332–59.

Shagoyan, G., 2007b. Leninakan ushel, Gyumri ostalsia (obrazy goroda do i posle zemletriaseniia) [Leninakan Has Gone, Gyumri Has Stayed (Images of the City Before and After the Earthquake)]. Available at <www.levonabrahamian.com> [Accessed on 1 November 2012].

Smith, V. L., ed., 1989. *Hosts and Guests: The Anthropology of Tourism*. Philadelphia: University of Pennsylvania Press.

Smith, V. L., 1989. Introduction. In: V. L. Smith, ed., *Hosts and Guests: The Anthropology of Tourism*. Philadelphia: University of Pennsylvania Press, pp.1–17.

Smith, V. L., 1992. Pilgrimage and Tourism: The Quest in Guest. *Annals of Tourism* 19, 1–17.

Tourism, 2003. Ministry of Trade and Economic Development of the Republic of Armenia. Available at <www.minted.am/en> [Accessed on 14 March 2007].

Tourism 2007. The Ministry of Trade and Economic Development of the Republic of Armenia. Available at <www.minted.am/ru/20> [Accessed on 14 March 2007].

Turner, V., 1969. The Ritual Process: Structure and Anti-structure. Chicago: Aldine.

Urry, J., 1992a. The Tourist Gaze 'Revisited'. *American Behavioral Scientist* 36, pp.172–86.

Urry, J., 1992b. The Tourist Gaze and the 'Environment'. *Theory, Culture and Society* 9, pp.1–26.

Urry, J., 2002. *The Tourist Gaze*. London: Sage.

Van den Abbeele, G., 1980. Sightseers: The Tourist as Theorist. *Diacritics* 10, pp. 2–14.

Van Gennep, A., 1999. Obriady perekhoda [Rites of Passage]. Moscow: Vostochnaia literatura.

Walle, A. H., 1998. *Cultural Tourism: A Strategic Focus*. Boulder: Westview Press.

Chapter 15
Corruption as Institution and Habitus: Georgia under Eduard Shevardnadze as Seen from the Perspective of Pierre Bourdieu's Theory of Practice

Barbara Christophe

In the last twenty years, those of us who are interested in political and social developments in post-Soviet space could not but end up frustrated in some kind of way. Whenever we opened a book, we learned a lot about deficiencies. We read about democracies with adjectives (see Collier and Levitsky, 1997), about 'failed states' and distorted variants of capitalism. When it comes to the South Caucasus, the picture gets even bleaker. A mere ten years ago, Georgia especially, was nearly without exception perceived as the mother of all miscarriages, as the epitome of a totally failed transition. With unsettled ethnic conflicts and corruption blossoming beyond all reason, it seemed that even embryonic forms of effective statehood, the simplest of preconditions for developing along the lines of an unrivalled Western model of societal organisation had not emerged. At the end of the day, we knew for sure, what was missing there but we had hardly any clear notion about what made these societies and those power structures that did exist function, despite all the cited defaults. None of the post-Soviet societies have slid into open anarchy and most post-Soviet regimes have displayed a remarkable capacity for stable reproduction, but we lack a theoretical language to describe the mechanisms that could account for this apparent miracle.

In the following, I will attempt to reverse the fatalist but dominant trend in post-Soviet studies to focus exclusively on defects. Taking Georgia as an example, I will try to offer an insight into the logic behind what appears to be a new but nevertheless surprisingly effective mode of exercising power. In doing so, I will refer to ethnographic data gathered during the fieldwork conducted in Georgia between 1998 and 2002 (Christophe, 2006). The immediate scope of my empirical and theoretical findings is thus restricted to the Georgia of Eduard Shevardnadze. But I am quite confident that at least some of my conclusions can be easily applied to other Post-Soviet societies as well.[1] And, recent developments in the new

1 Though formulated in a different theoretical language, Keith Darden's findings on the Ukraine do conform quite well to my analysis of Georgia (2001).

Georgia that is said to have emerged after the so-called 'Rose Revolution' (2003) that toppled the Shevardnadze regime in the midst of what began as public protests against election fraud (Miller, 2004) seem to cast serious doubts on the commonly held opinion, that the country is now on its way towards embracing Western standards of governance. The selective and politically motivated mobilisation of corruption charges against potential rivals to President Mikheil Saakashvili's (2004–2013) claim to power may thus also turn out to prove the validity of the following analysis, which is based on a two-fold agenda.

In a first step, I will scrutinise the discourse in scholarship on corruption, using empirical evidence from Georgia under Eduard Shevardnadze as a critical test for the plausibility of mainstream approaches. I will develop the hypothesis that the debate has actually been dominated by a hidden but questionable consensus. Notwithstanding rival views on its root causes, nearly all authors seem to subscribe to the assumption that corruption serves as an indicator of state weakness by institutional failure. I object to this line of reasoning on the basis of two interrelated findings. First, I will argue that at least the generalised corruption to be found in the Georgia of Eduard Shevardnadze must be construed as a complex institution[2] in its own right. Secondly, I will demonstrate that this institution, rather than having undermined existing power structures, actually contributed to their stabilisation.

In the next step I will tackle the question of what a system of rule, mainly based on the skilful manipulation of corruption, tells us about how power is transformed into domination. As almost all theoretical accounts of this process focus on the successful steering of the perceptions of the ruled as the one and only precondition for this miracle to happen, I will look into the interplay between institutional structures and cognitive standards in Georgia. Referring to Pierre Bourdieu's concept of 'habitus' (Bourdieu, 1979; Reckwitz, 2003), I will argue that the proper functioning of the institution of corruption is indeed dependent on the effective moulding of the subjectivity of social actors. But, I will also show that the casual link between objective structures and subjective perceptions is much more complex than a culturalist notion of traditional values as the legitimation formula of corruption suggests.

Corruption as Institution

Summing up the main lines of arguments in the debate on the root causes of corruption, we can distinguish, roughly speaking, between two competing models of explanation, referring either to institutional defects (see for an overview,

2 Obviously, this hypothesis is based on a rather broad understanding of the concept of institutions, which according to the by now famous definition provided by Douglass North (1990, p.7) can be conceptualised as 'a set of formal rules – and informal conventions – that provide the framework for human interaction and shape the incentives of members of society'.

Goudie and Stasavage, 1998; Collier, 2002) or a lack of legitimacy as the key factors. Both of them construct corruption as a compliance problem, as the result of deviance from officially recognised rules. Differences mainly pertain to the underlying reasons identified as being behind institutional failure. Although I will hardly describe anything new or exciting, I will nevertheless cast a closer look at the implications to be drawn from these assumptions – just for the sake of defining the background against which I will direct my empirical findings.

From the perspective of a public choice approach, rule infraction appears to be a rational strategy of action, always pursued by individuals when two conditions are met. Firstly, the institutional incentives for the breaching of rules must be high. This simply means that the costs for compliance with rules are artificially inflated by the too numerous and complicated legal restrictions. Secondly, due to weak capacities for monitoring, the probability of being punished for rule infraction must be perceived to be extremely low (see for example Easter, 2003). This assumption is clearly informed by the notion of the principal–agent–problem, which is regarded as the Achilles's heel of all organisations construed as chains of hierarchical relations between superiors in the role of principals and subordinates in the role of agents (see Solnick, 1996). As I will show in detail below, this line of reasoning clearly rests on less than plausible beliefs. On the one hand, it is taken for granted that the subordinate always has a winning lead over his superior in terms of disposing over relevant information. He is automatically suspected of utilising this advantage by concealing his behaviour, which by nature seems to tend towards opportunism. On the other hand, the principal is beyond doubt. He identifies himself one hundred percent with the official rules as defined by the organisation he serves. If he nevertheless fails to implement these rules, this must be due to being duped by his cunning agents, who take advantage of the principal's weakness in monitoring them. It goes without saying that these assumptions are sometimes far removed from the real picture.

Some of these false assumptions are avoided by a culturalist mode of explanation (for example LaPalombara, 1994; Olivier de Sardan, 1999). Here we are faced with an alternative notion of corruption, which is not necessarily equated with rule infraction but, rather, conceptualised as the product of fierce competition between two rival sets of rules, each of them endowed with diverging claims to validity. The erosion of rules embodied in formal institutions by norms of reciprocity incorporated into informal institutions is emphasised, the latter, being, moreover, said to rely on the superior potential of legitimation inherent to cultural traditions (Waldmann, 2002). Though corruption thus again turns out to be a rough challenge to the state's autonomous capacity of rule setting, this situation is considered to be affected less by an institutionally unconstrained opportunism. It is, rather, conceived of as being the ultimate consequence of the higher obligatory power of alternative mechanisms of social integration. According to this line of reasoning, these mechanisms owe their success in generating loyalty and compliance to their being anchored in traditional norms. As we can easily see, this model also gravitates towards the notion of a weak state. But, in contrast to the public choice model, state weakness is thought of as resulting from a conflict between two competing social logics instead of emerging in reaction to institutional defects. In this conflict, the universal norms of bureaucratic rationality succumb to the particularistic norms of tangible social networks of allegiance. To come to the crucial point, the social actor typically involved in corrupt transactions is here not the selfish free rider anxious to press home an advantage but the over-socialised individual deeply enmeshed in dense networks of social obligations.

Having reconstructed the inner logic and the implicit assumptions of mainstream approaches towards explaining the causes of corruption, I will now try to uncover some of their blind spots on the basis of an ethnographic case study on the practice of corruption in the Georgia of Eduard Shevardnadze.

The first episode to be scrutinised brings us to the Red Bridge (*tsiteli khidi*) at the border between Georgia and Azerbaijan.[3] Throughout the 1990s, the lion's share of smuggling with gasoline was conducted across this border. The first irritation one comes across concerns the geographical location of the customs facilities, which were at that time situated behind a crossing from which point several roads led into the interior of the country. Several years ago this more than obvious flaw was reported to the customs authorities by the inspector in charge of the checkpoint – with fatal consequences for his career prospects. Instead of being rewarded for his initiative, he was immediately dismissed. His successor was subsequently compelled to pay such high bribes to the customs department in order to get this appointment that he could not help but take part in the corruption – simply for the sake of getting a return on his investment.

What we actually learn from this quite mundane story is that in fact, none of the actors involved lived up to the expectations raised in the models discussed above. The roles attributed to the actors by the public choice approach are even turned upside down. The first act of the drama presents us a principal in the shape of the head of the customs department who could not care less about pushing through organisational goals. Quite the opposite – he decided to impose sanctions on an agent for taking too literally the norms of bureaucratic rationality. The second act comes as an assault against the certainties nourished by both the public choice paradigm and the culturalist model. The type of corruption we have encountered so far is hardly explainable in terms of deviation from officially endorsed standards of behaviour. It, rather, turns out to be a carefully designed sleight of hand, a *coup de main*, creatively performed by an authority that proves to be highly efficient. The extortion of bribes from subordinate officials, who do not only have to purchase their position but have to pass a crucial share of their incomes in bribes on to their superiors in hierarchical chains of looting, is an irresistible incentive structure that guarantees the stable reproduction of corruption-prone agents. But, neither does corruption follow from adherence to traditional norms and values, as expected by culturalists. It is, rather, consciously encouraged by mechanisms built into formal hierarchies.

3 The reconstruction of the following affair is based on Stier, 2002.

As challenging as these findings are to rehearsing patterns of thinking, they raise new problems as well. To begin with, we still have to unravel the mystery of how one can possibly create a sustainable demand for corruption. The next and even more pressing question concerns the mechanisms of control that have to be installed in order to assure for a minimum of discipline on behalf of the agents encouraged to take part in such corruption games.

Part of the solution can be found in a second narrative, which takes us to those engaged in the smuggling of flour in the Georgia of Eduard Shevardnadze. Since customs duties as well as value added tax was regularly incorporated into consumer prices for smuggled flour – notwithstanding the fact that the payment of both was evaded – this business once promised considerable profit. Despite the simplicity of the mathematical calculations behind these deals, the phenomenon nevertheless demands explanation. After all, one might have expected competition between rival bands of smugglers to contribute to a decrease in prices. But, this is what actually never seemed to have happened in Georgia. Obviously, a careful selection of those entitled to profit from smuggling effectively limited competition in prices to a minimum. And indeed, as my own field research has shown, the beneficiaries of the informal flour business were almost exclusively recruited from the Ministry of the Interior. Of course, the privileged position of the police alone does not sound suspicious at all. As in all illegal deals, they benefited from their dual capacity as perpetrator and prosecutor. But still, in Georgia it was the stability of the monopoly secured by members of the state administration on illegal markets that indeed deserves some attention. This is a striking peculiarity which clearly distinguishes the Georgian situation from, for instance, the much more heterogeneous Russian scenarios. It is to be explained as the result of a tremendously effective channelling of opportunities.

A closer look at the ways in which the smuggling of flour was regulated, reveals some of the mechanisms applied to that end. The first thing one comes across is the observation that the smuggler's clients, the hundreds and thousands of bakeries, were effectively tied to a circle of hand-picked suppliers by the formal instrument of the tax law. To have his expenditures on flour deduced from his payments of value added tax, the ordinary owner of a bakery needed to be able to produce a document signed by the seller during the act of purchase, the so-called *faktura*, which was then disbursed by the respective tax inspection. What looks like a safeguard against tax evasion at first glance turned out to be a clever instrument for steering the distribution of opportunities to take part in cheating. Notwithstanding the numerous rules governing the issuing, circulation and registration of these documents, the *faktura* were, actually, a kind of trophy, desperately sought-after by many, but accessible only to those few, who were embedded in the networks of power. Thus, it was a formally institutionalised incentive structure that directed purchasers' interests towards dealing with suppliers able to mobilise informal networks in order to get access to official tax formulas. Keeping short the supply with these documents, the apparatus of rule could easily control those who were eligible to seize the economic opportunities of smuggling. This construction was, moreover, quite efficient in imposing discipline on smugglers. As their access to the formulas of *faktura* was always kept precarious by bureaucratic rules growing more complicated with each day, the purchasers were strongly advised to invest heavily in securing the goodwill of their patrons in the tax inspections.

But even these inspectors were exposed to a certain risk. Due to a careful registration of *faktura* formulas, the deals could always be reconstructed if necessary. As a rule, they were issued in four executed copies, two of which were to remain with the purchaser and the seller respectively, the other two being returned to the tax inspections. Again, despite official statements to the contrary, these bureaucratic procedures were hardly designed to stall illegal transactions. Instead, they aimed at the accumulation of compromising knowledge that could be utilised for the purpose of exercising pressure at any time. Every agent that fell into disgrace in the eyes of his principal could easily be brought to his knees by criminalising the same behaviour that had been tolerated previously. As a result, everybody save for those sitting at the very top of the whole system were literally acting under the sword of Damocles. For the sake of insuring oneself against the risk of being exposed to punishment, everybody tried to please his superior as best as he could. In the end the interplay between the creation of uncertainty from above and the strategies of risk management from below created a kind of centripetal force that assured the coherence of the apparatus of rule.

This case is exemplary for the systemic nature of the mechanisms of corruption in Shevardnadze's Georgia. In many branches of the bureaucracy, officials were lured into situations that turned each possible option for action into a certain risk. As a rule this was achieved by the imposition of contradictory obligations.

Let me cite one more telling example. In 2000 a revision of the tax code had increased the minimum turnover rate for the payment of value added tax from 3,000 Georgian lari (GEL) to 24,000 GEL. In reaction to this legal change, the number of registered tax payers fell rapidly. In the western Georgian town of Kutaisi for example, this number dropped from 3,000 to 168. At the same time, the parameters of the tax plan that defined in detail how much money each tax inspector has to raise for certain taxes, was not adapted to the new circumstances. In the end, the staff of the tax inspections found themselves in a highly precarious situation. On the one hand, the obligation to fulfil the requirements of the plan weighed heavily on them. Failure was sanctioned by immediate dismissal. On the other hand, this obligation could only be met by redeploying returns from other types of taxes. But, according to an unwritten rule any insider could memorise by heart, a tax inspector could redeploy only a ten percent increase in plan requirements on his own. Everything that went beyond that margin had to be approved by the authorities. In the end, the interplay between all these instructions which clearly contradicted one another and thus made compliance utterly impossible, could not but create a strong compulsion towards rule infraction. At the same time, everyone caught in violation of the regulations stood a good chance of losing his job. In the end the ordinary tax inspector could not make any move without increasing his vulnerability.

Drawing a preliminary conclusion of my first argument, I would like to sum up my findings in three points: firstly, corruption in Eduard Shevardnadze's Georgia did not equal institution failure. Corruption needs, rather, to be grasped as a highly efficient institution in itself. The ultimate function and achievement of this peculiar institution consisted in generating insecurity. The definition of rules, which could not possibly all be adhered to, created a sustainable demand for corruption and rule infraction.

Secondly, corruption in Georgia did not prove the weakness of the state. The strength of the institution rested in the ability to sanction any rule infraction that was not explicitly approved from above – be it in exchange for bribes or loyalty. By carefully steering the selection of those entitled to invest in the purchase of a certain degree of security, the state assured its control over the chosen few capable of acting. It goes without saying that the maintenance of this steering capability required a certain ability to impose sanctions. In other words, it was dependent on the existence of an apparatus of rule coherent enough to function as a deterrent. As we know from the sociology of organisation, efficiency always presupposes the enforcement of hierarchical chains of command. In the Georgian context this was achieved by the application of two simple principles. On the one hand, compliance on behalf of the agents was reliably produced by the simple fact of their compulsory integration into the institution of corruption. If they wanted to benefit from corruption – and we have seen that they actually had no choice – they would sooner or later realise their dependence on the intermediate inputs of their principals. All the examples mentioned so far have demonstrated again that it was only the definition of contradictory rules by superior agencies or legislative bodies that enabled the subordinate official to turn his monopoly in selling dispensations from these rules into a profitable business. On the other hand, the subordinates' readiness to submit to the hierarchy sprang from the same kind of artificially constructed insecurity, which ensured not only a steady flow of bribes but could easily be turned into a mechanism of imposing discipline on corruption-prone agents. Although complicity in corrupt transactions appears to be an indispensable condition of the informal contract accepted by every official at the moment of his appointment, the same behaviour could be easily punished as a criminal offence according to the parallel code of rational–bureaucratic conduct of duty, which was never abolished.

Thirdly, corruption did not follow from compliance with traditional norms and roles as defined by informal institutions. Such an interpretation is refuted by the observation that the readiness of social actors to take part in corrupt transactions quite often had to be encouraged by carefully designed mechanisms of compulsion. These mechanisms owed their efficiency, as a rule, to a skilful combination of formal and informal incentive structures. In addition, in most cases the first impulse was definitely the work of formal rules. When tax inspectors decided to submit to the institution of corruption, they did not act under the pressure of traditional norms of reciprocity. They were instead caught up in trying to make their way through bureaucratic regulations and instructions designed intentionally by their superiors to make them stumble. Completely aware of the possibility that they could all of a sudden be called to account for an institutionally programmed infraction of rules, they simply had no other choice than to contribute to the stabilisation of inter-agency hierarchies. What is to be observed here is the complementarity rather than the competition between formal and informal institutions. On the one hand, the loopholes and contradictions built into formal institutions had defined the space into which informal institutions could be inserted. On the other hand, it was only the ability to selectively mobilise the sanctioning power controlled by formal institutions that guaranteed the power of social actors sitting at the top of informal institutions.

Corruption as Habitus

So far I have described the Georgian brand of corruption in the times of Eduard Shevardnadze as a complex institution, whose capability at stable reproduction resulted from a skilful manipulation of self-interest. In a difficult balancing act, it simultaneously exploited and constrained the selfishness of the actors involved. This perspective is obviously very much informed by a modified rational choice approach. In what follows, I will attack this position by returning the focus to the role played by culture. I will depart from the insight that all institutions have to interact with cognitive and symbolic structures of perception in order to be effective. According to conventional wisdom, institutions aim at reducing complexity. If the institutions are successful they define guidelines of action that can be taken for granted by the majority of members in a certain society. Individuals are thus released from the obligation to constantly weigh the costs and benefits of a certain option before acting. But, this can only be achieved when the normative and cognitive principles an institution is based upon are deeply internalised by the relevant social actors whose behaviour the institution intends to steer.

If we apply this insight to our analysis of the institution of corruption, this means that all the institutional incentive structures that seem to have been so successful in enforcing the rules of the corruption game on all social actors in Georgia could only function properly when and if they succeeded in tying in with the implicit knowledge these actors have previously accumulated. To safeguard against naive culturalist misconceptions, which are quite widespread in the discourse on corruption, I will take refuge in Bourdieu. Whereas the social sciences in general were long trapped in binary coded thinking, construing either institutions in terms of adaptation to pre-established cultural patterns or culture as a product of institutional incentives, Bourdieu made a strong point for stressing their interdependence. With the concept of habitus he emphasised the synchrony of two processes: the internalisation of objective structures and the externalisation of cognitive patterns. What can this perspective reveal about the interaction between culture and the institution of corruption in Georgia?

In the following, I will look into the patterns of perception as articulated by social actors in the conflicts triggered again and again by corruption. As I have already shown, the Georgian apparatus of rule was composed of quite heterogeneous interest groups. Its coherence had to be secured by the careful installation of incentive structures and control mechanisms designed to discipline its agents. Although this enterprise of imposing discipline seems to have been quite successful in the long run, that did not exclude the occurrence of considerable infighting over the distribution of the spoils. The question that naturally follows from that observation is of course why these conflicts did not threaten the reproduction capability of the institution of corruption.

At least part of the answer is to be found in the narrative of a conflict in a western Georgian municipality where the issuing of bad loans triggered a deep budget crisis at the end of the 1990s. The story that led to this crisis is a quite simple one: the local administration had to pay the interest for loans it had awarded to a carefully selected circle of clients without paying any attention to collateral securities. As was to be expected, those who had benefited from the generosity of the local administration could not have cared less about repaying their debts and in the end the money to cover the loss had to be taken from the administration's budget. Due to this financial burden, caused by a corrupt deal between the head of the local administration and his business friends, the teachers' salaries could not be paid any more. At this point, Merab, the chairman of the local council, appeared on the stage. It is his behaviour that is of special interest in the context of the argument I want to develop. At first glance, his constantly changing patterns of action appear to be highly contradictory. When he first intervened in the unfolding conflict, he seemed to be acting as the only true representative of the public interest. He had aggressively attacked Djumber,[4] the head of the local executive, as well as Djumber's partners on the level of the central state for having prepared the corrupt deal. Everything as to be expected, one tends to think: a legislature which takes seriously its obligation to control the executive. But as the whole affair gained momentum, it became apparent that Merab could not really maintain this position as selfless defender of the public good. Soon he turned to damaging the image of his personal rival, Djumber, in the eyes of the centre. At that moment he was already less motivated by authentic outrage over the selfish actions of the local head of the administration than by his highly personal agenda. Eagerly, he grasped the opportunity provided to him by the scandal to blame his rival for mismanagement and present himself as the better candidate for the job. This strategy was mainly addressed to the central agency responsible for making such appointments. Moreover, it was clearly based on a readiness to forget about the leading role central agents played in preparing the loan deal. But, this could obviously not be communicated to the local audience. In order to deflect local attention from his real interests, Merab thus decided to personalise the whole conflict. In the end, he came up with a narrative depicting Djumber's decision

4 All names in this chapter have been anonymised.

to suspend the payment of salaries to the teachers as a move that was first of all motivated by an interest to harm his, that is, Merab's reputation. To be fair, this interpretation was not totally baseless, drawing on the fact that Merab himself had given his word of honour to the teachers to defend their rights. But by recalling this promise, Merab tried to kill two birds with one stone. On the one hand, he wanted to present himself as the furious Georgian compelled by the dirty strategies of his rival to commit the most detestable of all sins, that is, to breach his promise. On the other hand, he obviously tried to conceal his own opportunistic motives. A man of honour is always measured by his ability to keep his promises. And, the effort to match this moral standard is an end that justifies the means. This is the hidden message transmitted by Merab's claim and it is understood by any ordinary Georgian who grew up with the implicit certainties of his culture. As a consequence, the highly questionable campaign Merab initiated for more than dubious motives against his eternal rival Djumber, was easily transformed into a desperate battle for the restoration of his stained honour, a battle he was simply obliged to wage for the sake of Georgian values.

What we can observe here is a permanent changing of meaning. What appeared at first glance to be a confrontation between a corrupt local administrator and a local politician fighting for justice is upon closer examination a fierce power struggle driven by highly opportunistic motives on both sides. In this reading of the conflict, everything seems to circle around the eternal play of prestige and honour. As a consequence, every version to be told about the events entails a certain dose of ambivalence. Nobody knows for sure what is going on; and nearly without notice, opportunism becomes a legitimate norm.

But in this case, the double game played by Merab came to the fore precisely at the moment of his partial success and his partial failure. He was successful in getting Djumber dismissed. But at the same time, he could not establish himself as the new head of the administration. Notwithstanding Merab's intervention, the central authorities appointed Giorgi as the new mayor. This resulted in another rather unexpected reversal in Merab's strategy. The first decree to be adopted by new mayor Giorgi concerned the resumption of payments to the teachers. In this situation, Merab, who had just waged a fierce struggle in the interests of the teachers, denied to give his approval to that decision. In justifying this surprising move, he openly boasted about his tactical skills. The first thing he referred to was the balance of power, which had overnight changed to his advantage. Proudly, he pointed to the fact that his advice had been sought after by the central power structures before appointing Giorgi. The awareness of having advanced his position in the networks of power obviously led Merab to take a fresh look at local affairs. This could be felt with utmost clarity in the interviews I conducted with him in that time. Whereas, he had talked about criminal machinations with regard to the awarding of loans to the clients of the administration before, he now stressed alone the necessity of repaying debts. Whereas, he had once accused the local administration of being involved in the illegal export of timber, he now emphasised his readiness to tolerate minor irregularities, openly appealing to the image of the typical Georgian who is known for his generosity and would never be so narrow-minded as to blame a fellow countryman for relatively inconsiderable infractions.

What was actually behind Merab's sudden change of agenda is brought to surface only by a closer look at the political context. Again, the political constellation had changed and Merab had to react. Most important for him was the fact that the governor had threatened every local boss with dismissal if he failed to pay the teachers in time. Immediately, Merab had seized the opportunity inherent to this new situation. If he could obstruct the fulfilment of this obligation, it might further his own career prospects. Again, he was quite successful in obscuring his selfish motives by laying the blame on his rival. He simply asserted that Giorgi, the new mayor, actually wanted to load the responsibility for inconvenient decisions onto him, Merab. But, even if this claim was primarily motivated by Merab's intention to justify his policy of obstruction, it was again to a certain degree based simultaneously on sound arguments. The teachers' salaries could only have been paid if the local council agreed to crucial cuts in budgetary spending on other social issues. Merab's actions were hardly driven by these considerations. First of all, he was clearly proud of seeing through Giorgi's dubious plans. He was eager to be perceived as the clever professional who is up on every trick and knows the dirty game of political intrigue better than anyone else in the local arena. He would be the one to spike his rival's guns. Again, he wanted to be seen as someone acting in accordance to typical Georgian values. He was boasting about his tactical skills and the formal elegance of his behaviour, both features that are highly valued in the context of Georgian culture.

It goes without saying that these references to traditional values were clearly motivated by tactical considerations. But, what follows from this observation? With Bourdieu we could state that this is the normal state of affairs. According to his model, norms of behaviour as inscribed into habitus always need to be translated by social actors into scripts adapted to specific situations. Due to an inevitable ambivalence they thus leave ample space for taking into account personal interests. One could even claim that all norms need to allow for this kind of flexibility in order to be observed. In the long run, flexibility thus contributes to the prolongation of a normative order. In this case we might conclude that cultural values had been used by Merab merely as an argument in his restless struggle for power. We could moreover state that corruption was not so much encouraged or even caused, by adherence to cultural values. Rather these values were appealed to in order to obscure Merab's opportunistic motives, providing him a legitimate justification. It follows the general argument that cultural values do not cause social action but served to legitimate it retrospectively.

But as convincing and plausible as this interpretation seems to be at first glance, it reflects only one side of the truth. This becomes apparent if we ask ourselves what Merab actually achieved with his tactical manoeuvring and by making instrumental use of culturally acceptable legitimation forms. Looked upon from this perspective, his performance appears to be less impressive. Neither did he succeed in getting the desired appointment to the position of a mayor, nor did he manage to gain any significant symbolic capital. Put another way, the symbolic capital he might have gained by presenting himself as a man, who lives up to Georgian values, was insufficient for helping him in his struggle for power. But, this is quite easy to explain if we take into consideration that in the Georgia of Eduard Shevardnadze, advancement to a position of power did not depend on legitimacy in the eyes of Georgian society but mainly on the benevolence of superior power holders. In the end, Merab had to abstain from scandalising the corrupt deals of his rivals without receiving any advantage at all in return. All his self-confident words on his cleverness appeared to be empty talk. Probably, its main aim consisted of helping him to adapt to a situation that was difficult for him to bear: his own lack of power and influence. By justifying his own behaviour in terms of legitimate Georgian values, he tried to come to terms with a constellation that forced him to take part in dirty power games that he was at the same time too weak to win and too weak to resist.

Closing the chapter on culture and habitus, we can thus state that the implicit appeal to traditional norms and values actually contributed to the stabilisation of power structures. Nourishing the illusion that at least the clever had a real chance at escaping the all-controlling grasp of the apparatus of rule, his pride in his cultural skills helped Merab to make his peace with a power game that had actually broken him. Although cultural stereotypes thus did not legitimate social actions in any clear-cut way, they nevertheless fulfilled an important function. This becomes obvious if we look at similar strategies of self-defence applied by any number of other members of the Georgian apparatus of rule. Even leading members of the administration, constantly portrayed themselves as potential victims of a state perceived as a foreign body. On a regular basis, the overwhelming feeling of being powerless was compensated for by assuring oneself and others of the ability to cheat the system, an ability that was moreover labelled as being typically Georgian. Tax inspectors took pride in their skills at manipulating figures and balance sheets, a skill that was said to keep them beyond the reach of the controlling arms of their superiors. The head of a local tax inspectorate wished that the previous governor, who had been too ignorant to see through his machinations, could come back. In a way, even Eduard Shevardnadze took part in this game. Quite often he portrayed himself as the powerless client of mighty international patrons in the shape of an international organisation that pressed for the realisation of reforms in exchange for financial aid. And, similar to Merab, he took pride in being able to cheat these aid organisations by means of simulating reforms. Although, one could say that this strategy was realised at the expense of Georgian society, which might have benefited from the implementation of coherent reforms, Shevardnadze obviously counted on gaining legitimacy by playing the role of the typical Georgian too weak to change the situation but at the same time he was clever enough to take as much advantage of it as possible. The reference to traditional Georgian values thus constituted a kind of normative link between the rulers and the ruled. Moreover, it helped to obscure sharp power asymmetries. A relatively powerless official like Merab, who constantly had to play games invented by others, could at least enjoy the feeling of reacting in the same way as people who – compared to him – disposed of much more power. As a result, the eruption of tensions and conflicts was effectively avoided. Cultural codes thus assumed the function of establishing plausible interpretations of social reality that facilitated the endurance of actually unbearable situations. They prepared the ground for a fatalistic acceptance of the prey-seeking state, an acceptance that rested on the belief that the state, though it could not be changed, could be outsmarted. As a result, everybody acted in accordance with the institution of corruption, even if he was convinced of his ability to offer resistance.

Summary: Corruption as Institution and Habitus

Thus, in the end I neatly return to my point of departure. I began by criticising two mainstream models of explaining corruption: the public choice model pointing to the crucial role played by perverse institutional incentive structures and the culturalist model laying blame on traditional, that is the cultural norms of solidarity that are said to undermine bureaucratic rationality. Against common wisdom, which as a rule would emphasise the opposing logics behind both perspectives, I have underlined how much they actually have in common. To be more precise, I have argued that both of them think about corruption mainly in terms of institutional default. I have highlighted the tacit agreement between adherents of the two opposing camps in corruption research mainly for two reasons. On the one hand, I could thus define more properly where and why I strongly disagree with mainstream approaches that constantly tend to underestimate how difficult it is to bring about or reproduce corruption. On the other hand, the alternative model of accounting for systemic corruption that I have outlined so far, however, is also based on a specific fusion of institutional and cultural arguments informed by Bourdieu's concept of habitus. As I have argued, corruption in Eduard Shevardnadze's Georgia can be conceptualised as an institution of its own rights composed of a great number of incentives and monitoring and sanctioning structures designed to compel bribe-paying clients as well as bribe-extorting members of the bureaucratic apparatus by means of the brute force of an artificially created uncertainty to submit to the rules of a highly hierarchical corruption game carefully controlled by top rulers. I have shown, moreover, that reference to cultural norms mainly serves the function of morally justifying patterns of behaviour triggered by the incentive structures of the institution of corruption. Last but not least, I have claimed cultural values help individuals to cope with the feeling of powerlessness imposed on them by the compulsion to take part in corrupt transactions. We can thus conclude that institutional constraints and selectively mobilised cultural values smoothly interact to produce the habitus of corruption-prone bribe-takers and bribe-givers. We can, moreover, claim that the prime function of culture consists of helping people to justify their adaptation to institutional constraints forcefully imposed on them in order to assure for their reliable participation in corrupt transactions.

References

Bourdieu, P., 1979. *Entwurf einer Theorie der Praxis*. Frankfurt am Main: Suhrkamp.

Christophe, B., 2006. *Metamorphosen des Leviathan in einer postsozialistischen Gesellschaft: Georgiens Provinz zwischen Fassaden der Anarchie und regulativer Allmacht*. Bielefeld: transcript.

Collier, D. and Levitsky, S., 1997. Democracy with Adjectives: Conceptual Innovation in Comparative Research. *World Politics* 49(3), pp.430–51.

Collier, D., 2002. Explaining Political Corruption: An Institutional Choice Approach. *Crime, Law and Social Change* 38(4), pp.1–32.

Darden, K., 2001. Blackmail as a Tool of State Domination: Ukraine under Kuchma. *East European Constitutional Review* 10(2), pp.67–72.

Easter, G., 2003. Building Political Compliance in Transitional Economies: Russia. Paper presented at a conference titled, Tax Evasion, Trust and State Capacities. St Gallen, Switzerland, 17–19 October 2003.

Goudie, A. W. and Stasavage, D., 1998. A Framework for the Analysis of Corruption. *Crime, Law and Social Change* 29(2–3), pp.113–59.

LaPalombara, J., 1994. Structural and Institutional Aspects of Corruption. *Social Research* 61(2), pp.325–50

Miller, E., 2004. Smelling the Roses: Eduard Shevardnadze's End and Georgia's Future. *Problems of Post-Communism* 51(2), pp.12–21.

North, D. C., 1990. *Institutions, Institutional Change and Economic Performance*. Cambridge : Cambridge University Press.

Olivier de Sardan, J.–P., 1999. A Moral Economy of Corruption in Africa? *Journal of Modern African Studies* 37(1), pp.25–52.

Reckwitz, A., 2003. Grundelemente einer Theorie sozialer Praktiken: Eine sozialtheoretische Perspektive. *Zeitschrift für Soziologie* 32(4), pp.282–301.

Solnick, S., 1996. The Breakdown of Hierarchies in the Soviet Union and China: A Neo-Institutional Perspective. *World Politics* 48(2), pp.209–38.

Stier, K., 2002. Entrenched Corruption Begins at Georgia's Border. *EurasiaNet* 26 June. Available at <http://www.eurasianet.org/departments/insight/articles/eav062702.shtml> [Accessed on 19 June 2012].

Waldmann, P., 2002. *Der anomische Staat:* Über *Recht,* öffentliche *Sicherheit und Alltag in Lateinamerika*. Opladen: Leske and Budrich.

Chapter 16
Marketing Reforms: The Dimension of Narratives in Georgia's Fight against Corruption

Lili Di Puppo

A particularity of Georgia's anti-corruption reforms after the Rose Revolution of November 2003 is the way they have transformed the country's image in a short period of time from the 1990s prototype of a corrupt and weak post-Soviet state to an anti-corruption model. This image change is illustrated in a World Bank publication with the title 'Fighting Corruption in Public Services: Chronicling Georgia's Reforms' which was released in 2012 (World Bank, 2012). The publication reveals how far the country has changed its image in the last nine years as Georgia is now presented as a model for post-revolutionary states in the Middle East. The bank's book which focuses on the reforms under the administration of Georgian President Mikheil Saakashvili (2004–2013) also marks the end of this era as it coincides with the coming to power of a new government under Prime Minister Bidzina Ivanishvili following the parliamentary elections of October 2012.

The chapter examines this process of building an image of success in the Saakashvili years and the government's attempt to establish an authoritative narrative on the country's reforms. I understand success as an 'interpretation' and will show here the mechanisms through which the Georgian government engages in this production of success. I ask the question as to whether the government succeeds or not in gaining an external approval of its representation of success and examine the factors that can explain its difficulty in securing this approval. In particular, I will examine how the government faces the challenge of alternative discourses that seek to unveil the 'hidden transcript' of its reforms.[1]

First, I will present my theoretical framework and my understanding of success as 'interpretation'. In the second part, I will analyse how the government has sought to frame its anti-corruption reforms into a narrative of success. Thirdly, I will examine the external validation of this narrative through the case study of the World Bank's promotion of the country's image of success. In a fourth part, I will study the challenges posed by alternative discourses to the government's

1 I apply James Scott's distinction between 'hidden' and 'public' transcripts to my study of the Georgian government's 'production of success' (1990).

representation of success by analysing the adoption of a national anti-corruption strategy and the reforms of the audit institution, Chamber of Control. Finally, I will analyse the election period in 2012 as revealing certain central features of the government's construction of an image of success as well as the way alternative discourses eventually bring to light the inner contradictions in this image. I will conclude by examining how the Saakashvili government has benefited from the inherent subjectivity of assessments of success on its reforms, but also has difficulties sustaining its narrative against alternative domestic discourses.

Understanding 'Success' in Anti-corruption Reforms in Georgia

The mainstream anti-corruption discourse is characterised by the notion of anti-corruption as a neutral and rational activity. The ideal of this discourse promoted by international anti–corruption organisations is one of a 'terra blanca' where anti-corruption instruments can immediately achieve their goal of reducing corruption. However, the fight against corruption usually does not take place in a vacuum of meaning; it is rather pursued in a particular cultural context that is characterised by a previous legacy of anti-corruption campaigns. Thus, the new Georgian government of Mikheil Saakashvili after the revolution was confronted not only with a legacy of corrupt practices, but with a legacy of anti-corruption practices and a rhetoric inherited from previous campaigns dating back to the Soviet era and the period under the presidency of Eduard Shevardnadze (1991–2003, see Barbara Christophe in this volume). Negative meanings were attached to the notion of the fight against corruption and to anti-corruption measures in the Georgian context. In particular, anti-corruption was viewed as a rhetorical activity and as being part of a political game between rival politicians that would not lead to any concrete results. Further, anti-corruption strategies and documents were seen as cosmetic acts that were only drafted at the request of donor organisations.[2]

The government after the revolution faced the challenge of changing the perceptions of corruption and anti-corruption activity in the country. Further, it needed to answer the high expectations of citizens and their demands for immediate changes. It sought to invest the fight against corruption with positive associations by creating a new narrative on Georgia.

In the following, I will apply an understanding of success as 'interpretation' and not as 'goal achievement' or 'impact' to examine Georgia's fight against

2 A Georgian analyst remarks on the attitude of Georgians to strategy documents: 'There is quite a cynical attitude to strategies, a strategy is something you draft for Westerners, sometimes you hire Westerners to draft for other Westerners, and you put it in your file and when someone asks [you to show it] … they [the Georgians] don't think it's important'. Interview with Georgian analyst, Tbilisi, May 2007.

corruption.[3] I view the government's reform steps as revealing an attempt to build a discursive representation and a particular frame of interpretation to read its activities in order to promote a new narrative on the country. In his examination of the social production of success in development projects, David Mosse (2003) identifies two major elements in this process: the building of an image of success and the validation of this representation of success by an 'interpretive community'. I will examine these two elements of the production of success in my study of Georgia's fight against corruption and will also apply James Scott's (1990) distinction between 'public' and 'hidden transcripts'. The validation of an interpretive community allows the consolidation of a narrative of success into an 'official transcript'. An external approval is needed or the 'hidden transcript' of these activities can be revealed. A further observation on the production of success that I draw from the literature on interpretive policy analysis is that assessments of success develop a dynamic of their own as they become 'success stories', 'narratives' and 'labels' whose effects may have political consequences that go beyond the simple evaluation of a particular policy's outcomes (Arend and Broekhans, 2010, p.12). 'Failure' and 'success' should not be viewed as technical assessments as the use of these labels can serve specific purposes, for example 'success' can be used to 'brand' a specific country or organisation and enhance its profile and reputation.

The Building of a Narrative of Success

The Rose Revolution of November 2003 in Georgia has been described as an 'anti-corruption revolution'. The new and young elite that came to power after the revolution named the launch of anti-corruption measures as one of its highest priorities. As already observed, this elite was confronted not only with a legacy of deeply entrenched corrupt practices, but with the negative meanings associated with anti-corruption activity.

The major elements in the reforms launched by the government after the revolution are their rapidity and the visibility of results. Further, these reforms were framed into a state-building and modernisation discourse that symbolised an 'irreversible' break with the Soviet past. Corruption was associated with the negative legacy of the Soviet era and the years of weak statehood under the former president, Eduard Shevardnadze. The rapidity of reforms signalled the importance accorded by the new government to the necessity of challenging perceptions. Indeed, the relationship between perceptions and actual corrupt practices is complex to the extent that perceptions tend to influence behaviours. The perception that an institution is corrupt encourages corrupt behaviours.

3 I borrow the distinction between a notion of success as 'goal achievement' and as 'interpretation' from van der Arend and Broekhans (2010).

After the revolution, the new government under Mikheil Saakashvili's ruling party, United National Movement (UNM), engaged in a strategy of producing success by framing its reforms into a particular discourse and by targeting certain reform sectors for their potential to quickly showcase results. 'Success' is thus not understood as the end process of an activity and as revealing the extent of the 'impact' of this activity on concrete corruption levels, but as 'interpretation'. Georgia's image as a 'successful reformer' and an anti-corruption model in the post-Soviet space is not viewed as the direct result of a series of sound and efficient anti-corruption reforms, but as the result of a conscious strategy of the elite in power to produce this 'success'. Georgia's reforms such as the notorious firing of the traffic police have achieved certain tangible results, for example the fact that the new patrol police do not take bribes from car drivers any more. However, Georgia's 'success' is also the result of a work of interpretation, of framing these reforms into a coherent narrative and of targeting certain areas where these changes can be made visible, while concealing other more problematic aspects of the country's modernisation. The necessity of rapidly achieving results and producing a quick image change has determined the type of reforms implemented and their sequencing. The measures that were implemented not only had the potential to effectively deter corrupt behaviours such as a rise in salaries in state agencies, but they also had the potential to 'showcase' these changes and alter perceptions of corruption by creating a new image as a means of further discouraging corrupt practices.

The centrality of the quickness of reforms is illustrated in the train metaphor used by Mikheil Saakashvili to emphasise the speed of the country's modernisation. Saakashvili used this metaphor in 2007 when referring to the opposition in Georgia: 'They want to catch the train, which has already departed and which is already so far away that it is even impossible to catch with a Formula 1 car'. and 'Tickets are still available on our train. We do not want to exclude anyone'. (Civil Georgia, 2007a). The visual image that is created is of a rapidly reforming country, this 'success' appears to precede the concrete and lasting changes that can be achieved by the reforms. Perceptions are changed by projecting the image of a new Georgia onto the minds of citizens and external observers before the reforms have actually achieved a lasting impact on the country's economic and social realities. The new elite thus compensates for its limited means to achieve wide-ranging changes in a short period of time by emphasising certain results in selected reform sectors such as the traffic police, education and the civil registry. These areas become flagship sectors that can showcase the building of a 'new, non-corrupt Georgia'. The speed with which these sectors are reformed as well as the immediacy of results mean the risk of disillusionment that was a typical side effect of the anti-corruption campaigns of previous eras is avoided.

The elements of rapidity and visibility are emphasised in the World Bank's publication of 2012 (World Bank, 2012). The importance of rapid successes is linked to the need of the government to establish credibility and gain legitimacy. The publication lists ten factors behind the country's 'success'. It says under the factor 'establish credibility early': 'early successes build support for further action, in a virtuous cycle of reforms' (World Bank, 2012, p.10). Immediate results allow for an extension of the window of opportunity gained by the government directly after the revolution through its strong popular mandate. This renewed window of opportunity gives an impetus for a new cycle of sometimes unpopular reforms.

The government's strategy of producing success can be seen as aiming at making corruption invisible by removing it from the public eye and the space of encounters between public officials and citizens, while rendering the results of anti-corruption measures highly visible. The government thus targeted as a priority these areas of daily encounters between citizens and state agents that were also perceived as being the most corrupt in Shevardnadze's era and as vivid symbols of the systemic bribery under its government. The notoriously corrupt traffic police were replaced almost overnight by brand new patrol police. About 16,000 police officers were fired and replaced with 2,300 new road patrollers. The number of staff in law enforcement agencies was reduced from about 63,000 in 2003 to 27,000 in 2011 (World Bank, 2012, p.8). Indeed, the police reform had the effect of rapidly changing citizens' perceptions of the institution.[4] Further, government officials of the Saakashvili administration regularly referred to the reform in international forums as an illustration of the country's 'success story'.

A major characteristic of the reforms was their immediate visual impact. Older and overweight policemen with Soviet-style uniforms were replaced within a few weeks with younger and thinner road patrollers with new uniforms and new cars. Further, new police stations were constructed with glass exteriors to symbolise a new commitment to transparency. The rapid changes in the architectural landscape of the capital, Tbilisi, render visible the process of nation- 'building' and of the 'construction' of a new, more transparent and modernised Georgia through the use of glass. Another notable measure of the new government was the restoration of twenty-four hour power supply. The 'darkness' characteristic of the Shevardnadze period, caused by daily power cuts, vividly symbolised the corruption of the previous system.

The old institutions were dismantled and even abolished rather than being restructured as a signal of a radical break with the past. For example, the Anti-monopoly Service, the Food Quality and Control Service and the agency

---

4 Attitudes towards the police in Georgia provide an example of rapidly changing perceptions. In an August 2003 survey, 70 percent of respondents stated that police officers are 'most or almost all involved in corruption' (the figure was 73 percent in 2001 and 70 percent in 2002). Police officers came second to customs officers (Georgian Opinion Research Business International, 2003). By contrast, a February 2007 survey of voters reveals that 66 percent had a favourable opinion of the police in February 2007 (70 percent in April 2006) and the police were the fourth most trusted institution after the church, the army and the Georgian media (IRI, et al., 2007).

responsible for motor vehicle inspections were abolished.[5] In the official discourse, these measures were aimed at limiting opportunities for corruption by cutting bureaucratic red tape. The number of permits and licenses were reduced from 909 in 2003 to 137 in 2011 (World Bank, 2012, p.54). The regulatory agencies were seen as being more effective in creating opportunities for bribery than delivering services. These measures also had the effect of supporting the narrative of a new Georgia without corruption. Citizens as well as foreign visitors to the country would no longer experience the bribe-taking practices typical of the Shevardnadze era.

The symbolism of a rupture with the Soviet and post-Soviet past and the new 'zero tolerance policy' was also communicated visually through the arrests shown on television of high officials from Shevardnadze's administration. These officials were allowed to repay large sums of money to the state treasury in order to avoid prison in a plea bargaining arrangement. The government further targeted the 'thieves-in-law' or Soviet-era criminals and sought to sever the ties existing between the criminal world and the state (see also Evgenia Zakharova in this volume). A new legislation was passed to allow the confiscation of property and money of illicit origin. Membership in the thieves' society was criminalised. The government's crackdown on the criminal world was also portrayed as the promotion of a new behavioural model in the form of a law-abiding and Westernised citizen with a strong work ethic against the romanticised ideal of the 'thief-in-law' that symbolised a certain resistance against the Soviet system, even while being at the same time a product of this same system. The 'thief-in-law' enjoyed a social reputation and cultivated ties with the Soviet intelligentsia as illustrated in the figure of Jaba Iosseliani who staged a coup against Zviad Gamsakhurdia, the first president of independent Georgia. The government's fight against the thieves' society was portrayed as an effort towards state-building and the cultivation of a new patriotism and pride towards the state in Georgian society.

Corruption thus became invisible in the post-revolutionary era and persisted only in the stories circulating about the links between high officials or deputies in the parliament with certain businesses as well as the problem of the existence of monopolies in the economy. An image was created of Georgia as a 'reformer' country driven by economic liberalism even if the economic climate was still characterised by insecure property rights, the lack of independence of the judiciary and cases of pressure from the ruling party on small businesses. These more problematic aspects of the reforms were concealed behind a narrative that emphasised market liberalism.

The government thus favoured radical and visible reforms over long-term structural measures that would not have the same effect of changing perceptions. Reforms were prioritised that could help create a new image of the country in a short period of time. However, the government faced a recurring problem in the form of a certain disjuncture between the discursive representation of the reforms and the

5 The World Bank publication refers to the term 'guillotine' to describe the shutting down of these agencies (2012, p.54).

social and economic realities of the country. Indeed, poverty and unemployment remained high in the Saakashvili years, while dissatisfaction with the repressive methods employed by its administration against the opposition grew. However, this disjuncture is different from the one existing in the Shevardnadze years, as certain concrete results are visible for all. Georgia's anti-corruption record cannot be so easily contested and its reforms portrayed as cosmetic changes, especially by countries such as Russia which do not score well in corruption rankings. Anti-corruption reforms appear to provide a more solid foundation than a democracy narrative on which the former government of Saakashvili could build an image of success. However, the risk still exists of the revelation of a 'hidden transcript' of the reforms, of the public unveiling of the 'true' intent behind these changes. While the Saakashvili government justified a concentration of power in the hands of a small elite as a means to achieve results, opponents of the government see this concentration of power as the actual end of these measures. The government thus needs to seek 'validation channels' to support its narrative against these counter-claims and attempts to reveal the 'hidden story' of its revolutionary project. It needs the support of an 'interpretive community' to sustain and reproduce its image of success.

Promoting Georgia as an Anti-corruption Model

The World Bank publication of 2012 can be seen as an illustration of the successful validation of Georgia's reform achievements. It can be viewed as an element in a broader project of publicising the country's reforms to an international audience. The publication indeed has the effect of upgrading Georgia's status to the one of a model for post-revolutionary states in the Middle East. Another important means of constructing Georgia's image as a success story is the country's rapid ascension on international governance indexes. Georgia quickly rose in the World Bank's 'Ease of Doing Business Index' from a score of one hundred and twelfth in 2005 to a score of sixteenth in 2012. Furthermore, Georgia ranks sixty-fourth out of one hundred and eighty-three countries in the Transparency International Corruption Perceptions Index of 2011 with perceived corruption being lower than in several EU member states including Slovakia, Italy, Greece, Romania and Bulgaria. By contrast, it ranked eighty-fifth out of one hundred and two countries in 2002.

In particular, the country's ascension on the Ease of Doing Business Index provides an illustration of the Saakashvili government's strategy of producing success. It shows how certain reforms were consciously targeted for their potential to sustain a particular image of Georgia as a fast reforming country and a frontrunner in the post-Soviet space. The country's rapidly improving scores in the period 2004–2007 that culminated in Georgia earning the label of 'world's top reformer' in 2007 can be linked to an effort by the Georgian authorities and USAID to promote this progression (Schueth, 2011). The Ease of Doing Business Index is particular in that the World Bank not only measures the competitiveness and regulatory quality of states, but the Index is intended to facilitate and stimulate reforms (Schueth, 2011, p.56). The project's website offers a 'user's guide' and details on the Index methodology that can be used to calculate what reforms will produce the greatest ascension in the ranking (Schueth, 2011, p.56). By learning from others what reforms produce the greatest results, states may be able to 'catch up' quickly with more advanced economies. The Index has the effect of setting an optimal development model that can be achieved by adopting 'best practices'. It presumes that states are equally positioned when entering the playing field (Schueth, 2011, p.57). The Index's particularities that stand for rapid progress over long and incremental reforms thus answered the Georgian government's wish to achieve quick results and obtain an immediate recognition of these in order to support its narrative on a 'new Georgia'. The country's ascension on the Index allowed a publicising of this image, while effectively masking those areas that would not fit into this narrative. The Index can be seen as an element in the work of interpretation of ordering the country's reforms into a coherent representation of success, while removing from sight other more problematic aspects of these changes. Similarly to other auditing practices, the Index reveals what it is intended to reveal, thereby concealing areas that cannot be grasped with its methodology (Schueth, 2011, p.61). It renders certain chunks of reality measurable, quantifiable and visible, while obscuring what it cannot measure. In particular, the Index does not shed light on insecure property rights and the lack of judicial independence even if these factors affect the quality of the business environment in Georgia.

The Index can be seen as a valuable tool in the country's strategy of constructing an image of success instead of a neutral instrument to measure and record the country's progress. It shows how assessments of success can be viewed as 'stories' instead of objective evaluations as they develop a dynamic of their own and have certain implications in terms of enhancing an actor's reputation. Georgia's ascension on the Index reveals the broader implications of the creation of a 'success story' as the country's label as 'reformer' and the external recognition of its reform progress resulted in increased foreign investments. The country tripled its volume of Foreign Direct Investment (FDI) inflows between 2004 and 2007. By 2007, Georgia attracted $1.6 billion with FDI exceeding foreign aid as a source of external finance.[6] Sam Schueth notes how a favourable rating from the credit-rating agency Standard and Poor's and the country's indexing as a 'frontier market' in 2007 marked 'Georgia's transformation from a failed state to a neoliberal vanguard state at the leading edge of capital market expansion into the periphery of the global economy' (Schueth, 2011, p.62). The country spent $7.8 million on its investment promotion campaign and secured the services of the international advertising firm M&C Saatchi (Schueth, 2011, p.68). The promotional campaign referred to Georgia's scores on the Index drawing favourable comparisons with advanced economies such as Germany and Australia under the slogan 'And the

6 See UNCTAD, 2008. Due to the war and the global financial crisis of 2008, the FDI dropped, while the country has again become more dependent on external aid.

winner is: Georgia' (Schueth, 2011, p.68). The campaign can be seen as a further means to produce success as it positions the country as an attractive investment destination against advanced economies. The methodology used in the Index to assess a state's competitiveness allows creating criteria by which success can be measured and made tangible as well as establishing a virtual space where Georgia is able to compete with leading economies.

The creation of this virtual space through the Index reveals another important feature of the Saakashvili government's reform project. The government seeks to project a virtual reality in which the country can escape its problematic geographical and temporal position as a post–Soviet state 'in transition'. Indeed, the government's project can be seen as one of demarcating the country from the post-Soviet space by emancipating it from certain geographic boundaries, in particular its proximity to Russia. Further, the country seeks to escape the various negative labels and concepts that are associated with the notion of post-Soviet 'transition'. 'Success stories' are a means of drawing these new demarcation lines. Georgia's status as a 'reformer' is helped by creating parallels with other far away countries such as Singapore or Taiwan and emancipating the country from its cultural and historical position on the margins of Europe. The new elite that came to power after the revolution views Georgia's cultural legacy and particularly the Soviet period as a possible hindrance to the country's modernisation and aspires to transcend this legacy. This rupture with the Soviet past and with the country's cultural legacy can be seen in the marginalisation of the old intelligentsia and the break with the romanticism associated with the figure of the 'thief-in-law' as well as the emergence of a new type of Western-oriented intellectual inspired by economic liberalism.[7] The Saakashvili government sought to cultivate closer ties to the United States than to the European Union as the latter's more bureaucratic and formalised approach did not suit Georgia's need for rapid successes. The new elite's modernisation project is sometimes perceived in Georgian society as representing a possible threat to the country's traditional values.[8]

The country's ascension on the Index reveals how the government manages to consolidate its narrative of success through the validation of other actors. The Index and its strategic use to sustain Georgia's 'reformer' narrative can be seen as a case of the convergence of two different anti-corruption actors in the common production of an image of success. The World Bank has an interest in sustaining the country's 'success story' as its progress validates its own methodology. Georgia's image as a pro-active country relying on its own resources to advance reforms is reinforced in turn by its rapid ascension on the Index and the World Bank's publication of 2012.[9]

7 See Shatirishvili (2003) on 'old' and 'new' intellectuals in Georgia.

8 Ghia Nodia refers to the concept of 'cultural security' in Georgia and the possible tensions between 'imported' Western values and national Georgian traditions as well as the struggle between new, 'modernising' and old, conservative elites (Nodia, 2005a, pp.73–4).

9 The bank's publication does not claim to assess the success of Georgia's reforms, but still has the effect of consolidating these claims of success by chronicling them and

The book has the effect of contributing to Georgia's image change from a 'recipient' to an 'exporter of knowledge' to other countries.[10] The two actors allow for certain contradictions in their representations of success to achieve this convergence. For example, the bank's publication does not refer to the use of external anti-corruption knowledge to explain the country's success. The report mentions the adoption of US and Italian anti-mafia legislation and the fact that several members of the new government had received their education abroad as examples of a transfer of international experience (World Bank, 2012, p.98). However, it says: 'Reformers drew on international experience. But, they are quick to point out; they adapted it to Georgia's unique circumstance and developed their own solutions'. (World Bank, 2012, p.98). Further, the Georgian government's preference for radical and quick solutions in the reform of institutions appears to contradict the mainstream anti-corruption discourse of organisations such as the World Bank that tend to emphasise the use of expertise and the institutionalisation of anti-corruption measures into a coherent sequence. However, the bank's publication mentions under the factor 'launch a frontal assault' among ten factors that can explain Georgia's success: 'rather than spending precious time strategizing, worrying about sequencing, or consulting on action plans, the government launched a rapid and direct assault on corruption in a broad array of public services. It acted quickly to keep vested interests at bay'. (World Bank, 2012, p.10) The contradictions between the government's approach and the mainstream anti-corruption discourse may explain Transparency International's more uneasy adherence to its narrative. For example, the Transparency International Georgia Integrity report of 2010 does insist on the use of expertise to combat corruption (Transparency International Georgia, 2011). It points out the necessity for the Georgian government to conduct research aimed at qualifying and quantifying corruption as a means to inform and trigger new policies (Transparency International Georgia, 2011, p.25). However, the organisation still validates the government's narrative partially, as it also depends on its approval to be perceived as a valuable anti-corruption actor offering expertise to governments.

---

presenting the country as a potential model. The World Bank's vice president, Philippe H. Le Houerou, says in the book's foreword to the publication: 'It does not seek to evaluate Georgia's approach to reducing corruption, but to identify the key political economy factors that contributed to the anti-corruption reforms in Georgia' (World Bank, 2012).

10 Georgia's 'export of knowledge' contributes to the consolidation of an image of success. The state agency Georgia Reforms and Partnership Enterprise (GRAPE) was created in 2012 with the aim of promoting and sharing the country's reforms worldwide. This new initiative shows how 'reform success' is being turned into a 'brand'.

Challenges to the Saakashvili Government's 'Reformer' Narrative

The Saakashvili government's attempt to establish an authoritative frame of interpretation to read its anti-corruption activities is challenged by alternative discourses that seek to unveil the 'true intent' of the reforms after the revolution. In particular, these discourses point to certain inherent contradictions in the government's representation. The government's actions are portrayed as being driven by an economic libertarian agenda that emphasises the benefits of market liberalism as a means to remove corruption. At the same time, this transition to liberalism is achieved through a strengthening of the state and a concentration of power in certain power structures such as the Interior Ministry. Saakashvili government's project of creating a 'new Georgia' can be understood as a 'cultural revolution' that aims at promoting a new type of Western-oriented and non-corrupt Georgia.[11] The new post-revolutionary elite can be seen as 'modernisers'. However, the modernisation project appears to result in a sometimes violent confrontation between the state and society.[12] Further, the image of success projected by the government appears to be increasingly distanced from the actual social and economic conditions in the country. The government's project can be seen as the building of a post-modern 'utopia', a modernising state whose path of evolution is not determined by its geographical location and cultural legacy.[13] Georgians can become Americans almost overnight and be inspired by Asian countries such as Singapore and Taiwan, countries that have managed to transcend their problematic geographic location near a powerful neighbour through the benefits of trade and market liberalism. However, critical voices portray the government's reliance on repressive methods against domestic opposition as a reminder of the Bolshevik period. The government in its forceful attempt to distance itself from a Soviet legacy of failure is being compared to this same era.[14] Indeed, the government in its modernisation project appears to increasingly evolve in a different timeframe to the rest of society, demanding from Georgian citizens a rapid transformation and

11 Nodia notes how the new elite that came to power after the revolution 'can be metaphorically described as those who speak English and work with computers' (2005b, p.48).

12 Nodia refers to the dangers of 'being carried away by a revolutionary Jacobin zeal' and 'a temptation to resort to authoritarian modernisation in the name of establishing liberal democracy' when describing the challenges faced by the new elite after the revolution (2005a, p.72).

13 For example, the World Bank report notes that Georgia's reforms have disproved the idea that corruption is a cultural phenomenon and as such difficult to combat: 'Georgia's success destroys the myth that corruption is cultural and gives hope to reformers everywhere who aspire to clean up their public services'. (World Bank, 2012, p.104).

14 The project of creating a new type of Georgian citizen as well as the planned construction of a new city from scratch – Lazika on the Black Sea coast evoke certain Bolshevik features in the form of the rejection of the determinism of culture or 'utopian projects'.

projecting an image of a rapidly reforming economy that does not correspond to their everyday lives.

A first contradiction in the government's narrative of success can be found in the fact that it seeks to gain the approval of external actors towards its reforms, while it conflicts at the same time with mainstream views of anti-corruption activity through its unconventional and *ad-hoc* methods. This conflict is revealed in the tensions that have characterised the relations between the Saakashvili government and international organisations in the post-revolutionary period with these organisations criticising the Georgian authorities' *adhoc* governing style and the lack of institutionalisation of reforms (interviews with representatives of international organisations, 2007–2008). The adoption of a national anti-corruption strategy following the recommendations of the Council of Europe and the Organisation for Economic Development and Cooperation (OECD) in 2005 illustrates this problem. The document has the effect of supporting the narrative of success of international anti-corruption organisations as it 'embodies' the belief in the need to use a specific knowledge to guide anti-corruption reforms and institutionalise these measures. However, it contradicts the government's image of success. Indeed, the adoption of an anti-corruption strategy is an acknowledgment that the problem of corruption still exists in Georgia and the government requires external advice and a special strategy plan to tackle it. Nevertheless, the government adopted the strategy in 2005 as the document represented a means to translate its anti-corruption record into the authoritative language of the global anti-corruption field. A refusal to adopt the strategy would have automatically raised doubts on Georgia's commitment to fight corruption. However, the strategy appears more as a document that allows the translation of the country's anti-corruption reforms to an international audience than as a strategic tool to guide these measures and combat corruption. For example, the Transparency International Integrity report of 2010 on Georgia comments on the 2010 Action Plan for implementation of the strategy, that it appears that the AP 'was compiled on the basis of general reforms that were already planned in different government agencies, rather than through an analysis of specific corruption-related issues' (Transparency International, 2011, p.28). Further, the World Bank publication of 2012 on Georgia's anti-corruption reforms does not refer to the anti-corruption strategy (World Bank, 2012).[15]

The reform of the state audit institution, the Chamber of Control of Georgia (CCG), reveals further contradictions in the government's representation of success as it has difficulties integrating the reforms of the audit agency into its narrative of success. Indeed, executive agencies were given a major role in the fight against corruption with the effect of marginalising independent control institutions. The Chamber's reform illustrates the government's difficulty in asserting a particular narrative of its actions, in particular to portray its activities as serving a notion of

15 The report insists on the importance of a 'flexible strategy' and pragmatism to implement reforms rather than a formalised approach that would be difficult to adapt to ever-changing circumstances (World Bank, 2012).

public good, as well as the potential for alternative discourses to raise the question of the accountability of its measures. The Chamber appears to pose a problem to the government in the sense that it does not fit easily with the promotion of a narrative of success. The government has chosen to prioritise the reform of state agencies that were perceived as the most corrupt in Shevardnadze's times and where improvements could be immediately felt by citizens. Further, the executive and agencies such as the Ministry of Internal Affairs and the prosecutor's office were assigned a prominent role in the fight against corruption or in the implementation of reforms. Independent control agencies such as the Chamber are viewed with suspicion as they are not seen as being effective in delivering public services. In particular, the Chamber was an integral part of the corruption system in Shevardnadze years as it fulfilled the two functions of accumulating *kompromaty* or compromising material on political opponents and of taking bribes from state agencies. In line with the government's libertarian agenda, the Chamber's abolition instead of its restructuring or the outsourcing of its functions to private companies was regarded as the potential solution to the problem of its reform after the revolution (interviews with government representatives and analysts, 2008).

The Chamber's role in the fight against corruption is indeed problematic to the extent that it is a potential source of alternative corruption narratives and a challenger of the government's own story. The institution fulfilled this role of a producer of corruption stories under Shevardnadze's administration and provided a resource for the control and subordination of officials. The Chamber did not expose cases of corruption; it rather actively created these cases by obtaining bribes from corrupt officials in exchange for the non-disclosure of compromising material. The agency's production of corruption narratives served the political game between different factions that competed for influence under the Shevardnadze regime. This exposure of corruption was not overtly damaging for the previous government as it was an element in an informal system of the promotion of corrupt behaviour for means of control (see Di Puppo, 2004). On the contrary, this function is more problematic under the Saakashvili government that has built its reputation and credibility on the integrity of public officials.

After the revolution, the government appeared to favour an inactive audit institution that would not risk challenging the anti-corruption narrative that it was seeking to establish. As already noted, the priority was to increase trust in state institutions as the belief in the integrity of these institutions did influence citizens' actual behaviour. A new law on the Chamber of Control was passed only in 2009 and reform steps were slow during the period 2004–2009. However, the absence of reform and the inactivity of the Chamber were also problematic to the extent that a passive audit institution also raised questions on the government's commitment to transparency. A scandal that broke out in 2007 further shows how the Chamber's ambiguous role created confusion in the reading of the government's actions and could challenge its narrative. The Chamber released a report on the Ministry of Education in 2007 accusing it of mismanagement of funds. The scandal revealed the existence of different narratives on corruption and the fight against corruption in Georgia. The Minister of Education, Kakha Lomaia, accused the Chamber's employees of incompetence, lack of professionalism and corruptness.[16] It depicted the agency as an old Soviet-style institution working with old-fashioned and inefficient methods. On the other side, opposition parties used the scandal to question the anti-corruption reforms in the education sector. They relied on the image of the audit institution as a modern agency producing impartial reports.

Another event in the Chamber's reform revealed the potential for competing discourses on the fight against corruption in Georgia. Following the scandal, certain steps were undertaken to reform the institution. In particular, about 600 employees were fired in 2007. The chairmanship of the agency presented the firing of staff as a necessary measure to remove corruption in the institution and allow the hiring and training of a new generation of professional auditors. The firing of employees was similar to the radical measures employed in other state organs, most notably in the police. However, the opposition portrayed this wave of forced resignation in the agency as a government attempt to 'silence' the audit institution following the Minister of Education's scandal. In the opposition's narrative, the government aims at controlling the audit institution rather than the agency fulfilling its role of controlling the government. The Chamber's uncertain status and its two 'faces' as a modern audit institution or an old-style corrupt Soviet agency create the potential for two competing narratives. The government's actions are directed towards the removal of corruption in the agency itself, while the opposition sees the institution as an instrument in the fight against corruption. The agency is seen as both an object of and a tool for anti-corruption reforms.

The opposition's vision of the Chamber as a modern audit institution converged with the representation of international organisations. Different donor agencies have implemented projects at the Chamber including the World Bank, the United Nations Development Program (UNDP) and the German Development Agency (GIZ). Their activities have focused mainly on the training of staff, the restructuring of the agency as well as the alignment of its auditing procedures with international standards. These activities were challenged by the slowness of reforms, the absence of a legal framework – as a law on the Chamber was passed only in 2009 and the firing of staff in 2007 since many of the former auditors had participated in trainings organised by the donor organisations. The lack of political will to reform the institution was criticised by these organisations. The Georgian government was eventually pressured by the European Union to undertake reforms at the end of 2008 in the context of large amounts of donor aid being allocated to Georgia following the Russian–Georgian war of August 2008 (interviews with donor representatives, 2008). A series of more rapid reforms undertaken after the war under the leadership of a new chairman can be seen as an attempt by

16 One article says: 'The Education Minister criticised the state audit agency for being staffed by many "non–professionals" who have been engaged in "corrupt deals"' (Civil Georgia, 2007b).

the Georgian government to converge with international organisations in a new reform narrative. These can be understood as a sign that the government realised the challenges posed by an unreformed institution to its anti-corruption narrative. New measures were introduced in this period to restructure the agency, bring its auditing procedures into line with international standards and train new auditors. The Chamber started to publish audit reports on certain government officials, albeit only at deputy level and not on the 'power ministries'. Georgia earned good reviews in external evaluations through these reform measures. Further, the new chairman's increased openness towards donor organisations and the demand for external advice to increase the agency's efficiency allowed both actors to sustain a more coherent and common image of their activities.

However, the election period of 2012 revealed the limits of the government's attempt to obtain the adherence of external actors to its anti-corruption narrative and improve the Chamber's image and reputation. Indeed, the institution's independence was questioned after the Chamber fined the new opposition party Georgian Dream led by oligarch and opposition politician, Bidzina Ivanishvili, at the beginning of 2012 for making illegal political donations. : Thus, the reforms that had been initiated to transform the chamber into a functioning and modern audit institution in line with the demands of international organisations were given another purpose. Hence, the agency started investigating inadequacies in the funding of opposition parties. The government rendered itself vulnerable to the public revelation of a 'hidden transcript' in its pursuit of reforms in the sense of the consolidation of power in a small circle of government officials.

The cases of the Chamber of Control's reform and the adoption of an anti-corruption strategy have shown how the Saakashvili government is faced with alternative readings of its actions. Further, it faces certain dilemmas in its attempt to converge with external actors in a common narrative of success. These contradictions in the government's representation were vividly brought to light in the election period of 2012 and may explain its electoral defeat.

The Limits of the Saakashvili Government's Narrative of Success

The election period of 2012 that culminated in the defeat of the ruling party, United National Movement, and the victory of the opposition coalition, Georgian Dream, can be seen as revealing both certain important features of the Saakashvili government's building of an image of success and the limits to this narrative. The arrival of opposition politician and oligarch, Bidzina Ivanisvhili, on the political scene in Georgia at the end of 2011 represented an important challenge to the Saakashvili government's narrative. Indeed, Ivanishvili immediately sought to challenge this image by relying on the services of public relations and lobbying firms in Washington and Brussels.[17]

---

17 See Egen (2012) on the 'PR battle' between Ivanishvili and Saakashvili.

The election period of 2012 reveals two aspects of the Saakashvili government's building of an image of success: the 'stickiness' of a 'reformer' narrative as well as the way this narrative finally succumbs to its inner contradictions and is challenged by alternative discourses. First, the 'strength' of the 'reformer' narrative in the form of the belief in the lack of viable alternatives to the Saakashvili governments modernisation project was revealed in the fact that the majority of external observers did not envisage the scenario of a victory by the Georgian Dream opposition coalition.[18] In particular, a survey published by the organisation National Democratic Institute (NDI) in the summer of 2012 found that the ruling party United National Movement (UNM) was leading ahead of Georgian Dream (GD). Saakashvili's UNM had succeeded in strongly identifying the process of modernisation and Westernization in Georgia with its own rule.[19] The example of the NDI survey shows how certain surveys and governance rankings became elements in the work of interpretation of the Saakashvili government that had the effect of consolidating its image of success, while obscuring certain more negative aspects of the country's modernisation, instead of serving as measurement tools and providing objective statements on the actual state of reform progress in Georgia.[20]

However, the increasing visibility of the disjuncture between a 'reformer' story and the actual economic and social difficulties of the post-revolutionary period as well as the increasingly authoritarian features of the Saakashvili government finally threatened the government's image of success. The narrative appeared to succumb to its inner contradictions, in particular the inner tensions between the image of a democratic and modernising country and the repressive methods by which this modernisation was brought about as illustrated in acts of intimidation against the opposition in the pre-election period. Further, the latent violence that was perceived as characterising the relation between state and society in the post-revolutionary period suddenly became graphically illustrated in the footage of an undercover video, showing acts of abuse by law-enforcement officials against

18 For commentaries on the false predictions of external observers, see Kirchik (2012), Adomanis (2012) and Cecire (2012).

19 Cecire (2012) remarks: 'the UNM and its leadership, which had long been enthusiastic partners to the United States and Western Europe, had become a metonym to many analysts – and especially the more casual observers – for modernisation and liberalism in a region traditionally hostile to both'.

20 For example, Adomanis (2012) notes on the effects of rankings in building an inaccurate image of Georgia: 'According to many international comparisons the Georgian government was an absolute rock star, slashing regulation, fostering foreign investment, and lowering barriers to entry at a historic clip. But, ultimately, very little of that mattered because of the small and inconvenient facts that the country remained poor, pensions remained paltry, and jobs remained scarce'. Cecire (2012) further quotes Georgian expert Mamuka Tsereteli on how the UNM leaders had fabricated a 'virtual reality': 'They were good salespeople of this virtual reality and sold it to the West as if it was the whole story.'

prisoners which was released in September 2012.[21] The video served as a catalyst for the underlying anger against acts of abuse of power by government officials, in particular in the Interior Ministry, and provoked a series of demonstrations shortly before the elections of November 2012.[22] The video scandal shows how the government's narrative is finally dented after corruption in the form of the unaccountability of government officials in Saakashvili's administration is made visible. However, the video was only a catalyst for the existing frustration experienced by citizens towards the government's repressive tendencies that ultimately relegated Georgia to the status of a typical post-Soviet state on the matter of democratic freedoms.

Conclusion

The analysis of the Georgian government's construction of an image of success after the revolution has revealed the paradoxes of this process. The government succeeds to both obtain external approval of this image and to consolidate this narrative, but is also confronted with certain dilemmas in obtaining this approval.

The government's attempt at image change can be explained by the central role of perceptions in anti-corruption efforts. The Saakashvili government wanted to alter these perceptions rapidly in order to change social practices and encourage more law-abiding behaviour from citizens. It needed rapid successes to emphasise the narrative of a 'new, non-corrupt Georgia'. Success is understood as 'interpretation' and the work of the government of emphasising certain reforms with rapid and visible results can be seen as a work of interpretation, of the building of a narrative. The understanding of success as 'interpretation' posits that assessments of success are inherently subjective. This subjectivity of assessments of success appears to play in the hands of the government, but also opens certain dilemmas.

In the analysis of the government's construction of a narrative, we observe that it is successful in creating certain authoritative references in the discourse of the country's reforms. Indeed, the Georgian case is particular in that the Georgian government appears pro-active in creating the labels, references and narratives that are used to assess its reforms. It is not a passive recipient of external labelling practices. With the rise in international examination and evaluation practices that are visible in the use of international governance indexes, developing and transition

21 Doubts were later voiced on the authenticity of the video with the suspicion that some of the abuse might have been staged, see Kirchik (2012).

22 The video showing acts of rape with broom handles by prison officials against prisoners, acts perceived as particularly shocking for Georgian conservative society, also illustrated the perceived 'violation' or disregard for traditional values of Saakashvili's team of 'modernisers'.

countries have become the objects of external evaluations and labelling exercises.[23] An authoritative language is created through the use of these labels that serve to measure a country's reform progress such as 'hybrid regime' or 'failed state'. The case of the adoption of an anti-corruption strategy in Georgia has shown how the government finally bows to the authoritative language of the global anti-corruption field and engages in a standardised commitment to fight corruption. However, the government also creates its own reference points in the form of a 'reformer narrative' that is supported by the World Bank. While there is no definite story of Georgia's success in fighting corruption, this story is still being reproduced and referred to even when contested. Georgia's successful reform becomes an authoritative label and creates certain obligatory references in a discussion of the country's path after the revolution. The 'stickiness' of Georgia's success story was revealed in the pre-election period when wide references were made to the Saakashvili reform legacy even in critical assessments of his rule. The co-existence of two different narratives on Georgia's Rose Revolution – a 'reformer and modernisation narrative' and a more critical 'democracy narrative' – are not necessarily to the government's disadvantage as commentators on Georgia still refer to the country's official success story even while criticizing the shortcomings of Saakashvili rule.[24]

However, the work of interpretation conducted by the government that skilfully makes use of modern communication means in the form of public relations agencies and governance rankings remains vulnerable to attempts to unveil the 'hidden transcript' of this project. It is precisely the reliance on producers of narratives such as public relations firms that enables the Saakashvili government's reforms to be easily portrayed as mere 'public relations exercises' or cosmetic changes even if the authors of these attacks themselves rely on the same means of producing counter-narratives through these communication agencies.[25] However, the government's narrative, while it is created as a means to project a new reality of a modern and developed Georgia even before reforms have had a concrete and lasting impact, is perceived on a domestic level as being increasingly distanced from the economic conditions in the country. Further, the government's narrative of success finally succumbs to a central important paradox in its modernisation efforts: the methods by which this modernisation is brought about. Indeed, alternative discourses portray the sometimes repressive methods

23 See Löwenheim (2008) on the rise in international examination practices.

24 For example, an article on 'the Georgian paradox' emphasises these two sides of the country's story, but makes wide reference to its reform achievements listed in the World Bank publication of 2012 (Caryl, 2012).

25 Cecire (2012) further remarks that the UNM itself and its advisers may have been 'blindsided' by these public relations firms and might not have understood that the electoral campaign needed to be centred around real domestic concerns rather than being portrayed as a geopolitical choice between the liberal West and pro-Russia supporters, a rhetoric that failed to convince the Georgian electorate.

of the Saakashvili's government, in particular of the Interior Ministry, as being precisely those inherited from the Soviet period. In these aspects, Georgia remains a typical post-Soviet state displaying certain authoritarian features.

In conclusion, Saakashvili's government has been successful in devising certain labels by which its reforms could be read and interpreted in external assessments, in particular by emphasising its reform success. However, Georgian citizens grew increasingly dissatisfied with the discrepancies between this image of success and the persistent poverty and lack of an independent justice that evoked the deficiencies of a standard post-Soviet country. At the same time, the projected image of a modern and successful Georgia as well as certain reform achievements from the Saakashvili era have raised expectations in the population for Georgia's image of success to become a tangible reality in the near future.

It remains to be seen what narrative the new government under Bidzina Ivanisvhili will devise, whether it will portray its new rule as a break with the legacy of the government under the ruling UNM party or build on previous achievements, while addressing the shortcomings of its predecessor. The new narrative could also place Georgia more firmly in its cultural legacy, for example by emphasising relations with the European Union rather than with the more distant United States.

References

Adomanis, M., 2012. How Were Western Experts 'Blindsided' by Georgia's Widespread Poverty? *Forbes*, 15 October.

Caryl, C., 2012. The Georgian Paradox. *Foreign Policy*, 31 January.

Cecire, M., 2012. How the West got Georgia Wrong. *The National Interest*, 9 October.

Civil Georgia, 2007a. Saakashvili's New Initiatives: Amid Political Standoff, 16 October 2007. Available at <http://www.civil.ge/eng/article.php?id=16038> [Accessed on 15 December 2012].

Civil Georgia, 2007b. MPs Angered over Minister's Assertive Speech, 29 June. Available at <http://www.civil.ge/eng/article.php?id=15356> [Accessed at 15 December 2015].

Di Puppo, L., 2004. Corruption as an Instrument of State Control in Georgia. In: Osteuropa Forum 21. Available at <http://www.oei.fu-berlin.de/publikationen_old/boi/21_boi/03_forum/08_di_puppo/index.html> [Accessed at 9 March 2014].

Egen, D., 2012. The Influence Industry: Georgian Power Struggle Becomes D.C. Lobbying Battle. *The Washington Post*, 16 May.

GORBI, 2013. *Corruption Survey in Georgia: Third Wave*. Georgian Opinion Research Business International. Tbilisi.

IRI et al., 2007. *Georgian National Voters Study. International Republican Institute*. Tbilisi: Baltic Surveys Ltd; The Gallup Organization; The Institute of Polling and Marketing.

Kirchik, J., 2012. Blindsided. In: *Foreign Policy*, 12 October.

Löwenheim, O., 2008. Examining the State: A Foucauldian Perspective on International 'Governance Indicators'. *Third World Quarterly* 29(2), pp.255–74.

Mosse, D., 2003. Good Policy is not Implementable? Reflections on the Ethnography of Aid Policy and Practice. Paper presented at the EIDOS Workshop on 'Order and Disjuncture: the Organization of Aid and Development', SOAS, London, 26–28 September 2003.

Nodia, G., 2005a. Georgia: Dimensions of Insecurity. In: B. Coppieters and Legvold, R., eds, *Statehood and Security: Georgia after the Rose Revolution.* Cambridge: MIT Press, pp.39–81.

Nodia, G., 2005b. The Dynamics and Sustainability of the Rose Revolution. In: M. Emerson, ed., *Democratization in the European Neighborhood.* Brussels: Center for European Policy Studies, 2005, pp.38–52.

Schueth, S., 2011. Assembling International Competitiveness: The Republic of Georgia, USAID, and the Doing Business Project. *Economic Geography* 87(1), pp.51–77.

Scott, J., 1990. Domination and the Arts of Resistance: Hidden Transcripts. Yale University Press.

Shatirishvili, Z., 2003. 'Old' Intelligentsia and 'New' Intellectuals: The Georgian Experience. *Eurozine* 26 June. Available at <http://www.eurozine.com/articles/2003-06-26-shatirishvili-en.html> [Accessed on 15 December 2012].

Transparency International Georgia, 2011. National Integrity System Assessment Georgia 2010. Tbilisi.

UNCTAD, 2008. United Nations Conference on Trade and Development, Country Fact Sheet Georgia (2008). Available at <http://www.unctad.org/sections/dite_dir/docs/wir08_fs_ge_en.pdf> [Accessed on 14 July 2010].

van der Arend, S. and Broekhans, B., 2010. Beyond Evaluation: Evaluating the Meaning of Success and Failure in Policy Practices, Paper presented at the 5th Interpretive Policy Analysis Conference, Grenoble, 23–25 June.

World Bank, 2012. *Fighting Corruption in Public Services: Chronicling Georgia's Reforms*. Washington.

Index

For Product Safety Concerns and Information please contact our EU representative GPSR@taylorandfrancis.com
Taylor & Francis Verlag GmbH, Kaufingerstraße 24, 80331 München, Germany

www.ingramcontent.com/pod-product-compliance
Ingram Content Group UK Ltd.
Pitfield, Milton Keynes, MK11 3LW, UK
UKHW011000180926
475701UK00004B/483

* 9 7 8 0 3 6 7 5 9 9 5 8 4 *